Father and Son

Father and Son

The Wound, The Healing, The Call to Manhood

Gordon Dalbey

Thomas Nelson Publishers
Nashville

Published in Nashville, Tennessee, by Thomas Nelson, Inc., and distributed in Canada by Lawson Falle, Ltd., Cambridge, Ontario.

The names of persons and certain details of case histories described in this book have been changed to protect the author's clients.

Unless otherwise noted, Scripture quotations are from the *Good News Bible,* Old Testament © 1976 by the American Bible Society; New Testament © 1966, 1971, 1976 American Bible Society. Used by permission.

Scripture quotations noted NKJV are from the NEW KING JAMES VERSION of the Bible. Copyright © 1979, 1980, 1982, Thomas Nelson, Inc., Publishers.

Scripture quotations noted KJV are from the KING JAMES VERSION of the Bible.

Scripture quotations noted NEB are from *The New English Bible.* Copyright © 1961, 1970 by The Delegates of the Oxford University Press and the Syndics of the Cambridge University Press. Reprinted by permission.

Scripture quotations noted NIV are from The Holy Bible: NEW INTERNATIONAL VERSION. Copyright © 1978 by the New York International Bible Society. Used by permission of Zondervan Bible Publishers.

Scripture quotations noted TLB are from *The Living Bible.* Copyright © 1976 by Tyndale House Publishers and are used by permission.

Scripture quotations noted RSV are from the REVISED STANDARD VERSION of the Bible. Copyright © 1946, 1952, 1971, 1973 by The Division of Christian Education of the National Council of the Churches of Christ in the U.S.A. Used by permission.

Library of Congress Cataloging-in-Publication Data

Dalbey, Gordon, 1944–
    Father and son : the wound, the healing, the call to manhood /
Gordon Dalbey.
      p.   cm.
    Includes bibliographical references.
    ISBN 0-8407-3450-6
    1. Fathers—Religious life. 2. Fatherhood (Christian theology)
3. Fathers and sons—Religious life—Christianity. I. Title.
BV4846.D35 1992
248.8'421—dc20   92–4975
                                              CIP

Printed in the United States of America

1 2 3 4 5 6 7 — 97 96 95 94 93 92

This book is dedicated to
John Miguel Dalbey (1991–   )
son of Gordon Dalbey (1944–   )
grandson of Earle Gordon Dalbey (1916–   )
great grandson of Richard Dalbey (1880–1939)
great great grandson of Richard S. Dalbey (1842–1896)
great great great grandson of Edmund Dalbey (1810–1848)
great great great great grandson of Isaiah Dalbey (1779–1822)
great great great great great grandson of Abel Dalbey (1754–1843)
May he remember always the Father of his fathers

Contents

Introduction

Early in the winter of 1991, shortly before my son John Miguel was born, I asked a conference of 350 fathers this question: When your first child was born, did your father reach out to you with support, encouragment, or helpful advice?

I paused as a strange hush settled over the men. "Maybe," I suggested, "your dad said something like, 'It's a little scary at first, but hang in there and you'll be doing fine before long' or 'Make sure your wife gets a break from the stress once in a while to rest'?"

The hush stirred to nervous shifting as one . . . then two more . . . and finally, a total of five hands went up.

Only 5 out of 350?

Stunned, I resolved to test this statistic at my other conferences around the country. Everywhere, the proportion came out roughly the same: one or two out of a hundred.

Clearly, in the most crucial occasion of father-son definition—when the son becomes a father himself—the American man is abandoned. He thus feels inadequate and afraid as a father himself, and therefore, all-too-ready to abandon his own son.

Most of us participate readily in activities we do well, but avoid those we do poorly. Invite me to play tennis, softball, or basketball, and I'm with you, because I compete pretty well in those sports. Suggest a sport I haven't played much, like surfing or hockey, and . . . sorry, but I've got other plans.

It's like that with fathering. The man in our society does not reach out to his son because his own father never demonstrated how. He feels inadequate as a father and withdraws from his children. He therefore struggles after manhood as if climbing a snow-covered mountain. Above him, a huge snowball of pain gathering size and momentum from generations before is rolling down as a Leviathan, ready to crush him in its destructive path even as it did his father.

The honest man has discovered that on his own he is as powerless to stand against that legacy of pain as was the boy it first overwhelmed generations earlier. Nor can he save his father or his own son from its curse and destruction. He may try to talk with his father, only to be rebuffed, ignored, or sidestepped. He may vow, "I'll never hurt my son the way my dad hurt me!" only to find himself later hurting his son similarly—or conversely, by not disciplining the boy when necessary for fear of being so hurtful.

This father-wound snowballing down the generations has today become a giant, common enemy of fathers and sons alike. Its crippling sense of rejection, alienation, and shame mocks godly manhood and leaves men—even godly men—trembling.

For so, "When the Israelites saw Goliath, they ran away in terror" (1 Sam. 17:24).

Even as in the ancient biblical story, this enemy common to men of all ages is not conquered by the adult male, whose vision is truncated by his "mature," wordly view of power. Rather, in a strange yet compelling truth, the boy—freed from any pretense of "manly" muscles and worldly expertise—becomes the avenue to saving power: "Goliath came forward and challenged the Israelites as he had done before. And David heard him. . . .

"David answered, 'You are coming against me with sword, spear, and javelin, but I come against you in the name of the LORD Almighty, the God of the Israelite armies, which you have defied. . . . [T]he LORD does not need swords or spears to save his people. He is victorious in battle, and he will put all of you in our power'" (1 Sam. 17:23, 45, 47).

Thus acknowledging the power of his God alone, the boy seizes a pebble for his slingshot and slays the giant no adult man dared face. And God's people are saved.

Only the Father God of all time can deliver a man from generations of destruction into manhood—that is, from being abandoned to being a son (see Rom. 8:14–16). This is what He has done in Jesus on the Cross, and will do for any man who invites Jesus into his father-wound. Indeed, He has stepped decisively into the path of the snowballing Goliath, letting it smash against Himself and thereby, breaking its power over fathers and sons.

Jesus came to restore relationship with the Father—that is, to remind men abandoned and unfathered for generations that they are beloved sons.

Quoting Joachim Jeremias, theologian Marvin Wilson notes that men in the Old Testament occasionally referred to God as "Father," but never as "my Father." Traditional Judaic prayers used the term, "our Father." Jesus, however, not only referred often to God as "my Father," but used the intimate Hebrew term *abba,* or "Daddy."

Thus Wilson declares,

> The same childlike closeness is central to the sonship that is at the heart of the Christian gospel; for those who, by faith, have been adopted into the Father's family as children may also address him as Abba (Rom. 8:15; Gal. 4:6). Jeremias sums up the striking significance of this theologically pregnant term used by Jesus: "with Abba we are . . . confronted with something new and unheard of which breaks through the limits of Judaism. Here we see who the historical Jesus was: the man who had the power to address God as Abba and who included the sinners and the publicans in the kingdom by authorizing them to repeat this one word: 'Abba, dear Father.'"[1]

The powers of the world, meanwhile, can know only the natural father of the flesh. Lacking the Father God's larger view, they can respond to men's wound today only by devaluing the earthly father and thereby, masculinity.

As if to de-claw the tiger, the world proclaims that fathers aren't that important after all. From TV sitcoms to the Dagwood and Drabble of newspaper comics, the father is often portrayed as a buffoon. Denying Jesus the common courtesy of asking why He called God "Daddy," the politically-correct universalists rush to proclaim instead the revisionist "Creator," "Parent," or even "Mother God." Media and advertising prey upon males thereby cut off from the root substance of manhood, diverting young men to focus instead on style.

But a disabled tiger only becomes a man-eater. However expedient such a notion, and whatever pain it may in the short run postpone, a man taught that the father is not important will act accordingly when he becomes a father himself. Emotionally, if not physically, he will abandon his own children.

He will not know how important he is to his son, because the wounded little boy in his psyche tells him it's safer not to know. That is, to know how important he is to his son, a man must remember and confess how important his own father was to him. And that, for today's unfathered man, means the boy within him must face the Goliath.

Without the Father God to uphold and guide him in that life-or-death rite of passage, he remains a boy—lost among the powers of the world, abandoned to his own fears and self-centered desires.

And the snowball rolls on down.

A man wounded unto death by the loss of father-love does not need to be told that a father's support and encouragment is worthless anyhow. He needs to know that the Father God of all men has called him to Himself as a beloved son.

This book is therefore not about becoming a father, but rather, about the prior and primal step of manhood in becoming a son. It is designed for the man

- who has been wounded by his father and is honest enough with himself to reject the world's quick fix of denying the pain and the need,
- who has dared to consider his dad's human limitations and has begun to sense that neither Dad nor any other man can now fulfill his deep and persistent father-longing,
- who nevertheless wants to grow up without forfeiting father-love, and indeed, senses that he cannot become a man without it, and
- who is ready to give thanks for whatever father-love God has been able to give him through his earthly father, to cease demanding any more from Dad, and to surrender his wound at last to the Father God who defines and shapes all men.

I had written about half of *Father and Son* when my own son John Miguel was conceived. Though the world might see that as a "charming coincidence," God quickly and deliberately revealed His hand at work. For John Miguel's birth itself portrayed dramatically for me the essential distinction between being Dad's natural child of the flesh and a son of the Father God.

The first child for both of us in our forties, John Miguel had been a surprisingly easy pregnancy, with only minor discomfort for Mary and no sickness. Our hopes for a similarly easy labor began to fade, however, when we discovered the boy was "posterior," or positioned such that contractions pushed him against Mary's spinal cord with excruciating pain.

We had resolved to avoid a cesarean section. From the outset, however, the doctor feared serious stress to the baby through such an ordeal, and declared that any consistently elevated heartbeat would dictate precisely such emergency measures. Reluctantly, we agreed to what seemed an ominous likelihood. Yet, to the astonishment of doctor and nurses alike, the boy's heartbeat monitor showed no significant variation from the norm throughout forty-two agonizing hours of labor.

The medical staff did not know, however, that we had established an elaborate prayer chain before going into the hospital. Like a frontline field commander to his supply corps, I was phoning out an update regularly between contractions. Furthermore, from the onset of labor—contraction after four-minute contraction, hour after hour—I had been laying hands on Mary's womb and praying very specifically.

First, I spoke directly to John Miguel. "Son," I said, "I know this is really hard, but many people are praying for you. If I could, I'd lift you out of it in a second, but I can't. I'll pray for you with all I've got. But this is your battle, and you've got to stay strong and fight through it. Whatever happens, I promise to stand here beside you and not go away. I am your father. I am with you, and the Father of your forefathers has never left us."

And then I would pray. "Mighty Jesus, victorious Lord Jesus, King of kings, Lord of lords, we give up to You. I have no power to win this battle, but all power is Yours. In the name of Jesus, Father, pour out Your Holy Spirit on John Miguel. Give him hope and determination and perseverance."

Finally, I would speak again to John Miguel. "In the name of Jesus, I, your father, speak courage and strength to you!"

Throughout the ordeal, I was praying for Mary as well. Sometimes, I sobbed prayers through tears; at other times, I could only repeat words mechanically. Overall, however, I felt a distinct confidence.

After forty-two hours, the doctor became concerned that Mary would have no strength left to push the baby out, and recommended vacuum suctioning. After a brief discussion, we agreed and she proceeded. Standing by the hospital bed, my hands on its side railing, I looked up at the boy's heart monitor and watched in hypnotic rest the steadily flickering 135 base range which had reassured me for forty-two hours.

Reaching to comfort Mary, I was jarred suddenly by an ugly, mucky "pop" sound. "I can't hold the suction," the doctor declared nervously. My jaw dropped as I saw the blood-streaked handle and suction cup in her hand. "It keeps breaking loose!"

Looking down, I glimpsed a shock of dark hair disappearing back into the birth canal. For a second, the doctor hesitated, then spoke sharply to the attending nurse, who turned and left. Quickly, the doctor inserted the vacuum suction again.

Startled by the sudden intensity of action, I glanced up and stared in disbelief. The boy's heartbeat had leapt to 215! Clothing swished ominously into the room and I turned to see several people in medical gowns closing in on us. Another, in surgical scrubs, rushed in fastening a mask across his face.

What is happening?

Beside me, the doctor worked feverishly with the suction handle. Another mucky "pop," and the gowns closed the circle.

My stomach began to churn.

"He's not coming out! The suction won't hold!"

No! Jesus, no! The words leapt into my mind as a wave of cold darkness swept over me. To my shock, my knees began to buckle.

The grey mask stepped closer, and my head fell forward. Desperately, I clutched the bed railing and fought to stay upright. "Jesus!" I whispered, wobbling. "Jesus!"

"Wait . . . he's coming!" The words pierced the darkness over me like a laser beam. "He's coming! Here he comes . . ."

Determined to see, I lurched upward. Slowly, the shock of dark hair emerged. Then faster, the head, shoulders, and whole body slipped out. Quickly, the doctor handed the little body, limp and blue, to the nearest gown, and grasped the scissors.

"No wonder!" the doctor exclaimed. "The cord was wrapped around his legs, holding him back!"

Steadier now, I pulled myself up as the boy disappeared into the circle of gowns, and then stepped close. Between busy gowns and prodding arms I glimpsed John Miguel lying listlessly in the center. Immediately, I pressed closer, leaned over sideways and slipped my right arm between two gowns. Feeling blindly for the boy's head, I tried to say again my prayer. "I'm your father and I'm with you," I began quickly. Suddenly, a small swatch of wet hair touched my palm. "I'm . . . your father," I said again, holding the tiny head in my hand, ". . . and the Father of your forefathers . . ." But I could say no more. And as the arms and gowns moved about me, I wept.

Minutes later, John Miguel emerged from the circle sleepy-eyed and wrapped in a small blanket. "Now at last, you get to hold him," the doctor said to Mary, and set him in her arms. With a deep, deep sigh, I leaned over the bed and put my arms around them both.

Even as we rejoiced at last over our son, Mary and I could not help asking God afterwards, "Why, with all our prayers, did we almost lose him?"

"You did lose him," we sensed God's reply, perhaps a week later. "You lost him to Me. Your prayers as his father are more important than any other person's. But I wanted you to learn from the outset that it is I who saved the boy, not you. In order to experience this, you had to reach the point of seeing your son's life in the balance and not be able to pray at all.

"John Miguel is Mine. I wanted you as soon as possible to recognize him as a son of the Father. He belongs to Me. If he belonged to you, if words from your mouth could have saved him, he would have died trapped in the birth canal while you were passed out speechless on the hospital room floor.

"You are John Miguel's father, and I will honor your prayers for him. But you are both My sons. My purposes for him are greater than you can know, and with your cooperation I will see to it that he fulfills My calling."

We are sons of our fathers, and sons of the Father God. May this book help you surrender to the God and Father of us all, that you might honor your earthly father, faithfully stand with your son, and become the man you are called to be.

CHAPTER ONE

A Spiritual Amnesia

Is he not your father who formed you?
Did he not make you and establish you?
Remember the days of old,
think of the generations long ago;
ask your father to recount it
and your elders to tell you the tale.
(Deut. 32:6b–7 NEB)

The best sermons, it has been said, are the ones you've already heard. The message, that is, has not simply been repeated from a previous Sunday, but rather, awakens understanding you already have that was previously dormant. "Yes, that rings true," you say; "somehow, I always knew that"—even if you have never heard anyone actually say it.

My goal in this book is not to teach something brand new, nor to conjure unheard-of ideas, but to recall what we already know, and have known long before this book was conceived. We've known it, in fact, since being formed in the womb.

But we have forgotten.

The problem with this broken world lies not in our imagination, that we cannot anticipate a future—from solar-powered cars to marriage vows—but in our memory. Like our biblical forebears addressed in Deuteronomy, we cannot confess the authentic past, that is, what God has already done in and among us.

Without such roots, the proud winds of desire and expediency blow, and we bend, we fall. Not knowing what we're made of, we can't know how we're designed to function; not knowing where we come from, we can't know where we're going.

Indeed, not knowing how God has acted in our past, we cannot know the character of the Father and therefore, cannot discern and surrender to His call today. Even as our biblical forebears, we have forgotten who we are—that is, whose we are.

From the Hasidic tradition of Judaism, Holocaust survivor Elie Wiesel tells this powerful story:

> Once upon a time there was a king who knew that the next harvest would be cursed. Whosoever would eat from it would go mad. And so he ordered an enormous granary built and stored there all that remained from the last crop. He entrusted the key to his friend and this is what he told him: "When my subjects and their king will have been struck with madness, you alone will have the right to enter the storehouse and eat uncontaminated food. Thus you will escape the malediction. But in exchange, your mission will be to cover the earth, going from country to country, from town to town, from one street to the other, from one man to the other, telling tales, ours—and you will shout, you will shout with all your might: Good people, do not forget! What is at stake is your life, your survival! Do not forget, do not forget!"[1]

Nowhere today is this call to remember more exigent than among men. Though we have been created male, with all the requisite hormones and body parts, we have eaten the "new grain" and forgotten what it is to be authentic men.

We have forgotten the Father. For the new grain of "modern" secularization has brought a spiritual amnesia among us.

We long for fathers to recount the story, for old men to tell us the tale.

Consider the new grain which television has borne. In the 1990 movie *Avalon,* for example, an entire extended family of immigrants waits anxiously after World War II for the arrival of the family patriarch from Europe—a grey-bearded, story-telling old man around whom the children and adults sit warmly.

Television debuts as the second generation of men are fighting over a perceived snobbery when one moves from the city to the suburbs. The third generation of men sell televisions, and as the patriarch dies and the older men split, we see the family leaving the fellowship of the dinner table to watch TV instead. Ultimately, the men, women, and children of all generations are gathered together about the wondrous picture machine, and those who once sat in delight learning about themselves from the patriarch and his stories, now sit silently before glowing test patterns and canned laughter.

Today we men, who have forgotten the God who has called us with power to restore His kingdom to our families and this world, are too often busy eating the new grain—safely watching others do our manly thing for us in TV cops-and-robbers shows, ball games, adventure shows, and beer commercials.

Men who safely watched the TV coverage of other men fighting the Persian Gulf War in 1991 were afforded the ultimate in vicarious masculinity when Barbara Walters asked General Norman Schwartzkopf how he felt about his part in the victory over Iraq. With a tear in his eye, the Allied Commander said, "My dad would have been proud of me."

In recent years, our loss of masculine roots has crystallized for me in a poignant, compelling new question which, as an author speaking around the country on men's issues, I often hear from women—whether at churches, conferences, or on radio phone-in shows: "What can a woman do to help a man become stronger?"

This question, and the urgency with which each woman begs it, can only amaze a man in his late forties like myself. Twenty-five years ago, with shoulder-length hair and a passion for change, I joined countless other young men to protest and righteously renounce all traditional arenas of masculine strength, from war-making to corporation success ladders.

As men, we rejected the ancient "macho" model of alienation and violence and sought instead a new focus in "love and peace."

The sensitivity required for such a journey could only have been called forth and nurtured by women—who, out of their own wounds from men, understood all too well that the alienated, violent male is not in fact a real man, but rather, a frightened person. Much of what had passed for masculine strength—from muscles to missiles—was thereby revealed to us men as, instead, a frantic effort to mask our inner wounds and insecurities.

Insofar as we refused to confess our brokenness, we could only project it onto women, wounding and keeping them insecure. Since a man cannot recognize and respect the pains and longings of a woman—or any other person—until he becomes sensitive to his own, women began to cry out, "What can I do to help a man become softer, and more sensitive?"

As women urged us to "get in touch with your feelings," a whole new and glorious world opened in our masculine souls. With direction and encouragement from female mentors—often girlfriend, wife, or woman therapist—we learned at last without shame to cry, hold babies, cook, and even to encourage and nurture the woman in her life agendas.

When in 1973 pro football linebacker Roosevelt Grier wrote a book entitled *Rosy's Needlepoint for Men,*[2] clearly the times were a-changin'.

By the late 1970s and early '80s, however, we began to sense something was wrong—that, indeed, the forgotten masculine root could not be tapped in or among women. Poet Robert Bly, the grandfather of today's growing men's movement, declared that men had so well adapted our energies to the woman's needs—perhaps even as a little boy to his mother's—that we abdicated the vital but often difficult task of recognizing and pursuing our own needs. Catholic priest Father Richard Rohr, who lectures nationally on male spirituality, taught us that more is required of manhood than just being sensitive to others: we also need self-discipline, the courage to risk rejection by speaking the truth, and a readiness to accept individual and social responsibilities. Feminists acknowledged that they had wanted men to become sensitive, but not passive.

My own professional pursuits reflected graphically this ominous trend. As a pastor, I discovered that only about one-third of church members today are men; as a writer, that hardly 15 percent of my publisher's books are bought by men; as a counselor, that less than one-fifth of my clients were men.

Once, I called a large Christian radio show to host me as an author-guest and was connected to a female administrator. When she instructed me to send a copy of my book to their editorial staff, I noted that of course, I hoped a male staff member would review it. Immediately, she noted that they had no male editorial staff; furthermore, if the material in my book was not wholly understandable to women, I would not be considered for the show, since the majority of their listeners were women.

As virulently as we rejected the traditional macho image, as righteously as we fled from it to feminine models, we men clearly have found no new and appropriate masculine model to replace it. A generation of young men who built a lifestyle around challenging power and authority have grown up not only suspicious of it in others, but afraid to exercise it ourselves. We were so anxious to discern and reject a self-centered *authoritarian* spirit that we abdicated the essential life task of discerning and embracing a genuine *authoritative* spirit—as one called and gifted, humble yet deliberate.

Predictably, where godly models are not sought, demons rush into the vacuum. By the eighties, a progressively gory series of *Rambo* movies burst forth to proclaim the even more alienated, more violent "man." Their immense popularity seemed only to confirm the underlying hypothesis of the sixties' "liberation" movement, namely, that masculine strength is intrinsically destructive—and thus, to be scorned.

From a Christian view, however, such cinematic excess only confirms that the powers of the world, being divorced from the Creator God who alone defines a man, cannot redeem manhood in the image of the Creator—but can only distort it further in the image of the Destroyer.

The most sincere critics of male behavior have often failed to see that men have clung to the macho image and remained violent and alienated not because these traits define masculinity, but rather, because they mask an embarrassing wound in men today which crosses all socioeconomic, ethnic, and political boundaries.

That wound is caused by an epidemic alienation from the father, who is every man's masculine root in this world. This breach in the masculine soul is the gateway for destruction both in and through men today. The powers of the world, however, do not want to recognize it, because they have no power to heal it. The father-wound can only be healed by the One sent by the Father God to do just that, namely, Jesus, whom the world "did not recognize" (John 1:10).

In a word, the boy today has not bonded with Daddy. Lacking that essential external connection to the larger world of men cripples his identification with the masculine in himself; his masculine courage and strength, associated negatively with the absent or destructive father, focus negatively. Muscles designed to protect, serve, and uplift are wasted in fistfights, anesthetized by alcohol and drugs, or paralyzed by fear. Manly presence and its call to truth and accountability—from meeting the girlfriend's father to facing a congressional ethics committee—is often simply gone: the girlfriend's father may be lost to a TV ballgame or divorced and living elsewhere; the congressmen themselves may lack ethics.

"How many men today," Rohr laments, "can say like Jesus, 'I and the Father are one' (John 10:30 RSV)? Tragically, very, very few."[3]

In speaking to men's groups of all kinds—at a prestigious university alumni association downtown, an inner-city storefront church, a suburban middle-class church—I have discovered that inside every business suit, every pair of faded overalls, every stay-press sportshirt, lies the wounded heart of a boy longing for his daddy.

The man is hurt—and often, angry. As one burly, flannel-shirted contractor in his forties demanded at question time after a small-group sharing at my men's retreat, "I want to know: are us guys in our group just that off-base, or what? I mean, not one of us could name two positive things about our fathers!"

Thus, in a feature titled "How Fathers Figure," *Los Angeles Times Magazine* writer Paul Ciotti quotes clinical psychologist Ken Druck:[4] "I see many men walking around in mid-life with a sense of yearning for things that they can't get from their wives and can't get from their jobs and can't pull from inside themselves. Having listened to thousands of stories in workshops around the world, I'm convinced what the men are missing is a sense of their own identity: a very primitive and very deep sense of validation that passes from father to son."

"It's the basic plea of the male child," Ciotti concludes, quoting columnist Asa Baber, " 'Dad, show me how to be a man.' "

Every male child—now as always—longs to be one with his father, like Jesus with His Father God, and thus receive fatherly protection, affirmation, encouragement, affection, provision, guidance and strength. However painful or frightening, that longing in each man is the impetus to seeking and receiving the Father God's saving power. Every man must therefore recognize, confess, and deal with this need.

Unattended, the father-son wound can only become infected and, ultimately, destructive. Surrendered to Jesus, it becomes the avenue for knowing at last the true Father God of all men—and oneself as His beloved son.

That is, precisely at the point where his earthly father fails him, a boy/man is forced to seek and discover the Father God who fails no man. But, because this encounter is painful and thus fearful, most men avoid it—and thereby, avoid the Father God. The man's true self, which God created and now calls him to be, remains forever dormant and elusive.

The need for healing the father-son wound is the key to understanding the biblical faith. Thus, in the closing verses of the Hebrew Canon—the threshold of the New Covenant and springboard to the coming of the Messiah—God proclaims,

> But before the great and terrible day of the LORD comes, I will send you the prophet Elijah. He will bring fathers and children together again; otherwise I would have to come and destroy your country. (Mal. 4:5–6)

Every good Jew, including Jesus, knew these verses well, for they define the new Kingdom to be ushered in by the promised Christ. The focus of God's saving action in this world, the job of the Messiah, therefore, is to reconcile the broken relationship between fathers and children—which reflects the broken relationship between us adult children and our Father God.

Certainly, the biblical faith affirms the maternal character of God (see Ps. 131:2; Isa. 66:10–13; Matt. 23:37), who comprises both feminine and masculine (see Gen. 1:27). But men today need desperately to recognize, respect, and bond with the masculine dimension of God's character—which I call *Father God*.

Significantly, God does not proclaim, "When I reveal My saving purposes among you in the Messiah, at last you will see mothers back together with their children again!" In fact, mothers are already together with their children, and in most cases, far too much, because the father is not present and taking his proper responsibility for the children's emotional and spiritual welfare.

Indeed, as this text declares, when fathers are not together with their children according to God's will, powers of destruction are beckoned and a "curse" (RSV) is loosed on the land.

In a graphic instance, Richard Rohr tells of a nun friend working in a men's prison.[5] One spring, an inmate asked her to buy him a Mother's Day card to send home. She agreed, and word traveled fast; soon hundreds of inmates were asking for cards. Resourcefully, the nun contacted a greeting card manufacturer, who obliged with crates of Mother's Day cards, all of which she passed out.

Soon afterward, she realized Father's Day was approaching and, thinking ahead, she again called the card manufacturer, who responded quickly with crates of Father's Day cards. Years later, the nun told Rohr, she still has every one of them. Not one prisoner requested a card for his father.

Clearly, men in prison lack fathers. They therefore lack proper boundaries and the encouragement to channel their masculine energy creatively instead of destructively.

In another example, award-winning filmmaker and former college football player Robert Carmichael asks in a *Los Angeles Times* sports feature, "Is the Price Too High? Payment for Playing Football Can Be Debilitating Injuries, Lingering Physical Problems."[6] Suffering still-painful injuries from his thirteen-year playing career—including a cracked sternum, torn ligaments in his hip, shoulder, and neck, and a totally reconstructed knee—Carmichael at forty-two continues to require knee surgery and lives "in constant pain."

Amid detailing the destruction which football caused his body—unto its effects today on his children when he cannot run or play sports with them—Carmichael notes, "My father had been an athlete, and it was through sports that I won his approval and made him proud of me. It was our only common ground."

After years of Pop Warner football as a boy, in his high school junior year Carmichael began to realize the toll football was taking on his body, and thought of quitting. But he "couldn't face the shame of being a quitter. . . . When I told my father, he created a scene and bullied and shamed me into continuing. He didn't want a coward for a son."

I have no ax to grind against football itself. But I denounce any activity which becomes a desperate and enforced striving to win the earthly father's approval, because I know it must eventually lead a man away from the Father God and thus to destruction.

Prison inmates and crippled ex-football players such as Robert Carmichael are merely a fraction of the men who have been "caught" or disabled by the destructive power of the father-wound. For the vast majority of men in our society today are imprisoned and crippled by a condemning voice that tells us we do not measure up as men—thus haunting the vacuum left in the masculine soul by the absent father and will-o'-the-wisp community of men.

Indeed, his relationship with his father defines the first, most elementary masculine community for every boy; without that relationship, as today, the adult community of men simply will not exist, for the man has not been taught as a boy to anticipate and thus seek it.

Perhaps it is easier to repress the "memory" of something that never happened. One pastor I know started a church men's group and divided weekly discussion topics to include a discussion of fathers during one session and of mothers the next. "All of us were amazed at the radically different tone or spirit between those two nights," he reported. "The 'fathers' discussion was pretty sober and low-key, with some good ideas coming out, but basically a lot of head stuff. But during the time about mothers, guys were getting angry, crying, laughing, arguing. It was a different world from the week before."

He paused, knitting his brow. "I guess so much more came out about our mothers because there's more to respond to, since we just have a lot more interaction with them growing up."

To suppress, however, is not to forget. A boy may interact more often with his mother, but he still longs to be one with his father. Absence can kill. Indeed, a plant may be destroyed not only by squashing it, but also by not watering it.

I saw most clearly the boy's impetus to bond with the father when a good friend invited me to his home for a dinner party. After dinner, the dozen-or-so adults were enjoying a lively game of "Pictionary"—a visual charades that requires a picture drawing board.

While my friend's eighteen-month-old son was playing off to the side by himself, the guessing became so animated that several of us were standing up. Unable to see the picture board, my friend took off his shoes and hopped up onto the couch behind us. For several minutes, he bounced from one side of the couch to the other, trying to glimpse the game board, until finally one person guessed correctly. A cheer went up, and we retired to the kitchen for refreshments.

As we left the room, a guest turned and exclaimed to my friend, "Hey, would you look at your crazy boy!"

We all looked, and were startled to see this little fellow—eye-level with the couch—muscling himself up onto the cushions. Once there, wobbling, he righted himself, hopped several times, dropped to all fours, crawled to the other side of the couch, stood, and hopped again.

"How about that!" another man exclaimed, teasing my friend as his son went back and forth across the couch, crawling, standing, hopping, dropping. "What in the world is he doing?"

We all laughed—until one woman spoke up. "I know what he's doing. He's just doing what his daddy did!"

My jaw fell in amazement—as did my friend's.

Certainly, no one had instructed the boy to climb up onto the couch. Indeed, he did not have enough language ability to understand such an instruction. Something preverbal, even primal, had been sparked.

Even if he could have understood, it would have made no sense to tell the boy, "But the game is finished." For the ultimate Game—the focus of the male child's energy and attention to be one with the father—is never finished.

Indeed, if the boy had been asked, "Why are you doing that?" he most likely would have proclaimed simply—with no trace of apology—"Because Daddy did it." Because that, for any son, is enough.

It was enough for Jesus:

What I say . . . is what the Father has told me to say. . . . I love the Father; that is why I do everything as he commands me. (John 12:50b; 14:31)

Similarly, after a visit from his father broke a frustrating slump, tennis star Michael Chang declared, "My dad knows my game inside and out. He knows my weaknesses and strengths. Basically, everything I do is what he has instructed me to do. He knows how to correct me, how to get my timing back. He knows my game really well. Lots of times I can call him up and say, 'My forehand isn't smooth,' and he already knows it."[7]

Such is the Father God, who already knows our weaknesses, strengths, and needs and comes to save us unto victory when at last we surrender and call Him.

When Jesus talks with His disciples the night before His death, telling them that He is the only way to the Father, Philip speaks for the other men in response: "Lord, show us the Father; that is all we need" (John 14:8).

Of all the wondrous powers they might ask Jesus to demonstrate and impart before leaving them—to heal, teach, exorcise, correct the Pharisees—the men want finally only one thing, the bottom line of all power, of life itself: to bond with the Father.

Jesus' response to Philip heralds the fulfillment of God's promise in the final verses of the Old Covenant. For if God's ultimate saving act, proclaimed in Malachi 4:5–6, is to bring fathers and children together, we should expect that Jesus, the anointed Savior, would literally embody father and child as one. And indeed, when the men ask for the Father as sufficient to their every need, Jesus is amazed—if not dismayed:

> "For a long time I have been with you all; yet you do not know me, Philip? Whoever has seen me has seen the Father. Why, then, do you say, 'Show us the Father'? Do you not believe, Philip, that I am in the Father, and the Father is in me?" (John 14:9–10a)

Men today who long for their true Father, therefore, must begin to know Jesus—personally, deeply, truly. This is the healing which no other remedy can offer men, no matter how understanding, compassionate, or even spiritual.

For Jesus is the way to the Father (see John 14:6). A man who wants a higher position in the company must see the manager; the one who wants the ladies' attention must see the woman. But the man who wants the Father must see Jesus. Other spiritualities may bring a man to a particular standard of morality, enlightenment, or knowledge. But only Jesus can bring him to the Father.

Tragically, this has not been recognized in many churches today, where too often men hide from the Father—and thereby, hide from true manhood—rather than meet and surrender to Him. In fact, churches are too often run by men who seek the appearance of well-being as a way to avoid facing and dealing with their painful father-wound. Regardless of its theology, therefore, the church has offered men not healing, but anesthesia.

And so most men turn instead to the world, whose painkillers are more polished and effective. A TV ball game and a beer readily make a man forget his inadequacies and longing for a father; a church where people talk about a Father God, but never talk honestly with Him or each other, only exacerbates the wound.

Male leaders in the liberal/mainline churches, afraid of oppressing women, have abandoned men and self-righteously abdicated to secular universalism. "I'm not like other men," the "liberal male" would have us believe—and he bonds with many feminists who as wounded daughters are equally anxious to avoid the pain of their own father-longing. That is, he hides from his father-wound behind the women—even as a boy hides from a hurtful father behind his mother—and rejects the Father God as "sexist."

Male leaders in the conservative churches, on the other hand, afraid of being oppressed by women, have rendered the Father God so particularly masculine as largely to discount women—thereby losing the more feminine characteristics of mercy, compassion, and grace, which are so essential to the character of God and the biblical faith.

"I'm not like women," the conservative male would have us believe. Then he hides his pain by proclaiming a Father God tailored to his own, exclusively male image.

Whether liberal or conservative, the man in church today has lacked a father to call him away from the mother, to protect the boy's fragile sense of masculinity long enough for him to grow and individuate as a man. The liberals give up on the father altogether and meld with the "gentler" matriarchal view; the conservatives grasp rigid patriarchal structures as a surrogate father.

Meanwhile, the crippling father-wound cries out from a generation of men (and women), only to be muffled by shouts designed to avoid meeting the true Father God. "Inclusive language!" cries the Left; "Scriptural language!" cries the Right—while, deep in the masculine soul of all, in the simple language of the human heart, a little boy whimpers, "Daddy?"

And nobody in church listens. Therefore, the man himself is afraid to.

Nobody, that is, except Jesus—who may Himself weep for the man, but does not rush to eradicate his pain. For Jesus respects men enough to wait on our own will.

When a man finally reaches toward the Father, however, the great "liberal/conservative" theological debate is revealed as a sham, a conspiracy of the flesh in both camps, designed to avoid the humbling, terrifying surrender required for relationship with the Father.

The problem with the classical liberal/conservative polarization is not that it separates us from each other, but that it separates us from Jesus, and thus, from the Father—who alone can overcome our carnal differences and bring us into true fellowship as His children.

A man on his knees, confessing and crying out to Jesus his true and painful longing for a father, is simply too engaged with reality to indulge theological/political fabrications. Indeed, a man surrendered to the

—11—

Father God is, by definition, like Jesus: neither oppressive of nor oppressed by women, but rather, freed at last to be a true and manly son—which includes bearing the Father's heart for His daughters as well as for himself as a son.

"Lord, show us the Father." This is the ultimate cry of the human spirit, revealing the painful truth about ourselves as men today which political or theological differences can obscure and postpone, but never obviate.

Certainly, the Malachi text does not focus on sons alone. The term "children" includes daughters as well. But I focus herein on sons, because only sons grow up to be fathers and are thus called to such awesome accountability. If the boys are healed, they will become healthy fathers, and in the next generation we shall see healing for their daughters as well as their sons.

Furthermore, while the wound between fathers and daughters is quite real, painful, and destructive, daughters are statistically less likely to grow up and, for example, start wars, molest children, buy pornography, or promote racism and sexism. The wounds of the male child are more likely to manifest in pathogenic social patterns.

This all-important role of the father has been underscored in an increasing number of psychological studies which conclude that "it is the father who is the primary influence regarding sex roles for both boys and girls."[8] That is, the father not only calls forth masculinity in the boy, but femininity in the girl as well.

Genetics confirms this. The human sex chromosome has two components: the male, an "x-y," and the female, an "x-x." Only the male parent, therefore, can contribute a variation, since both the mother's components are the same "x." When the egg is fertilized, the mother's "x" is always the first component; if the father's sperm gives an "x," then the child is "x-x" and a daughter; if his sperm gives a "y," the child is an "x-y," a son.

It's easier to understand the father's confirming sexual identity in the son, the same-sex child. But women across the country have told me that, on reaching puberty, they looked to their fathers to confirm their femininity.

I once ministered to a woman who experienced persistent anxiety when dating. After several sessions, I had found no particular trauma with men in her past. When finally we prayed and asked Jesus to come with the Father's Spirit of knowledge, wisdom, and healing, she sat quietly, and then knit her brow.

"I remember when I was about fifteen and had my first date," she said finally. "He'd called me the week before, and I'd been in a fuss for days getting a new dress with my baby-sitting money, a new hairdo and everything. That Saturday night, he was coming over to pick me up at 8:00. I was all ready by 7:00, and decided to go downstairs to the living room and let Dad see me.

"I remember going into the living room, and Dad was behind his newspaper, pretty much as always. I ruffled my dress, sat down, got up, went out to the kitchen, even dropped a plastic cup. But Dad just sat there.

"Finally, the doorbell rang. My heart was racing. Was my hair okay? What about my dress? I turned to Dad, but he was still behind his newspaper. The bell kept ringing, so I went and opened the door. 'I'm going out now!' I called to Dad. 'Okay,' he said, still behind his [expletive] newspaper. Feeling nervous and awkward, I turned and walked out the door."

Noting that her memory was sparked after we asked Jesus for help, I encouraged her to hold the memory of standing in the living room all dressed up, with her father behind his newspaper, and to ask Jesus to be there with her.

As I prayed quietly in support, praising the Father God and surrendering to Jesus, she reported that she could sense Jesus present in that living room.

"Is Jesus doing anything?" I asked, careful always to give Him free hand to lead in all things.

"No," she replied. "He's just standing there with me. I feel a sort of peace . . . but I'm still upset with my dad."

Since Jesus had appeared, clearly He wanted something to happen. But since He was choosing not to act Himself, I invited her to trust in His comfort and strength, and at last speak out her true feelings to her father.

Hesitantly, she took a deep breath. "Dad," she said, "I . . . I'm going out on a date soon and . . . I'm nervous. . . . I'm scared, Dad. . . ." She paused, and took another breath. Then it all poured out.

"Dad! Look at me, Dad!" she shouted. "Dad, I need you to look at me! Tell me I look okay, Dad! Tell me I'm okay! Why do you think I'm so bad to look at, Dad? Dad . . ." Her voice trailing off, she fell sobbing into her hands.

Moments later, I invited her to ask Jesus to do whatever He wanted in this scene. She did, and told me this:

"Jesus walks over to my dad and puts a hand on his shoulder. Dad drops his newspaper, looks at Jesus, and then looks at me. 'I'm sorry, Sally,' he says. 'It's not that I think you look bad, but that you look so good it makes me scared. You used to be a nice little girl and now . . . you're a real woman.'

"Dad's smiling now. 'And a beautiful woman, Sally,' he says. Oh, and he really means it! 'A beautiful woman, and you'll make some man very, very happy some day. I'm sorry I got scared and didn't tell you.' Oh, Dad . . . I forgive you!"

As Sally sat beaming, I prayed for Jesus to let this newly revealed truth set her free from her fear of looking bad to men, to heal where her earthly father's fear of her womanhood had wounded her feminine soul, and to pour out the love of the Father God upon her.

In the presence of Jesus, Sally could hear God speak His Father-heart of love and know at last the truth that would set her free as a woman. This is the bringing of fathers and children together as prophesied at the end of the Old Testament. The healing of men, to becoming godly fathers of daughters as well as sons, is therefore a clear priority on God's agenda, if not the major focus of His ministry in Jesus.

Once, just before teaching at a denominational conference, a participant rushed over to me and blurted out, "Quick! In ten seconds, tell me: What's your teaching about?"

"You have a Father who loves you," I replied, "and He's come in Jesus to show you."

Only this Father God can shape us into the authentic men and women we were created to be. His endless love for us is the essential kernel of old grain, the great truth that every human being, because of our spiritual/genetic makeup as children of the Father God, knows deep in his—or her—soul.

But we have forgotten.

We have eaten the new grain offered by powers that would keep us feeling unloved and thus, dependent upon the world for painkillers and counterfeits—from drugs and sex to fame and fortune.

I respectfully leave it to women themselves to articulate their father-wound and their relationship with the Father God who would heal them.

Meanwhile, what women can do to make men stronger was unwittingly shown me by the instructor where my wife and I took dance lessons recently. "The dance happens as two partners each do their parts in harmony," he explained at the first lesson. "Though the man 'leads' and the woman 'follows,' if the dance is to be successful, the woman must keep her own balance, know the steps well herself, and maintain her own center. She cannot lean on the man to do it for her, nor can she push him."

I believe that today a woman can follow a man's lead, but she cannot teach him to dance. She can recognize, and in that limited sense, confirm a man's strength, but she cannot make him stronger. Only the Father God can do that, through fellowship with other men who have surrendered to Him. As men, we must therefore begin to let the Father strengthen us by surrendering to Him and to one another.

But how can we men remember—and in that sense, know at last—the Father from whom we come, in whom we become true men?

Why, indeed, did Jesus call God His "Father"? He could have said, "Mother," "Brother," "Sister," "Friend," "Higher Power," "Life," or a host of other names. But of all recognizable relationships and concepts on earth, He chose "Father."

Why? What characteristic of God does the male parent bear so essentially, that his relationship to his children becomes the fulcrum of the biblical faith, upon which hinges God's ultimate saving action in this world?

We men are far too wounded, too alienated, and therefore, too engaged in bearing the prophesied curse of destruction to the land, to waste our time and energies hiding from God and this question. Neither "liberal/universal" substitutes such as "A Higher Power," nor "conservative/religious" substitutes such as "Just read the Bible," can heal the terrible brokenness we men bear today. Both are necessary, but not sufficient. We need The Highest Power. And indeed, Jimmy Swaggart, like the Pharisees, knows the Bible well—but he, like many other men less famous but equally wounded and alone, fell.

What Philip declared to Jesus two thousand years ago is true today. Men want to see the Father. Only relationship with the Father God will suffice our terrible need as men in our families, in the church, in this world.

To allow God to meet that need, we must resist the parallel temptations either to speculate about the future or to reminisce about the "good old days." Rather, we must begin to sift the past for signs of the living Father God at work.

We must heed the Father's ancient call in Deuteronomy and dare to tell the story, even our own stories. For our lives, our survival, are at stake. The curse of destruction among and through us broken men is well at hand.

But where, without fathers and old men, do we begin?

Where, indeed, if not by remembering?

CHAPTER TWO

Seeking the Brown Ooze

What does a boy uniquely gain from having a father present that men today must remember? Apart from such "manly" skills as business, carpentry, and auto repair—which a knowledgeable mother might teach equally as well—what does the male parent communicate or impart to the male child that the female parent cannot?

The most intriguing answer came to me after a long session of prayer and healing with a thirty-year-old man whose father had severely rejected him. "Sure, Dad hurt me terribly at times," he sighed. "But I remember once, when my brother and I were about six and four, sitting on the bed with Dad, one of us under each of his arms as he told us a bedtime story.

"I don't remember what the story was, but I'll never forget feeling there was something different about him that I'd never felt from Mom—something hard to describe, but definitely masculine, like a kind of brown ooze coming out of him and going into us little boys."

Fascinating! I thought—then wondered: *Where have I experienced the "brown ooze" myself?*

Praying later, I thought of years ago, when I was a small boy and my father was a Navy officer stationed aboard a ship. When the fleet went to sea, I missed Dad as deeply as I rejoiced on seeing him in his khaki uniform open the door, squat down with arms open, and call to me, "I'm home! How's my boy?" Heart racing, I sprinted to him and threw my arms tightly around his neck as he lifted me high off the ground in his secure embrace.

Once, to my wonder and delight, he pulled from his huge uniform pocket a blue and yellow Captain Marvel T-shirt, just for me.

To that little boy, the Lord's return could not have been more glorious.

When finally my sisters and I gave him a chance, he set his hat on the table and embraced Mother—whereupon I turned with awe and approached the table reverently, to do what my mother and sisters could not. Slowly, with both hands, I lifted The Hat. As if to crown myself, I angled its thick band and strong, hard visor sharply off my forehead and down the back of my neck; otherwise, laid squarely on my head, it covered my face down to my chin. In the embrace, in The Hat, I was one with my father—certified as a man-to-be, anointed with the brown ooze.

In later reading Robert Bly, I found this notion aptly portrayed:

> When a father and son do spend long hours together . . . we could say that a substance almost like food passes from the older body to the younger. . . . The son's body—not his mind—receives and the father gives this food at a level far below consciousness. The son does not receive a hands-on healing, but a body-on healing. His cells receive some knowledge of what an adult masculine body is. The younger body learns at what frequency the masculine body vibrates. It begins to grasp the song that adult male cells sing. . . .[1]

I especially looked forward as a boy to my father's taking me to the barbershop—the one place in town where only males went.

I remember the circular red, white, and blue pole turning out front, and asking my father how the stripes came out of the bottom of the pole and disappeared into the top. His explanation eluded me, and it remained a humbling mystery to me—like the fellowship of men inside.

There, surrounded by walls covered with high school football schedules and large photographs of fish and game birds between the mirrors, we would take turns approaching The Chair. Significantly, this was no flimsy aluminum perch as in today's salons, but might more properly be called a throne. Its huge ceramic armrests, thick leather padding, and heavy steel rim frame beckoned each man. When my dad arose from his cut, Sam would whip-crack hair from the white bib-cape, call out my name, and reach for the "boost plank"—a leather-covered piece of wood laid across the arms to seat small boys, whose heads otherwise would not extend above the chair back for cutting.

I always sat on the plank, until one day—a day etched deeply on my heart, though the memory remained dormant for almost forty years— Sam cracked the cape, called my name, reached for the plank as usual, and then paused strangely. "Wait a minute there, son," he said, and turned to my father.

Puzzled, I stopped in front of The Chair and looked up uneasily at these two giant men towering above me—the very men, in fact, who had the power to name and define me as a male. At three feet tall below two six-foot men, I felt then as I might today if standing, at almost six feet myself, below two twelve-foot men.

As I stood powerless and waiting in this land of giants, one—the guardian of the male place in the village, spoke to the other—the namesake guardian of my male heritage.

"I do believe this boy's growin' up," Sam declared to my father, who nodded in agreement. With a hint of ceremony, Sam turned and replaced the boost plank against the wall. "I don't think you'll be needin' this anymore." Matter-of-factly, he whisked his barber brush crisply over the broad leather seat and stood back. "You get right on up here now, son," he proclaimed.

Awestruck, I looked high above at my father, who nodded.

Like mighty angels from heaven, those two giant men beckoned me, and without another thought, I climbed onto the heavy steel footrest and then scrambled up to the seat. Cracks in the old leather scratched my legs below my shorts, but all discomfort was lost in the wonder of that moment. And then, at last, I sat where my father sat—indeed, as men sit. Deliberately, I strained my neck and stretched my back as high as possible. Lifting my elbows gingerly to the thick ceramic armrests, I glanced in the mirror and basked in glory as there—behind and before me—sat my father, smiling proudly.

Remember the days of old. . . .

Days of barbershops . . . days of the father.

Too easily, we men forget the deep impact of such boyhood experiences, often discounting the father-son longing as mere childishness. Yet it persists into adulthood, and no worldly achievement as an adult can preclude it.

A few years ago in Los Angeles, the Dodgers celebrated a World Series victory. Though the major news stories focused on the triumphant team that wasn't supposed to win, a significant story highlighted Jose Canseco, star player for the opposition, who in his nineteen Series at-bats got only one hit: a grand-slam home run.

When interviewed afterward, Canseco—with forty home runs and forty stolen bases, the millionaire muscleman at twenty-four and hero of men around the country—told a *Los Angeles Times* sportswriter how it felt to get this, his first grand slam. This one was for Jose's father.

"My dad was here today," Canseco said. "Of all the power hitters we've got in Oakland, I'm the only one who's never hit a grand slam. My father's always telling me, 'When you gonna hit one? When you gonna hit one?' 'Sure, Dad, I'll hit one tonight.' When I hit it, the first thing that went through my mind was, 'Grand slam, national TV, my father's here to see it, I'm covered.'"[2]

Lord, show us the Father; that is all we need.

The longing to be one with the father is intrinsic to masculinity. No universalistic sympathy or legalistic command can erase or fulfill it. If the father-son longing is not recognized, confessed, and submitted to the Father God through Jesus, a man's soul remains wounded unto death. He either surrenders to it and idolizes his father as a god, or curses it and condemns him as a demon. Caught in such extremes, he is thus denied genuine relationship with the father, and with himself as a man.

In either case, the earthly father remains the fixed standard which dictates the man's life responses—whether positively or negatively—and the unique person the Father God calls the man to be is lost, either in running after or away from the earthly father.

That is, a man may ape his father's lifestyle and values in an effort to win the father's approval. Ultimately, this retreat from his true and higher self into comparing himself against the father condemns him never to measure up as a man, simply because he is not his father, never can be, and has not been called to be.

In the other extreme, the man may sense his inner longing for his father, but find it too painful to confess and pursue. Perhaps the father wounded him especially deeply as a boy. Often in such cases, the son rebels, desperately trying to cut himself off from his father and thus, the associated pain. But this, too, ultimately leads the man to a lie, for he is his father's son.

Furthermore, the man who curses his father instead of surrendering his pain to Jesus for truth, forgiveness, and redemption, curses the preface to his own manhood. Thus, he cannot embrace and celebrate its unfolding as an adult. Indeed, whatever of his father he shuns or denies, and thereby consigns to the darkness, becomes a foothold for the powers of darkness to rule him subconsciously.

Frank, a fifty-five-year-old man married with several grandchildren, came to me for help, noting that he had been a practicing homosexual until becoming a Christian several years earlier. He had recently taken a new job which required considerable travel, and being alone on the road was beckoning many old sexual temptations.

I suggested to Frank that God might be allowing such temptations as a call to seek deeper healing, now possible with his firmer grounding in several years of faithful sexuality. With no further preconception, I invited him in faith to confess his powerlessness, surrender his fears to Jesus, and ask the Holy Spirit to surface and heal any deeper wounds. As he did so, I prayed quietly in support.

"This is weird," Frank said after a moment's silence, "but for some reason, I've got in my head a scene from when I was a boy, maybe five or six."

Reminding him that we had just asked the Holy Spirit to bring up whatever might be necessary, I encouraged Frank to tell me about the scene.

"Dad was yelling at Mom," he began, "in the dining room. I was off to the side, terrified. He wasn't hitting her, but he was yelling so loud she was holding up her hands as if he might hit her."

"Let your Father God be with you," I said. "Call on Jesus."

Frank prayed quietly. "Yes, Jesus is there with me now."

"What's Jesus doing?" I asked.

"Wow! He's picking me up . . . and holding me against His chest. He's strong and He's just . . . holding me against His chest."

"Let Him," I offered simply, and prayed quietly in joyful agreement for several minutes as Frank rested gloriously in the arms of Jesus, and thus, of his Father God. Then I invited him to ask Jesus if He wanted to do anything more.

Frank prayed further, then shook his head. "I don't know if Jesus is saying anything, but it's like there's still something jumpy inside me when I'm around my father."

"As long as you're securely in Jesus' arms," I suggested, "why don't you just go ahead and speak out to your father there in the dining room as he yells at your mother? Tell your father honestly how he makes you feel."

Hesitantly at first, then with growing confidence, Frank spoke up. "Daddy . . . please stop yelling like that. . . . You scare me, Daddy . . . stop . . . stop! Stop yelling, Daddy! Would you just stop yelling and just . . . just . . ." Frank's voice trailed off. "Just . . . hold me, Daddy . . .?"

Suddenly, a flood of tears burst forth, and at last, in the secure arms of his Father God, fifty years of pent-up longing poured out as Frank continued between sobs to beg his earthly father, "just hold me, Daddy . . . please . . . just hold me. . . ."

Later, as we asked Jesus to complete this work, Frank began to sense that in such rage against his mother, his father was acting like his grandfather, out of wounds never submitted to Jesus, but simply repeated down the generations from father to son. This sense brought Frank to compassion for his father, and ultimately, forgiveness.

Eventually, Frank realized that he had bonded in sympathy with his mother against his violent father. He hereby identified wholly with femininity and rejected masculinity. Thus, he had yielded readily when his wife resisted any masculine assertiveness in him. In fact, he had vowed, "I don't want to be a man"—that is, "like my father."

I led Frank in a prayer to renounce this curse against himself and claim instead the Father God's blessing of godly manhood. I prayed aloud that God would seal in Frank's heart the "memory" of being held as a boy with Father-love in Jesus' arms. I asked God to teach Frank to love his wife with the strength of his convictions as well as the tenderness of his heart. I prayed for such a trust in the Father God that he need no longer fear the woman as one keeping him from his manhood, as his mother had protected him from his father.

Finally, when Jesus held Frank the boy against His chest, Frank the man saw graphically that his longtime "sexual desire" for other men was, in reality, the boy's frustrated natural longing to be one with the father, in Daddy's arms. That is, the pain associated with closeness to the father was too much for the boy himself to face and bear, so his father-longing had to be suppressed. Unable to focus properly on Daddy, his longing became distorted and misfocused on other men in homosexual fantasies.

When he finally trusted Jesus enough to protect him *in* that pain—not necessarily from it—Frank could surrender in faith. This allowed the Father God to remind him in Jesus of what he had longed for his earthly father to do, namely, to hold him. The distortion then became unnecessary, and Frank could let the Father God begin to shape him as a real man—that is, one who walks in truth, in full awareness of his deepest feelings.

After allowing the Father God such full rein to heal deeply in Frank, I could at last pray according to 2 Peter 1:3–9 for his enduring victory against sexual temptation and his enjoying full relationship with his wife.

Frank continues at times to struggle with sexual temptation and is still learning to affirm his masculinity. But he has reached the legitimate and basic goal of Christian counseling: He knows whose he is. He has come to realize that life in this broken world is a struggle, and he has chosen to struggle with the Father God after righteousness rather than against Him in sin.

The question, then, is not "Can homosexuals change?"[3] but rather, "Can God change homosexuals?" If not, we worship a cruel God indeed, who commands certain behavior without providing the power to practice it.

From this perspective, those who affirm homosexual acts have a stake in keeping men broken. Nobody—neither men nor women— wants to face the painful father-wound. If a man acting out homosexually decides to stop and face that wound in himself, then the rest of us must stop our own denial and face whatever compulsive behavior it has prompted in ourselves. As long as we can keep men acting out homosexually—whether we cheer them on from the Left with "Gay Pride" parades and denominational "statements of affirmation," or curse and thus bind them in sin from the Right—we never have to recognize the awful father-wound in ourselves. Thus, we never meet the true Father God.

The burgeoning gay movement reflects graphically an entire society's conspiracy to deny the truth of our deepest inner pain and longing—our willingness even to bind others in compulsive behaviors in an effort to avoid facing our own.

Indeed, this denial recalls the Malachi 4:5–6 "curse" from broken relationship with the father—which is therefore overcome not by further cursing or denial, but only by returning to the true Father.

Obviously, although all men suffer from the father-wound, not all act out homosexually. In fact, most of the men out of that lifestyle I have ministered to were molested or seriously abused as boys by older men— who thereby took advantage of that wound in the boy. We respond differently to the wound, according to our circumstances.

Here we must understand: The father-wound is intrinsic to life in this broken world. Therefore, it must be recognized and treated deliberately, with both compassion and diligence. I recognize and celebrate that some men today have had better relationships with their fathers than others have had. But no matter how good his relationship with his father, the man who has not dared confess the father-wound within himself has not responded fully to the Father God's call in Jesus to godly manhood.

For Jesus came to restore relationship with the Father.

The man who has confessed honestly his longing for a healed relationship with the father will welcome and proclaim Jesus. The man who flees from the pain of his father-wound will find ample means of avoiding Jesus—from regimented religion to alcohol.

That is, the earthly father is not the heavenly Father, and thus, must at some point disappoint and wound the son. If this were not true, a man would never need Jesus, for the earthly father would suffice.

The natural man, separated from the Father God, can only deny that pain or rage against it. He thereby condemns himself to hold the god-or-demon view of his earthly father. He lives forever alienated not only from his father, but from his own intended manhood in the Creator/Father God as well.

The man of the Spirit, however, knows that the work and character of God in this present age is, by the power of the Holy Spirit, humbly to bring the self-centered flesh to death in ultimate surrender—thereby enabling a man to cry "Abba, Father" to God (see Rom. 8:14–16). Thus, the man of God confesses his longing to be one with his earthly father, while recognizing the latter's human shortcomings and his own pain which that causes. Instead of either yielding himself to or rebelling against his earthly father, he takes his longing to the cross, yields himself there to Jesus and confesses his wound, pouring out his pain. There, at last, he can begin to meet and be shaped by the Father God into his true and intended manhood. Indeed, by the light of the Spirit's truth, a man can discover his wounds to be his father's, and, by the Spirit's compassion, he can forgive—and truly let go of his pain.

In surrendering to the living Christ and not to his earthly father or his own natural, rebellious self, a man discovers that his father-longing, which no human father can fulfill, beckons not hopelessness and death but true life. It calls him out at last from the world's compliance/rebellion cycle into the arms of the heavenly Father.

I learned this truth in ministering to Lewis, a thirty-five-year-old man whose wife had been committing adultery and whose professional life was in shambles. As we talked, he clearly lacked any positive sense of himself—to a pathological degree that suggested his current problems were not the cause, but rather, the effects of that lack. Uncertain how to proceed, I prayed with him, calling on the Holy Spirit as Counselor to show us any root wounds.

Lewis soon reported that he had an image in his mind of a fishing rod, but nothing more. Stepping out on faith, I invited him to thank God for showing us that, and ask Jesus to show him more. Soon Lewis also saw a reel. Again, he thanked God and gave Jesus permission to show him still more. Eventually, after several such prayers—the Father goes slowly and gently where pains are deep—a full image emerged of himself as an eight-year-old boy fishing with his alcoholic father in a small rowboat.

At last, Lewis remembered trying unsuccessfully to put a squiggly worm on his hook as his father yelled, "You're doing it all wrong, you dummy! Can't you do anything right?"

I urged Lewis to call upon Jesus to be with him in that boat as the true Father God's presence. Out of that security, I urged Lewis to tell his drunken earthly father how he felt in that rowboat.

"Stop yelling at me, Dad!" he shouted. "When you put me down like that I feel like I'm nothing but a worm myself, Dad. You just crush me inside, so I feel worthless and unable to do anything for myself."

This was the burden Lewis had carried into his adult self-image.

When he had released his anger at last and spoken the most immediate level of truth to his earthly father, I invited him to seek the deepest truth by asking Jesus to show him his father with God's eyes.

"Lord, show me Dad the way you see him," Lewis prayed—then suddenly dropped his head into his hands and began sobbing. He cried for several minutes and then said, "When I asked to see my father with God's eyes, all of a sudden I saw a little boy on crutches, and somehow I just knew that was my father—a broken, crippled little boy—and I remembered how Granddad had pretty much put him down the same way he's done to me. I guess . . . I just felt all my dad's pain somehow."

"And that," I noted, "had become your pain, too—until you released it just now to the Father God."

By definition, a boy cries *from* his father's wounds, that is, from wounds which the father inflicts upon the boy, as in a spanking. A man, however, cries *for* his father's wounds, that is, compassionately, for the wounds which his father bears.

The man who dares to withhold judgment and retaliation long enough to see his father as God sees him—in the full truth of the father's brokenness—can begin to see his own wounds as, in fact, his father's wounds passed down to him. He can then bear those wounds to Jesus, thereby ensuring that he does not pass them down yet another generation to his own son.

The man is thus freed no longer to worship the earthly father as a god or curse him as a demon, but at last to love him as a man, in full and realistic view of his strengths and shortcomings, without expecting or demanding that he change.

Furthermore, the man can then decide to affirm the good in his father, accept and forgive the bad, and begin treating himself—and his own son—with that same mercy.

Clearly, this entire process requires the man's trust in Jesus, namely, that the Father God is real, present, caring, and powerful enough to know and meet his needs. Often, however, such trust is hindered precisely by the man's experience with his earthly father. That is, the man projects onto the Father God the very character traits of his earthly father which inhibit relationship.

As Christian counselors John and Paula Sandford note,

> People have many times come to us saying, "Don't talk to me about a loving God. Why doesn't He stop all the wars, or at least prevent some of the bestial things men do to men, sometimes in the very name of religion? Or doesn't He care?" Paula and I never try to defend God. We avoid theological debates (1 Tim. 6:20). We know the answer is not a mental one, but it is a matter of an impure heart. We merely ask, "What was your father like?" Invariably we uncover a history similar to what the counselee has imputed to God—cruelty, insensitivity, desertion, criticism, etc. No matter what the mind may learn in Sunday school of a gentle and loving God . . . the heart has been scarred and shaped by reactions to the earthly father, and projects that onto God. Not until such people forgive their natural fathers can they in fact see God as gentle and kind, lovingly present for them.[4]

If I ask a man, "How's your relationship with God?" all too often, he replies, "God's out there with other people, but He's not here with me." When I then ask, "How close was your father to you?" in nearly every case I hear stories of how "Dad was never there for me."

Christian psychologist Paul Vitz, in a teaching entitled "The Psychological Roots of Atheism," declares that when the father is not present, the child naturally concludes there is no God.[5]

For many men, talking directly to God honestly and openly, expressing anger as well as joy, is uncomfortable and even frightening, because they have never dared talk that way with their earthly fathers. Again, I often hear men say after some misfortune or tragedy, "I guess God's paying me back for the times when I sinned." Such a punitive view of God prompts me to ask, "How did your father discipline you as a boy?" Predictably, the man reports harsh punishments.

The most common false views of God's character—that He is absent, distant, harsh, unapproachable, uncaring, weak—can often be traced to corresponding images of the man's earthly father.

I have prayed with men whose fathers were harshly punitive, and when the man called upon Jesus in a particular memory, He not only held the boy, but restrained the father, took him aside, and essentially taught him how to act properly as a father.

John, for example, found it difficult at forty-four to let go and enjoy life. He was often accused by those close to him of being a "wet blanket." As we talked, clearly John associated having fun with fear, even condemnation. When we prayed, the Holy Spirit recalled to him a scene at age three, when a playmate had suggested they climb up onto the family car and dance on the hood. John's father saw the boys, came out, and spanked John harshly.

When John invited Jesus into that scene, Jesus went to the father and demanded he stop hitting the boy, explaining, "He's just a child and doesn't understand." In the prayer, John then felt encouraged to speak out. He told his father, "I was just having fun and didn't know it was bad. Don't hit me so much, Daddy! I feel like you'll never love me ever again!"

Eventually in the prayer-vision, the father broke down and told John how as a child his own father had beaten him and given him no understanding. With that, John could forgive his father and pray for him to be healed of the father-son wound that made him act so harshly. After that encounter, John no longer associated having fun with the father's disapproval. He no longer needed to disapprove of fun, and could give himself—and others—permission to enjoy life. Finally, Deuteronomy 14:22–26 and Matthew 11:19 helped John see that his heavenly Father is no killjoy, but indeed, likes His children to have fun.

Obviously, Jesus had not totally restrained John's father years before, or John wouldn't have had any painful memories later. But that does not mean the vision was false, any more than a dream can be discounted just because it portrays something that didn't "actually happen." Rather, in such a prayer Jesus portrays appropriately the character of the true heavenly Father—in John's case, as Protector and Advocate. This encouraged John to be his true self at last, to speak out his feelings, and to know the ultimate truth about his father needed to set him free from his fears and resentments. Jesus was not changing past events, but witnessing to a deeper truth in vision form, perhaps as a dream.

Still a man might ask, "But why didn't Jesus restrain my father back then—as the vision demonstrates He wanted to? Why did He allow me to be hurt so badly?"

Perhaps God allows evil so we will be motivated to seek and know Him—even as John saw his Father God's character distinctly different from his earthly father's when he invited Jesus into his pain. How is a man to know the Father God is powerful, unless or until he cries out for Him in his own weakness?

Certainly, the biblical faith understands that we live in a broken world. On the Cross, God says clearly that His sons are stung by the world's brokenness, but never abandoned to it. Indeed, precisely insofar as we surrender to Jesus in the grip of that brokenness, we come to know the Father's true power to save and renew us unto life eternal.

Richard Rohr offers the hypothesis that on the Cross Jesus experienced the father-wound, insofar as His Father God subjected Him there to the wounding of the world. The Savior of a broken world must meet that world in its brokenness.

Beckoning men of all times, Jesus' surrendering His father-wound on the Cross drew Him to His Father God—and thus, into fulfilling His created purpose.

At his best, then, the earthly father models fragments of the Father God's character, prompting the son to want forever from the Father God what Dad has offered for a season. Whatever the earthly father's behavior, we see the heavenly Father's character and desire for us in Jesus—who has respectfully given us free will to reject Him. And we may trust that our surrendering to His mercy and grace will produce His character in us and in other men.

I saw a graphic example of Jesus' demonstrating His will through a man to correct another man as father, almost exactly as in the prayer vision above.

I had just stepped outside my office for a stretch one afternoon when I was startled to hear an angry shout.

"Who the [expletive] do you think you are!" I turned and looked out to the street, where one man was shouting loudly as he shook his fist and strode threateningly toward another, standing an arm's length from an old car with its hood raised. "Shut up and get the [expletive] out of here and mind your own business or I'll beat the [expletive] out of you!"

"Tell him off!" a female voice screamed. I turned and saw behind him a woman grasping the hand of a young boy about three, whose face was awash with tears. Uncertain—fearful of violence, but knowing there was no time to call the police—I eased toward the men and stood by the curb praying, unnoticed by either.

Standing his ground in the face of the other's fury, the second man reached out both his arms, turning his palms down. "Just calm down and get ahold of yourself," he said. "I know you're upset, or you wouldn't have been doing that to your boy."

Eyes blazing and fists raised, the first man stopped several feet from the other. "I told you to shut up and get out of here!"

"Believe me, I wouldn't even be here if my car hadn't broken down," the second man said. "But I told you to stop, because hitting and yank-

Father and Son

ing on your boy like that can really hurt him bad. If you keep it up, it's
going to make it real hard for him to get it together when he grows up.
That's all I've got to say."

Lowering his fists slightly, the first man paused. "Well, just stay out of
my business," he huffed. He then turned and walked back to the woman
and boy, and they disappeared into a nearby apartment.

Standing alone in the street, the second man sighed deeply, shook his
head nervously, and turned back to his car engine. Immediately, I
walked over to him.

"Excuse me," I said, "but I saw what just happened there, and I want
to thank you for one of the best examples of manly courage I've ever
seen."

"Huh?" Wiping a greasy hand on his shorts, he turned and looked at
me. "Oh, well, that guy was pretty hot, wasn't he? Still, I guess I just
couldn't let something like that go by. I mean, that guy was dragging his
boy around by one arm, hitting him over and over again and shouting.
He was really out of control."

I confessed that watching the angry guy had frightened me, and
noted that most guys would've just looked the other way.

"It may not have done much good for that guy," he offered, seeming
grateful for the chance to talk. "But, you know, my dad used to do that
sort of thing to me a lot when I was a kid, and it's been real hard for me
to get over it. I guess not much more can scare you after that. I just wish
somebody'd said something back then to make my dad stop."

I reached out and shook the man's hand. "You're a real man," I said,
genuinely awed. Outside my door, I saw my next appointment waiting.
"Want to use my phone for your car?"

"No thanks. The old heap acts up like this every so often, and it just
takes a little bit to get it going. I'll be out of here in a minute."

"I'm a Christian," I said finally, turning to go. "So I'll just say that I'll be
praying God will bless you tremendously for what you did." For indeed,
there before my eyes was the heart and strength of the Father made
flesh in a man.

If God's greatest desire for men is to bring us into relationship with
Him as Father and son, surely He will do whatever is necessary toward
that end for any man who wants it. If the man's image of his earthly
father is the major impediment, God's major focus—as declared in Malachi 4:5–6—will be to restore true and proper father-son relationship—
that is, to heal a man's image of the father.

This process most often requires a man to face and feel fully his own wound, to see his father with Jesus' eyes and thereby, to see that wound in his father as well. He can then forgive, let go, and allow Jesus to lead him at last to the Father God to fulfill his needs.

A mature letting go—as opposed to vengeful rejection—is characterized by obedience at last to the Father God. The adult son must therefore pray, "Lord, show me how to keep your commandment to honor my father and to worship only you." Certainly, the Father God longs to answer such a prayer, just as any earthly father would respond if his son asked him, "Dad, would you show me how to behave better?"

Of course, God will answer that prayer appropriately—that is, often differently at different times for each man, who can check out any answer by seeking other men as witnesses (see 1 Cor. 14:29). One man I know sensed he was to write his father a letter once a week. Another, a school teacher previously filled with anger and vowing never to humble himself before his father, called and asked his father—a retired carpenter—to advise him on a remodeling project at home.

But what about actually calling or visiting your father?

I do not recommend such a visit if the man is still just coming to recognize how his father has wounded him. After the man has surrendered his father-wound to Jesus and allowed Him to lead through pain into forgiveness, however, an actual visit might be good for both father and son.

Such an encounter must be motivated not by the vengeful human spirit, which would say, "I want to unload on you at last how bad you were to me, Dad!" but rather, the Father God's Holy Spirit of truth: "Dad, I want to be closer to you. I don't really know exactly how to make that happen, but I'd like for us just to spend some time together."

This approach, of course, renders the son quite vulnerable to the earthly father—and thus requires greater surrender to and dependence upon the Father God. It is, in fact, the way of Jesus. A lie is always safer; we lie because we fear the consequences of the truth. Indeed, as Jesus demonstrated on the Cross, the deeper the truth, the more dire the consequences—and the more we need the Father God with us.

When you do get together, surrender to Jesus all judgment of your father and all right to vengeance—for that, indeed, is the Lord's and not ours (see Deut. 32:35). Ask Him for an open heart genuinely to know your father as a man. You might simply say, "Dad, what were things like for you when you were my age?"

Still, the man who prepares himself and reaches out to his father in this way may be assured that in doing so, he is not so much going after something he wants for himself as yielding to God's ultimate purpose: to bring fathers and children together. He is not laboring to row a boat, but positioning it on the crest of a wave.

Most men balk at actually meeting the father in truth because they fear he will only abandon them yet again, and say, "Oh, no, that's okay, there's no need for that sort of thing." If that happens, a son may want to persist in his vulnerability and reply, "Maybe not, but I feel like we're missing a lot of good stuff we could have if we were closer." Could the man even say, "Dad, I love you, and I miss you. I feel like I hardly know you and yet you're so much a part of me"?

No one dares promise a man that his efforts will meet with "success." If the father were so open to such intimacy, he and the son would have been close already. Reaching out in vulnerable love can get you crucified. The witness of the Cross promises us only that the man who risks himself in love will find his true Father with him, no matter how painful the situation.

If the father persists in wounding by rejection, the man can call on Jesus and feel his pain, trusting that his Father God weeps with him. He thereby learns at last that his father-wound no longer has power to destroy him. Perhaps through some supportive brothers, he can let the Father comfort and pat him on the back for such courage to risk himself in love. Then he can get on with his life—honoring his father as God directs, but maintaining appropriate distance and not allowing the father's brokenness to preoccupy, and thus, drag him back from the Father God's calling.

Often, the father balks at engaging the son because he knows how he has sinned against the boy, but does not know the boy has grown to forgive him. That is why a man should not approach his father for a deeper level of openness until he has worked through his wound unto forgiveness.

At some point—perhaps at the father's own bidding—it may be appropriate to say, "It hurt me back then when you did that." This may be a by-product, but should never be the goal of the encounter. Indeed, a man is mature enough to seek deeper relationship with his father when knowing the man becomes more important than getting an apology.

This, at last, is the true Father's love: that He did not come in Jesus seeking vengeance or demanding an apology for our sins against Him. Instead, the Father God sacrificed on the Cross His right to punish and destroy us—even to smite the land with a curse, as in Malachi 4:5–6—in order to win us to Himself, and thus restore the father relationship.

No matter how painful the relationship with his father, the boy still longs for the brown ooze from the very man who has wounded him so badly. This is the excruciating predicament of men today, from which there is no natural exit. Only by surrendering his wound to Jesus at the Cross can a man meet the true Father of men and be delivered into true manhood.

Thus, the brown ooze begs comparison to the blood of Jesus, which comes from the Father's body bearing wholeness to His sons.

Certainly, the pain of such surrender, and its root fear that the Father God will not be there as he lets go, may intimidate a man into seeking another, albeit counterfeit, exit from the father-wound. The mother offers the most accessible avenue of escape, and later, the girlfriend/woman. "I don't need to deal with the pain from Dad," a man may fancy, "because Mom's love made up for it" or "because I've got a wife now who really loves me."

Indeed, for the average man today, distance from the father has already caused overbonding with the mother. Unable to remember even his need for the father, he can only focus his yearning for freedom on breaking away from the mother. Therefore, he wonders later why he seems to sabotage his own efforts to bond with a woman.

Here, then, we must begin to ask: How does a boy's bond to his mother affect his later growth as a man?

CHAPTER THREE

Cutting the Cord: A Second Postpartum

In a recent *Los Angeles Times Magazine* cover story entitled, "Mothers, Sons, and the Gangs,"[1] several mothers of young gang members pondered sadly why their sons had gone astray. As a man, I was startled by what they didn't say. "I don't understand why he goes out on the streets," was the gist of each woman's grief. "I'm a good mother. I keep a clean house, I go to church, I don't run around with men, I cook for the boy, wash his clothes, and provide a good home. Why doesn't he want to stay here?"

No matter how righteous and fine a homemaker his mother may be, however, any man can recognize in gang members the innate male longing and need to break away from the mother, bond to the father, and be joined thereby to the company of men. Without the father to engineer that process, the choice for such young males is ominous: either join a gang and get killed or go to prison, or stay with Mom and starve in a cell of femininity.

Certainly, these are good mothers, wholly worthy of honor and respect. In fact, I suspect their sons genuinely know that. But these mothers are not fathers, nor can they be. And therein lies the rub—not just in the inner city, where its effects are most graphic, but throughout our country today.

The finest woman's best is not good enough to usher a boy into manhood. That is men's work, properly done by the father and the community of men. Our "modern" civilization, however, has forgotten that this must be done. Furthermore, it must be done to ensure the health and welfare of the village itself, to avoid a "curse" (Mal. 4:6) upon the land.

A boy who does not grow to see himself as a man among men lacks an inner-directed maturity, a sense of his own identity. He will let anyone define him. Indeed, he seeks someone to do it. If men of God are not fostering a godly fellowship of men and devising ways to usher boys into it, the male child can only yield eventually to the world's self-centered, destructive definitions. Hence, the gangs—and the inner, self-destructiveness among men today, reflected in the high rate of male suicide, regardless of socioeconomic status.

"When the father isn't present either physically or emotionally," Ciotti says, "boys tend to be more aggressive and less compliant. They have greater problems in preschool. They don't obey their mothers as well. They have problems in peer relationships, tending either to play alone or with younger children."[2] That is, they don't grow up confident in their calling to become responsible, productive members of society.

The more graphic statistics in black families bring this nationwide problem into sharp focus. Noting that over fifty-five percent of black families with children are headed by women, black clergyman Prentice Tipton declares,

> When mothers lead the family because the fathers fail to lead—either by absenting themselves from the home or by taking a passive role—boys are deprived of the most important natural model of manliness. Growing up mainly under the supervision of women, many of them experience insecurity over their identity as men.
>
> One tendency for boys growing up in such circumstances is to rebel against the women who are authorities over them and become socially disruptive—irresponsible in family and work commitments, overly assertive about their manly prowess, especially in sexual areas, or leading lives characterized by violence and crime, alcoholism, and other addictions.
>
> Another tendency for young men is to identify with the adult women who are the authorities in their lives and learn to behave or react in ways that are more appropriate to women than to men.
>
> To the extent that young males take either option, they do not learn the discipline, the responsibility, and the character involved in being a man. They are left groping for manhood in a variety of socially disruptive ways.[3]

As a Peace Corps Volunteer in rural Nigeria, I saw in the tribal rite of passage how another, ostensibly "primitive," culture was far more advanced than our own in recognizing, affirming, and making certain that this need for fatherly validation was met in every male.

Granted, this society didn't know how to manufacture potato chips that fit neatly on top of each other in a can, or how to transmit pictures into machines to watch passively. But they knew something about manhood that we have forgotten: To become a man, every boy must eventually break away from his mother, and no boy can do it himself, any more than a mother can truly let go of the boy by herself.

As observer Tipton concludes,

The approach that many Christian pastoral leaders take to this situation is to minister primarily to women, because they find them more responsive, reliable, and easier to work with. The hope is that by strengthening and Christianizing the women they can strengthen and Christianize the black community, and thus gradually overcome the problems with men.

However, such pastoral efforts have little effect on the problem because they rely on women to influence men, yet it is the failure of men to form men that is at the root of the problem. Like it or not, men are key to changing society. It is impossible to change society without changing the men, and only other men are able to change the men.[4]

Certainly, any honest pastor can identify with this statement. As Robert Bly puts it:

How firmly the son's body becomes, before birth and after, a good receiver for the upper and lower frequencies of the mother's voice! The son either tunes to that frequency or he dies.

Now, standing next to the father, as they repair arrowheads, or repair plows, or wash pistons in gasoline, or care for birthing animals, the son's body has a chance to retune. Slowly, over the months or years, that son's body-strings begin to resonate to the . . . older masculine body.

Sons who have not received this retuning will have father hunger all their lives. . . . Such hungry sons hang around older men like the homeless do around a soup kitchen. Like the homeless, they feel shame over their condition, and it is nameless, bitter, unexpungeable shame.

Women cannot, no matter how much they sympathize with their starving sons, replace that particular missing substance. The son may later try to get it from a woman his own age, but that doesn't work either.[5]

Nevertheless, the power of the mother in a generation of young men lacking fathers is not lost on organizations which seek young men. A recent full-page Army recruiting ad in *Time* magazine,[6] for example, centers around a middle-aged woman smiling broadly and embracing cheek-to-cheek a well-trimmed young man in green-and-khaki uniform, seen from his back. Blurred in the background, a grey-haired man in white shirt and tie smiles at them both.

"LETTING MY SON JOIN THE ARMY WAS THE HARDEST THING I'VE EVER DONE. IT WAS ALSO ONE OF THE SMARTEST," reads the bold caption across the young man's shoulder and mother's arm. The mother ostensibly continues:

Russ has always been the baby of our family, so I was terribly upset the day he left us for the Army. Even though I knew he had good reasons for joining—especially the money he'd be earning for college—I also knew how tough the Army could be. And I worried about how he would cope.

Then, three months later, I was invited to Russell's graduation from basic training. As I watched him standing there—looking so strong, so mature, so self-confident—I realized the Army had done something really important for my son. It had helped him grow up.

The ad concludes with a number to call and "find out what the Army can do to help your son or daughter."

Significantly, this Army ad aims not at the men themselves, but at their mothers, who have the power to "let my son" join up and, after basic training, confirm manhood. This focus reflects a profound shift in the locus of masculine authority and identity away from the father, who today is seen at best unclearly and in the background.

Again, the *Los Angeles Times* welcomed the first soldiers home from the 1991 Persian Gulf War with a front-page three-column photo: A tall young Marine has his arm around a trim, shorter woman, smiling with her head on his shoulder and holding a sign which the caption notes is "emblazoned with his name, a large arrow, and the word Mom."[7]

Early in 1991, William Kennedy Smith, nephew of Senator Ted Kennedy, was charged with battery and rape by a young woman he met at a local bar near the Florida Kennedy estate. Under the front-page headline, "Kennedy Nephew Surrenders," the *Los Angeles Times* ran a full-color picture of the accused talking to newspersons as his mother stands beside him. "This is very upsetting to me," the mother says in the adjunct article. "Anyone who knows him knows he didn't do this." Significantly, the article ends, " 'He's doing very well, he's very strong,' said Jean Smith of her son."[8]

William Kennedy Smith is no minor as he hides thus behind his mother's skirt, but fully thirty years old. He is not black, underprivileged, or marginal in any sense.

The father-wound today is no respecter of men.

Indeed, whether guilty or innocent of the charges, with proper fathering Smith would likely not have been out womanizing in a bar in the first place. Sadly, he was taken to the bar by his uncle Ted, a senator and older male who should have provided him with a better masculine model. But if we are to believe the tales of brother JFK's exploits with women, we must look for the roots of such immaturity to the father, Joe

Kennedy—who, according to one reporter, "thought high office did not need to crimp party-going and pursuit of sexual conquests."[9]

Army ads and fatherless youth notwithstanding, calling the boy out and away from the mother remains the job of the father, together with the elder men of the village, who alone can make the necessary "cut." Any such cut the mother presides over and "lets" happen cannot be genuine.

Western psychology textbooks acknowledge freely the postpartum grief of a mother when the umbilical cord has been surgically cut; the child has been born and thereby, individuated from her physical body. At first, he was in the woman, and thus, one with the mother. As much as any organ in her body, the boy literally was the mother; now, he is another person, namely, the mother's boy.

To be one with the mother is the natural condition of the flesh from its very genesis in the womb. To be one with the father is a condition of the spirit (see John 3:4–6). The impossibility of this in the flesh drives men to the heavenly Father. That is, a second postpartum looms—equally momentous for the male child and painful for the mother—in which the male child must move from being mother's boy to being father's son.

The American woman does not know this, because the American man has not taught her—because he has not dared to recognize and affirm his own unfulfilled need.

For example, one distraught single mother of a ten-year-old boy told me he was skipping school, coming home drunk at night, and throwing up on her floor. The boy's father, she noted, had been an alcoholic and died from a drug overdose when the boy was four. When I asked her how she had been responding to the boy's behavior, she raised a fist. "I tell him, 'You're just like your father!'"

Matter-of-factly, I acknowledged her anger toward the boy's father and offered to work with her in overcoming that. Then gently, but deliberately, I urged her to listen to me as a man. "Every male child longs to be one with his father, whether Dad is President or a derelict," I said. "When you tell your son that his father was a drunk, the next question in his mind will be, 'Where's the nearest liquor store?' You must give your son something positive about his father to bond with, or he can only continue to bond with—and thereby act out—the negative."

The boy who has not broken from his mother nevertheless knows the break must be made. Without a father to do it properly, the boy will try to do it himself, often in a clumsy, even destructive effort, such as with the gangs.

In a chilling confirmation of the "destruction" prophecy in Malachi

4:6, one sixty-year-old widow came to me upset by her thirty-year-old bachelor son's "awful anger" and wanting "help for us just to get along better." The son, who told about his recent trip to Europe and daily phone calls there from his mother, at one point burst out, "If you won't just let go and let me be, I might as well kill myself!"

A younger boy still living with his mother may force the "cut" by disobeying her deliberately, or in some way goading her into rejecting him. As a teenager, he may push her into kicking him out of the house—only to beg later to come back, because his breakaway has been short-circuited by the absence of the father. Like a flying trapeze acrobat, he has thrown off his grip on one end, only to discover in midair that no man has come reaching to him from the other side.

Often, the mother may fuss over the son's repeated antics, and even engage his energies in loud fights that can become seductive. But she lets him come home because she is lonely without him. Indeed, she finds sympathetic company with the son: Both boy and mother miss the man.

This turning to the woman for masculine character during his early stages of manhood stirs terrible confusion in a boy. Later, he will look to his wife to compensate for his own lack of strength. Nevertheless, he will resent her when she becomes strong, because she reminds him of what he doesn't have, but should have as a man. Yet again, in the next generation, the family—both husband and wife—miss the man.

This underlying sense of inadequacy causes a man to fear women, that is, to associate the woman with failure as a man. These fears are commonly prompted even in intact families when the father leaves town, perhaps on a business trip, and tells the boy, "Now, you be the man of the house while I'm gone!" The boy knows he cannot fill his father's shoes, and in fact, feels less confident and capable when his father is absent. His natural insecurity in the father's absence is compounded by the fear of being expected to do something he cannot—namely, fulfill the woman's needs as "the man of the house." Later, he carries this sense of inadequacy with him into his marriage, thinking, "I am not able to be man of the house."

To men struggling today with these fears, I say: The woman does not cause you to be inadequate; her needs merely reveal your sense of inadequacy. When that happens, don't waste time fighting her. Go to your Father God and confess your own needs as a man, asking for His wisdom and strength. And then get together with other men for support, encouragement, and prayer.

Meanwhile, tell your wife that you recognize your need for healing and how you're taking responsibility to meet it. Ask her to tell you what she genuinely needs from you. Listen, and try to meet those needs. Then tell her what you need from her, asking that she listen and try to meet your needs also. Then, take the initiative and ask her to get on her knees with you at the foot of your bed. Surrender to the Father, wait on His Spirit, and then pray aloud for each other.

Demonstrate spiritual leadership in the family by going like Jesus to the Cross. Confess your sins first. Tell the Father what you want Him to change in you, and offer yourself to Him to do that in whatever way He chooses (see Rom. 12:1–2).

Trust the Father to honor such bold humility in His son.

If, however, a man does not recognize his need to break from the mother, he cannot bond with his wife and will wound her deeply.

Alice, for example, was embarking on a new career and needed her husband Larry's support. She came to me distressed by a dream in which she was strangling him. We asked the Holy Spirit to reveal the cause of her anger, and as we prayed, she remembered a scene from shortly after their honeymoon several years earlier.

As a boy, Larry lived with his mother after his parents' divorce, and grew to hate his mother's chain smoking. Indeed, as an adult he refused to smoke himself, and avoided all smokers. At twenty-nine, he married Alice, who shared his aversion. The two agreed that they would not allow others to smoke in their home.

Shortly thereafter, Larry's mother visited the couple, and surprised them by pulling out a cigarette. "Did I hear someone say you had a rule against smoking in your house?" she asked, holding her lighter ready. "I'm sure that wasn't true, now, was it? I mean, surely you don't mind if I smoke here?"

Larry hesitated, then murmured, "Well . . . no, Mom. We don't really have any rules like that."

As the mother smiled and lit her cigarette, Alice stood shocked and crushed. "I guess I haven't trusted Larry to stand together with me in anything since then," she said. "Now that I need his support, I guess all that anger is coming back."

Without a father to enforce proper boundaries, Larry grew up seeing his mother as head of the house—even his own house years later. He therefore could not bond with his wife as a man.

Our collective ignorance of the boy's need for the father's call has harmed not only boys and wives, but mothers as well. Without the father's cue, the need to break from the mother surfaces most graphically when the boy becomes physically as large as his mother. Then, his inner anger at not being called out by the father suddenly finds the intimidating authority; the boy begins to threaten his mother physically, and at last, desperately, she seeks help.

Once, the single mother of a fourteen-year-old boy came to me both furious and afraid. "He actually lifted his hand as if to hit me!" she declared, and then detailed the tongue-lashing she gave the boy, which led him to stop. "He dropped back, but I'm afraid of what he'll do in the future."

When she noted that the father and she had divorced years earlier and he now lived several hundred miles away, I asked if nevertheless she had contacted him to report the son's behavior.

"Of course not!" she exclaimed. "His father has never cared about us!" At the same time, she allowed, the man was sober, working, and otherwise living responsibly.

Gently, but directly, I began to speak to her "as a man myself," and noted that the boy needed his father. I urged her to contact the man.

Fiercely, the mother dug in. "Oh, but he wouldn't understand Ronnie the way I do."

I persisted, allowing that indeed, a father's understanding often is different from a mother's—then declared that her son needed something from the father that she as a woman was incapable of providing. I pointed out to her that the boy's threat of violence indicated clearly that he now needed first not a maternal understanding of tender sensitivity, but a paternal understanding of proper boundaries and focus for his masculine energies. I explained that the boy might well be angry at his father, not her, but that he had to work that out with his father himself.

The mother resisted, and finally I simply asked her, "Do you love your son?"

"Of course!" she replied.

I then noted that love requires putting the other person's needs and best interests before your own. Obviously, she had deep anger toward the boy's father, and I would help her deal with that as a separate issue. But if she truly loved her son, she would contact his father and tell him humbly but deliberately that their son needed something only he, as a man, could give.

This all-too-common anger at being abandoned on the threshold of manhood, in the boy's critical time of need, focuses originally and properly on the father. Today, however, the father is often either physically absent from the home—as in the above examples—or present but punitive and intimidating. The boy, therefore, is either unable or too afraid to express his anger directly and appropriately at his father. He then must either deny it with compulsive behavior, such as drugs and sex, or project it instead on the one who is present and weaker, namely, the mother.

Such a boy, when he grows up, will carry that anger and likely continue to misfocus it upon the woman, that is, his wife. Like his father, such a man is likely afraid of and cut off from other men. Without the masculine fellowship of accountability and encouragement to seek healing, he often lashes out physically at her. The episodes of beating, followed by tearful apologies and confusion, are all too common in the annals of domestic violence.

I once ministered to a man who had struck his wife several times and, recognizing his wrongdoing, had sought help. Hours in psychotherapy spent beating a pillow and shouting his anger toward his possessive mother had given him a reality point from which to restrain misfocusing further violence on his wife. But he was still angry and confused, until he began to see his deeper hurt from the father who had abandoned not only him, but his mother as well, thus predisposing her to cling to the boy.

Again, as a guest once on a radio show for men, I was seized by the theme song, in which the singer recalls being his "mother's pride and joy" when a boy. As he grew up and became more independent, however, he saw "the fear growing in her face." At last, he proclaims his joy at overcoming his later confusion and kow-towing toward women. Knowing at last "where I stand," he finishes with the chorus that he's now "glad, glad, glad, glad, to be a man."

At once, the song struck me as a powerful testimony to the mother's hold on a boy. But as I proceeded with the interview, a strangely unsatisfied, even suspicious, sense hovered nearby.

Later at home, I realized why: One does not become a man simply by rejecting and breaking from his mother. The larger masculine—the father and the community of men—must be reckoned with, hearkened unto, as well. Otherwise, an edge of resentment, even hostility, remains and focuses eventually on women.

Because the mother is present and accessible, the boy's most focused emotion says, "Let go of me, Mom!" But his more primal cry is rather, "Come and get me, Dad!"

When misplaced on the mother, a boy's anger at being abandoned by his father fuels much woman-hating in our society—from Alfred Hitchcock *Psycho*-type movies victimizing women to rape, job discrimination, and sexism in all its forms. Even if the mother has been punitive or otherwise behaved inappropriately toward her son, the boy's deeper cry is to his father, "Daddy, where are you? Why don't you come and stop Mommy, and save me?"

Fred, a thirty-two-year-old engineering assistant, came to me nursing a bruised fist which he had pounded into his door after a girlfriend had left him. Questioning revealed an alcoholic mother, who had told him from his earliest memory, "I never wanted you. You were a mistake." His father had died when Fred was two.

After chronicling years of ugly physical and verbal abuse by his mother, Fred punched his sore fist into his other hand—and winced.

Anger toward the mother seemed to be the obvious issue, and when Fred fell silent, I suggested we pray and ask God's help. To my surprise, he jerked upright, eyes blazing. "If God were here right now," he said, "I'd strangle Him to death!"

"You mean, for what He allowed your mother to do to you?" I responded, matter-of-factly.

"No!" Fred shouted, raising his swollen fist. "For taking my dad from me!"

I sat stunned, awed at the truth I saw etched in fury before me: For a man, the pain of what the woman does, no matter how violent and evil, cannot cut as deeply as losing the father—who presumably would have drawn the boy to himself and thus protected him.

A boy's overbonding with the mother, therefore, reflects a weak or absent father. Still, this is no excuse for the mother to hold onto the boy indefinitely.

At one conference where I taught this maternal letting go, an angry mother demanded, "What's in it for the mother?"

I explained that a mother who does her part in letting go of her son frees him to love her. But a son held on to and thus restrained by his mother from becoming himself, can only fear and resent her. He may grit his teeth and keep the Law by not dishonoring her, but he cannot live in the Spirit, that is, in free relationship with her. He cannot trust and enjoy being with her, and therefore, will not seek her company. "Whoever would gain her son would lose him; whoever would lose her son would gain him," might be an appropriate paraphrase here of Jesus' words (see Matt. 16:25).

On another occasion, a mother of a teenage son wrote to me after hearing my teaching and affirmed, "This message is the key to coming to the Father God." Referring to a teaching by Christian educator Cliff Custer, she noted how Mary became upset when Jesus at twelve, the Hebrew age of accountability, preferred to be with the men at the synagogue than with her: "Didn't you know that I had to be in my Father's house?" (Luke 2:49).

Significantly, both the community of men and the Father God are linked here. As my correspondent therefore continued,

> How can a child . . . be about his Father's business with his mother choking him with her umbilical cord—even though she says it is out of love? When a mother cuts the cord, the child is free to move closer to his father and, ultimately, to Father God.
>
> It seems so simple, yet women come up with more excuses than you can imagine for why they can't and won't. One excuse is, "Well, what about me? Am I just out of the picture after my children turn twelve?" God's answer is, "No. You become as the Holy Spirit. You become 'Comforter,' a constant prayer warrior for your child."

This mother prayed when her son and daughter each were twelve, and imagined herself holding a large pair of scissors. "I asked Jesus to hold my hands," she said, "and help me cut the cord between me and my son and my daughter. He did, and they have been free and truly 'about their Father's business' since that time."

Still, she allowed, "It is a process that must be relived from time to time. When my kids get upset with me, it is in every case because I have crossed over the line and 'pulled the cord.'"

Often, a mother's good and natural desire to protect her child can short-circuit the necessary relating between father and son. Certainly, in the case of an abusive father, she must exercise that desire diligently. But even in a normal home, at times the father will wound the boy. When a reasonably mature boy comes running to his mother crying because "Daddy hurt me," she must be willing at times to say, "Then you need to go back and talk to your daddy about it, and work it out between the two of you."

A mother must beware of "explaining" or making excuses for a father's hurtful behavior to the child, thereby patronizing the father and undercutting the boy's image of masculinity. At some point, when the children mature, she may need to ask if her efforts to protect the children from their "insensitive father" are actually designed to preserve them for herself.

Under the guise of maintaining relationship with the father by smoothing over hurt feelings, she actually short-circuits and precludes the necessary honest encounter required for true relationship. Instead of crying in Mommy's arms, a boy may need to be saying to his father, "Daddy, don't hurt me like that!"

Once, a single mother came to me distressed that her thirteen-year-old son wanted to leave her to live with his father, who was an alcoholic, though not physically abusive. The mother resisted, but after praying, I encouraged her to consider the boy's request seriously. Eventually, she yielded.

A year later, she called me. "I want to thank you," she said. "All my criticizing of his father only made Jimmy defend his father and get us into fights. After he went and lived with his dad awhile, he learned for himself what his father's like, and can see now why I had to go for the separation. How he works stuff out with his dad now is his business; all I can say is that now Jimmy and I sure get along a lot better."

When the mother mediates relationship with the father, the son grows up unable to relate directly to a man. Indeed, he looks to the woman— often his wife—to mediate his male friendships.

Paul, at forty-one a successful executive, came to me with deep feelings of loneliness. The son of an alcoholic father and a doting mother, he had no male friends—although at a couples' party with his wife, he'd met one guy he "really enjoyed talking with."

Very casually, hoping to defuse his fear, I suggested he give the guy a call to get together.

"Yeah . . . good idea!" he exclaimed. I smiled inwardly at my apparent success—then drew up in surprise as he continued. "I'll have to ask my wife when we could have them over."

"But . . ." I said, hesitating, "I meant just the two of you men doing something together."

Paul knit his brow, and shook his head in dismay. "That honestly never occurred to me," he confessed. Then he listened intensely as I suggested that his father's abuse had caused him to fear other men, and turn to the woman for protection when relating to men.

Richard Rohr tells of a woman whose husband came to her distraught over his new job, complaining that his superiors treated him unfairly. Night after night he came home with stories of his critical boss and gossiping fellow workers. His wife listened patiently and sympathetically, until finally she said to him, "Listen, talking to me isn't changing anything. Why don't you just go to these men and talk with them as a man about what they're doing to you?"[10]

The line between understanding and mothering the husband must be drawn when the wife's understanding keeps the man from fulfilling his responsibility to work things out directly with other men—even as his mother likely stood between him and his father.

Most churches today do not teach about the boy's need to break from the mother, perhaps for fear of offending women, who often comprise a majority of the congregation. Yet such denial and fear ultimately cause more destruction and pain than the truth they avoid. Indeed, the Father God wants so badly to communicate this truth today, that at times He takes matters into His own hands.

A friend told me that two weeks after his wife came home from the hospital with their baby son, he returned from work one evening and found her in tears. As he held her, she told him how earlier in the day she had been diapering the boy and praising God aloud, saying, "Thank You, God, for Bobby. You know how badly I've wanted a child of my own, and now You've given me one!"

In the midst of her joy, however, she heard "like a voice" speaking back to her, saying, "Bobby is not yours. He's Mine." At first, she dismissed the voice as her imagination, but it persisted, interrupting her praise.

"Finally, I just began talking back," she told her husband. "I said, 'No! He's mine! I've prayed for him, waited for him, been through all the doctor's tests, worked hard, and carried him all these months!' But I just heard, 'He's not yours. He's Mine.'

"I couldn't believe what was going on. I begged. I pleaded. 'Lord,' I said, 'I just got home from the hospital. I've only had him two weeks!'

"And then I 'heard' in my mind, 'You never really had him to yourself, not even these two weeks. I created him, and I have called you to be his mother, to love and care for him for a season. But he belongs to Me.'"

After they had talked further, my friend and his wife got on their knees and praised God together. Then she lifted the baby up and away from her body, confessed, and asked God to heal her possessiveness in the flesh and give her all she would need to serve Him as a mother in His purposes for Bobby.

Obviously, not all mothers receive such graphic revelation of their true role with their sons. I believe that most often, God wants to bring this revelation to women through men.

But the American man has not taught his wife that she must face a second postpartum, because he has not dared to recognize his own need for it. That is, he is afraid to face the awful, gaping wound in his own masculine soul from not having been called out by his own father into the company of men. Instead, with protective bravado, he pretends he never needed that—and thereby abandons his son and cuts himself off not only from his own true need as a man, but from the true Father who has come in Jesus to fulfill it.

Jesus reflected this spiritual postpartum to Nicodemus, who puzzled over how a man can be born again, that indeed, he cannot go back into his mother's womb and come out again. We are born physically of the flesh, but spiritually of the Spirit, Jesus explained (see John 3:6).

The Spirit, that is, initiates the call to manhood—even as the Nigerian Igbo "nmoo" spirit-mask begins the midnight rite of manhood by leaving the father and elder men gathered at the edge of the mother's yard and approaching the mother's hut alone.

Granted, this is the wrong spirit, for these men do not know Jesus. But it is the right man. Sadly, we who know the right Spirit have forgotten the true man within us, who longs for the Father.

The earthly father, therefore, must be the heavenly Father's mouthpiece in calling the boy out and away from the mother, into new life as a son of the father in the company of men. This is the next step toward the ultimate goal of fellowship with the true Father of all men, and the stage before bonding to the woman in marriage. To skip it, as American men do, condemns a man to idolatry of women, that is, to seek from his wife the masculine identity and strength that can only germinate in fellowship with other men and the Father God. The man who persists in this confusion can expect the woman eventually to push him away in frustration, saying, "You need something I cannot give you—something that, indeed, I need from you!"

For the man who was never called out by his own father and thereby taught how, doing this for his own son is no easy task. But in the absence of historical or cultural precedent, a man need not despair. Instead, he can trust that his Father God has come in Jesus and is here now in His Body the Church, calling him out together with other men into the fellowship of His Holy Spirit.

Occasionally, Christian men who have never confessed their own father-wound ask me to lead a retreat for them and their young sons. I always say no, and urge the adult men instead to go on a retreat themselves first. Before a man can call out his own son, before he can be the father, he must first know the true Father—by letting Jesus deal with his own inner wound as an adult son.

A man must beware the temptation to hide behind his son from his own hurts—and thereby, avoid meeting the Father. For indeed, his inner hurts are where he needs the Father most, and will therefore be most receptive to His workings. We best learn the character of the Father—and therein, how to be godly fathers ourselves—by daring to trust Him with our most fragile, vulnerable parts.

This we must do in fellowship with other men, for this is ultimately what makes the true and godly community of men to which our sons need to be called.

Granted, it's frightening to trust your wounds to other men—especially for a man who trusted himself to his father as a boy and was painfully abandoned or betrayed. But this is precisely the courage required of men today if, indeed, the next generation of men is to unite powerfully as sons of the Father God.

Men today must begin to dare regenerate a trust in the masculine—lost as boys when abandoned by the father—by surrendering to the Father God and moving together in the fellowship of His Spirit at church.

A man properly learns to be a father only by learning first to be a son of the "Father from whom all fatherhood in heaven and on earth derives its name" (Eph. 3:14 NIV footnote). A man can only break the generational cycle of paternal abandonment and fear by surrendering at last to Jesus, and thereby, to the Father God's call.

"Now that you have known me," as Jesus told His earliest followers, "you will know my Father also. . . . Whoever has seen me has seen the Father" (John 14:7, 9).

Still, even the most healed man in the most harmonious marriage cannot expect his wife to respond cheerfully when he begins to seek more time alone with their son. Even the woman who can faithfully pray a "scissors" prayer, must do so often to overcome her natural tendency to continue holding onto her child.

The lioness, that is, will bare her teeth when the lion comes for "her" cub. But this is only natural, and not to be feared. What man could respect a mother who said, "Ah, go ahead and take him away"?

American men, so often confused by anger and fear with mothers who have not let go, must realize that a good mother holds onto her boy—not because she hates him or the father, but simply because that is a mother's job.

But a good father calls his son out. When he does, the mother is naturally hurt, and has every right to resist. But the father has the responsibility to insist, for he is announcing the call of the Father God, to whom both the mother and he must answer.

Clearly, a man who fears the woman's anger cannot do this. Indeed, in such cases we see the generational effect in a man who, as a boy himself, was intimidated by his mother and abandoned by his father. Such a boy, lacking a father strong and loving enough to call him out, grows up not trusting masculine energy to be sufficient before the woman. Hence, when his wife protests, he yields and withdraws from the boy—and thus perpetuates the awful cycle of fear and abandonment yet another generation.

Although it is entirely natural for a mother to hold onto her son, any compulsive clinging to him will be largely precluded if she has a man who loves her, to whom she can legitimately cling in times of need. One major gift a man can give his son is to be present to his mother emotionally as well as physically, to respect her feelings and stand by her, even as he holds her accountable.

The man who abandons his son has usually abandoned his wife as well. That is, the man who is not strong enough to stay centered and act faithfully in the face of the woman's anger likely has not been strong enough to recognize and serve her genuine need for him.

"But a boy just naturally goes to his mother when he needs comfort," a radio host once protested to me, citing his own child as an example.

"Only if the boy has learned that his father will not comfort him as he needs," I countered.

Shortly thereafter, a father listening to the show called in and told the audience how his six-year-old had come running into the house crying, bypassed him in the living room, and ran to his mother in the kitchen. He thought nothing of it—until he overheard the boy between sobs with his mother saying, "Why is it always better around here when Daddy's not home?"

"That really hit me hard," the father said. "Soon after, I took my son aside and asked him to tell me what he didn't like about me. When I kept asking, he finally did. Soon we were holding each other and crying. I said I'd do my best to change.

"Then the other day, my wife and I were sitting together on the living room couch and heard a bike go down. My son came running into the house crying and this time, made a beeline for me. He just jumped in my lap, and I held him as he cried it out."

Ultimately, the mother simply cannot handle the task of a boy's growth into manhood and thus needs to hand the boy over—no matter how painful that may be to both. But all too often today, the father is not present and calling the boy to him.

After ministering to many women, I believe that within every clinging mother is a lonely, frightened woman. Often she has tried to fulfill her need for masculine attention and affection, lacking in the husband, by turning to the son. Thus, when the boy leaves, she must face her emptiness and take it to the Cross. If she does not trust Jesus to meet her in that emptiness and lead her into fulfillment as a person herself—a beloved daughter, in fact—she will hold onto the boy as an idol, her source of saving power.

In a sense, she becomes addicted to the boy, insofar as serving his apparent needs "saves" her from having to face her own needs. Just as an alcoholic might take a drink, she devotes herself to her son—denying and avoiding the painful, lonely truth about herself, and likely, about her inadequate husband as well. In such fear, she gives God no chance to be "like a husband" (see Isa. 54:5) and reach to her with comfort and strength.

A Jenny Craig Weight Loss Centers newspaper ad hints at this misfocus, picturing a middle-aged woman, smiling and trim as she twirls in her stylish dress above the caption, "Success is having a son who says I look awesome."[11]

The burden of Mom's self-esteem is far too much for any son to bear. Let the woman say instead, "Success is knowing I am loved by my Father God. Because I feel so good about that, I take care of myself accordingly—and my husband thinks I look great!"

Even as the man is accountable for withdrawing, the woman is accountable for clinging—for each, in doing so, proclaims that "God is not present, available, and powerful enough to meet my needs."

In approaching his wife to call out their boy, the man is like an emotional/spiritual obstetrician. He must cut the woman—not to slash and destroy, but to separate and heal. The person has changed and must grow. Neither the mother nor the boy can remain truly themselves if they continue in the dependent boy-mother mode.

Thus, her resistance is not primarily to the father, but to the natural pain of losing someone dear to her. But both must grow. As with any operation, the pain is outweighed by the healing it promises.

The father must himself know, as a son and man, the healing promised in the mother-son cut and its genuine necessity. Otherwise, he will be swayed by his wife's immediate pain and withdraw from the operation, leaving the son stuck in the birth canal. Thus, he abandons both mother and son to their unhealthy relationship.

The man may need to help his wife express her pain, asking her how it feels and listening respectfully, even compassionately. But eventually, he must proceed to call the boy to himself and to the fellowship of men—knowing as he does so that ultimately this is good also for his wife, who must get on with whatever new calling God has for her.

Certainly, this is an awesome job for the man, especially for one who lacks a model of being called out by his own father. In fact, it's more than any man can handle by himself. That is why he must yield to Jesus, and thus go to the true Father who calls and empowers men—first as sons, then as husbands, and then as fathers.

Even the son may resist at first, especially if the father has only recently come to understand his role and has not previously established relationship with the boy. Often today, the boy has lived only with his mother, because of divorce, and has heard many negative things about the father. In such cases, the father must engage the fellowship of other men for wisdom and prayer to know how best to approach his son.

Yet, no matter how fearfully the son might stall, the father must bank on the boy's natural father-longing and not give up. For divorced fathers whose sons reject them, I recommend the discipline of a weekly letter to the boy—every Wednesday, for example, written without anger and without placing responsibility or expectation on him. A simple, caring, sharing letter is fine.

For the father who is not divorced, but has simply been emotionally distant from his son, a regularly scheduled time together, clearly set aside on the calendar, is essential for restoring the relationship.

Whatever the circumstances of an estrangement, the man's self-discipline must now stick, for the boy will very likely resist at first, to test the father's previously lacking commitment. Up to a year is not unusual before seeing change in the boy, depending on the circumstances and the depth of his pain.

Granted, it's hard, and it can hurt. Indeed, the father's pain now at being rejected by his son is akin to the boy's pain on being rejected earlier by the father. But this, at last, is the father's chance to cry out for and know graphically his own Father God's heart—for his steadfast reaching out to the son characterizes the love of the Father God, who never abandons His son, even through pain unto death. Such a father may well need to spend time on his face before the Cross, crying out, even as Jesus, "This hurts me! Father, stand by me and give me Your heart, because I want to forget the whole thing and run!"

The mother, therefore, is accountable to let go of the boy. But a man can hold "possessive mothers" accountable only when he has himself reached out to the boy as a father.

When the father does not fulfill his responsibility to call out the boy, I believe the mother must confront him—not vengefully, out of anger toward the father, but humbly, out of love and concern for the boy. In the church, single mothers of sons must call the body of men to take proper responsibility not just for their own sons, but for all the boys of the village/congregation as well.

Granted, in cases of divorce, the woman must bear her share of responsibility for the marriage breakup, and thus, for her son's dilemma. But the men of God cannot waste energy judging her—or the boy's father, by saying, "Let him clean up his own mess." The father-wound among boys today is so critical, so destructive a curse upon the land (see

Mal. 4:5–6), that the issue of the parents' sin must yield to the boy's need and the men's larger, social responsibility.

Often, the single mother wants to ask men in her church to reach out to her boy, but fears they will mistake her request as a sexual advance. Godly men must therefore take the initiative.

In one church, the men responded to this teaching by organizing a Christian Big Brothers program, calling upon the married fathers as well as single men to serve.

Aubrey Beauchamp, founder of Hospital Christian Fellowship, tells in her autobiography about overcoming her difficulties as a single mother of an adolescent son:[12]

> Sandy was fourteen now, a tall, energetic young man. . . . He was an average student, lively, not able to sit still for long with a short concentration span. He seemed to be an emerging leader but needed more supervision and guidance than either his schoolteachers or I could give him. There were spells of rebellion and disobedience at home with an occasional tantrum. I felt the acute vacuum of a father figure in his life. How can I handle this, Lord? I prayed, I can't be a father to him.

Before long, a friend told her about a boy's ranch in the Texas panhandle, and Aubrey felt natural misgivings:

> Send my son away? That's kind of drastic, I thought. All the way to Texas? Was that really necessary? All [Sandy's teachers] seemed to think the ranch would be good for him . . . [but] Sandy was strongly opposed to the idea.[13]

Eventually convinced it was best for her son, Beauchamp sent him to the school. At first, he begged her in his letters to let him come home, but she resolved only to write him regularly and to visit him at Christmas recess. "It's up to you whether you are going to be miserable or happy," she wrote.

Three months later, Beauchamp was getting optimistic reports from the boy's teachers as he joined activities and made good grades. "Yes, I missed Sandy very much," she says, "but I knew he was in good hands and in a better environment than I could provide."[14]

As Dr. Bobbie Reed declares in her *Single Mothers Raising Sons,* "When Dad is not there, find a substitute":[15]

> Because the boys' father lived too far away for frequent visits during the early years after our divorce, I knew [they] needed additional men in their lives. I hired male sitters, signed them up for Little League, swimming and diving teams with male coaches, and found a man in the

church with sons who would include one or both of my boys in some of their "men only" activities such as camping, fishing, and hiking.

Far too many mothers and churches have balked at this need in boys. Yet, as long as we allow the addictive fantasy that a woman, whether mother or wife, can heal or even patch up the father-wound in males, we avoid surrender to Jesus—and thereby, avoid meeting at last the true Father who alone can heal us.

Certainly, a mother can and must teach her boy to respect a woman, by setting boundaries on his behavior around her. If she does not, another woman—namely, her son's wife—will pay for it later. But she cannot teach him to respect a man—that is, for the male child, self-respect. This can only be imparted to a boy as he respects the man with whom he identifies.

If, with eyes of flesh, we observe that the father is absent and conclude that no father can be present to the son, then indeed, we must defend the mother's ability to fill in the awful gap. After all, someone must do it.

But if we dare see with eyes of faith, we cannot tolerate anything but the truth, no matter how painful, even lethal to the flesh. And in truth, no woman can heal the deadly wound left by the father's absence. Therefore, the man must die.

Now the man has two choices.

In the sure death of his natural manhood, he can surrender to the powers of alienation and destruction, and conclude that he can never bond with other men, a woman, or his children. Capitulating thus to the world, the man readily buys whatever the world—and many a church—sells to prop up a facade of manhood, from cigars to legalistic religion. The very intensity of counterfeit masculinity in the world testifies virulently to every male's deep hope that "somewhere, somehow, I really am a man."

Or the man can take a chance on Jesus. He can fall on his face and surrender to his Creator, the God of life who has come in Jesus to reveal Himself at last as Father. He can confess:

"My father has not called me out to himself and other men, and the pain from that terrifies me. I don't feel like a man at all. In fact, I confess I have wanted to remain a boy with my mother because I haven't trusted You, my Father God, to be there for me if I let go of her. And so I can't honor and respect her as You command. Instead, I just feel guilty or angry around her.

"But now, Father, I want You to make me Your man.

"Therefore, in the name of Jesus, I take the Sword of the Spirit and cut the bonds of the flesh with my mother. I put her in Your hands, and confess that I cannot fulfill her needs. Only You are her Savior. I put myself in Your hands, Jesus, and ask You to move me out into fellowship with my Father God and other men."

Most men today, on praying such a prayer, will feel a burst of release, followed by a sense of guilt. But a man need not feel guilty for "abandoning" his mother to Jesus. Indeed, having made the necessary spiritual cut, he can now honor his mother as a man, not as a clinging boy, because he is securely anchored in his masculinity with the Father among the men. The mother is no longer a threat to his manhood.

Ask the Father God how to honor your mother. One man I know prayed and sensed he was to write a letter to his mother once a week. Another asked the Father to show him his mother's best character traits, and wrote her a letter thanking her for what she had given him.

May every man today confess his longing for his father to call him out from his mother into the company of men. May he take that pain to Jesus and hear in Him the true Father calling him even now to be healed and empowered. May he surrender and let the Father lead him into true and godly fellowship with other men, and thus equipped, go at last to his son and wife as the man they need.

After I had offered this benediction one evening at a church conference, a woman came up to tell me how she had cut off her apron strings with scissors, and gift wrapped them for her son's twelfth birthday present. I celebrate such faithfulness among mothers, for this is perhaps the finest thing a mother can give her son at that age.

But the mother's letting go can never by itself suffice the boy's need. And so, long after my benedictions have faded from sanctuaries and retreat centers, I pray and wait.

I wait for many, many men to tell me how they have bonded together under Jesus and called boys to themselves in godly fellowship—as indeed, Creation itself "waits with eager longing for God to reveal his sons" (Rom. 8:19).

CHAPTER FOUR

Beyond Fig Leaves And Cooties: Loving a Woman

There are four things that are too mysterious for me to understand:
an eagle flying in the sky,
a snake moving on a rock,
a ship finding its way over the sea,
and a man and a woman falling in love.
(Prov. 30:18–19)

A hundred and fifty men sat waiting for me to teach on "Loving a Woman," and since I had taught on "Fathers and Sons" the previous session, I took a quick poll.

"How many of you men," I asked, "had a father who, when you were around twelve or maybe a teenager, took you aside and said anything like, 'Son, I notice you're checking out the girls these days, and that's fine, but I want to talk with you some about what's going on in your body and spirit as you do that'?"

Of the hundred and fifty, two men raised their hands—about the same proportion I find everywhere I teach, around the country. A third lifted his arm slightly and said aloud, "I don't know if this counts, but once my dad . . ."

"It counts!" I interrupted, looking around the sea of men's faces, their brows knit and heads shaking slowly. "If anything happened even to make you wonder, that's more than the rest."

"That's a sad commentary!" exclaimed Dr. James Dobson when I shared this during a "Focus on the Family" radio interview.[1] Indeed, it's disastrous. Anyone reading Malachi 4:5–6 could predict that men so alienated from their fathers would bear "a curse over the land" as they relate sexually to women.

In any other enterprise worthy of masculine energy—for example, starting a new job—a man would expect, if not demand, training and guidance from older men who had been on the job themselves for some time. Yet in relating to the woman—an enterprise comprising the very life mysteries of creation itself, upon which the future welfare of the species depends, requiring more of his true self than any other life investment of time and energy—a man is sent out utterly empty-handed.

Something spiritual happens when boy meets girl. Any boy young enough not to have eaten the world's "new grain" knows that. If I reach out my hand and touch my desk, I feel my desk. That's something physical. But a man can see a woman from across a room and, without ever touching her, feel something powerful stir inside him. That powerful "something" has not been transmitted physically, but by some means beyond the power of men to engender or control. Thus, the father writing to his son in Proverbs confesses that sexual attraction is simply "too mysterious" for him to understand.

That's scary—no matter how pleasant the initial feeling. Indeed, the good feeling comes in a package labeled, "Warning: Contents cannot be mastered by human powers."

A man can't always turn it off. A high schooler gets excited during algebra class when nearby Janey crosses her legs and the bell rings; embarrassed, he sits at his desk buying time fumbling with his notebook as his classmates rush by him for the door. A middle-aged executive, married with children, has a fleeting fantasy about another woman, feels shame, and puts it out of his mind; that night, the woman appears in his dreams.

Nor can a man always make it happen. Often when a couple decide to get pregnant, the most readily excitable man can experience anxiety—and nothing else—as his wife holds her ovulation timing kit and stopwatch and says, "Now!" Another man may struggle with chronic impotence, from which no amount of muscles, money, or technology can save him.

For the young man whose body is beginning to stir with sexual feelings, the world of attraction to "girls" is an awesome forest, filled with terrors even as it beckons delight. Around the ninth grade it suddenly seems as if girls are everywhere; skirts, blouse buttons, legs, and lipstick cry out to be seized.

In the grip of such power and mystery, any man in touch with reality would humbly take his shoes off. But we who have eaten the "new

—54—

grain" arrogantly clomp ahead in hobnail boots. And so the world hails the bold womanizer striding into the holy of holies, like Elvis in the movies—who in reality died alone of a drug overdose, divorced from his wife and lost in sexual perversion.

A people who have forgotten the Father God as Author of authentic femininity and masculinity harbor deep fears, and seek saving power to confirm sexual identity. Like the ancient pagans, they can only worship the one who conjures the most powerful spirit of lust, genuflecting before the television and showering the Sex Queen and Hunk with adoration and money.

Lust compels us into physical gratification in order to short-circuit the mystery, "saving" us from the humbling unknown and thereby, from trusting relationship with the Father God and His confirmation of sexual identity.

Not long ago, I was driving out Sunset Boulevard in Los Angeles for an appointment, and as the road crested before Hollywood, I was startled to see stretched high above me against the sky a giant billboard picturing twin women, tanned and blond, in bikinis. Presiding over the Los Angeles basin, the sign bore no words. Presumably, any man who had eaten enough of the media "new grain" to be "in the know," would recognize the women.

I did not. But I did recognize at once the age-old spirit of lust which they projected—like the lust goddess Aphrodite, hailed as spiritual patroness of Corinth with a giant naked statue high on the mountaintop overlooking that Greek harbor. "In Corinth, let the sailor beware,"[2] warned ancient wisdom—transmuted today, "In America, let men leap in wherever it feels good."

When such thundering voices call from the forest, a young man cries out for a secure voice of wisdom. He seeks an older man who has lived in the forest and can tell him, "That stream over there looks good, but it's poison; wait 'til further down the trail for the good stream. Over that way is a fantastic view, but it's a rough climb up—watch your step, and don't get too close to the cliff edge. The cave is good for protection once in awhile, but stay near the opening, since it drops off further inside."

Too often today, however, the older men themselves are lost in the forest, having never surrendered their sexuality to Jesus—who is Lord of the forest—and allowed Him to bring them to the Father God for His guidance. They are guzzling the poisonous stream of pornography, falling from the cliff vistas into adultery and fornication, lost in the caves of alienation and fantasy.

And so alone, the boys stumble ahead into the dark woods.

"I can remember in the back of the school bus when I was a freshman in high school," one forty-year-old clergyman told me. "Some older kid—at least seventeen!—was telling us how he'd had sex with a girl in the back of his car one night. There must've been a dozen of us guys packed around him, like fervent disciples listening to this denim-jacket guru.

"Frankly, I felt kind of repulsed by what he was saying. It didn't sound that good to me, actually—kind of dark and sneaky and dangerous, like stealing something. I was definitely disappointed, and confused. I felt ashamed for wanting sex. If that's what sex is like, I thought to myself, I hope it's a long time before I have to do it."

Most men today can tell of going out in the woods years ago as young teens with other boys to look at pornographic "men's magazines"—a graphic example of being lost in the forest without an older mentor.

Contrast these crude stories of darkness, shame, and fear with the loving intention of the Father God—who sees that it is "not good for the man to live alone" (see Gen. 2:18–25), and takes the initiative to meet His son's need. Significantly, the Father first brings the animals to the man, perhaps to surface his deepest needs by meeting his most accessible ones first.

We can imagine God's saying, "I know you've been lonely, Adam, so look what I've got just for you. Here's a couple of dogs to befriend you, some rabbits to hunt with the dog, horses to ride, fish in the waters—you'll have a great time fishing!—some birds to sing in the morning, and all the other animals to keep you company. Enjoy!"

So Adam ran with his dogs, rode his horses, chased his rabbits, caught his fish, sang with the birds, day after day after day—until we can imagine one day God's coming upon Adam downcast in the Garden. "What's the matter, son? How come you still seem lonely? Didn't you like the dog and horse and . . ."

"Yes, Father," Adam interrupts. "I . . . appreciate the animals. All of them. I really do. They do things for me, and they do okay by themselves. It's just that, well, they don't . . . really need me all that much. I . . . don't want to sound ungrateful, Father, but is that . . . all you've got?"

So the man named all the birds and all the animals; but not one of them was a suitable companion to help him.

"Just . . . what else did you have in mind, son?" God asks, suppressing a father's knowing, loving smile.

"Well, I like the way they all have eyes and noses and legs, kind of like mine. But have you got anything that's more . . . like me, Father?"

—56—

"How do you mean?"

"I'm . . . not exactly sure. All I know is something's still . . . missing somehow. Maybe if it walked and made sounds more like me? It's really . . . hard, Father. The animals all go off by themselves to sleep at night, and I just lie there awake, feeling . . . kind of empty."

"Can you describe what you're wanting then, at night?"

"It's strange—I thought it would go away when the animals came, but it's even worse now. It feels like . . . something inside of me that's not there. I just don't . . . have a name for it. Father, I need You. I know it sounds crazy, but I need . . . something like me, but different from me."

Then the Lord God made the man fall into a deep sleep. . . .

Because the man is now ready. Until he has experienced all other creatures and found them lacking, he cannot appreciate the depth of relationship which the woman beckons, even out of his own body and soul.

But for the best, the price is highest. Hence, the "deep sleep," the general anesthesia. A local novocaine, a light nap, would suffice to get another animal; for a pig or a fish, God could take a part of the man's ear or tooth. But for a truly "suitable companion to help him" fulfill his calling as a man, something essential to the whole man must be extracted. Hence, a major operation is coming, a deep cut required.

Relating to the woman faithfully exposes deep wounds in a man.

For so the Surgeon would heal.

And while he was sleeping, He took out one of the man's ribs and closed up the flesh. He formed a woman out of the rib, and brought her to him.

How many men, when dating a woman, are oblivious to the bond being formed between them? "I couldn't believe it," as one man exclaimed to me in genuine awe some months after his wedding, when he and his wife began talking about having children. "I happened to mention we'd need to think of names for a child, and right away she pulls out boy and girl names she said she'd picked out for our children after our second date—almost a year before I asked her to marry me!"

"Adam? . . . Adam! Wake up, Adam!"

"Huh? Wha . . . what happened?"

"I've taken a part of you and made it into another, one you may now reach after to draw back to yourself. Don't try to understand it; just come over here. You thought the dog and the fish and the horse were something? Take a look at what I have for you now, son!"

Then the man said, "Wow! Oh, Father! Yes, yes . . . Oh, my Father! At last, here is one of my own kind—bone taken from my bone, and flesh from my flesh. 'Woman' is her name, because she was taken out of man."

Wholly submitted to the Father, trusting His power and love, Adam is not overwhelmed by the spiritual mystery of sexual attraction. The Father covers his inadequacy, protects him from fear, and thereby, releases him to joy. "Therefore a man leaves his father and his mother and cleaves to his wife, and they become one flesh" (Gen. 2:24 RSV).

Hallelujah! Through unbroken relationship with the Father, a man can be set free from boyhood parental wounds and rejoice in his marriage.

Furthermore, the story concludes with a promise for the son thus in unbroken relationship with his Father: "The man and his wife were both naked, and they felt no shame" (Gen. 2:25 NIV). That is, they could be vulnerable and wholly exposed to each other—sharing their deepest needs, hopes, fears, brokenness—and still feel fully loved and accepted, without shame.

But the man decided to sin along with the woman, and thus break relationship with the Father. And the bright Garden became a dark forest.

Sadly, at least ninety-eight percent of men in our society today have learned about their sexuality shamefully—as in the back of the school bus and in pornographic materials—instead of through caring relationship with godly fathers. Virtually every man among us today therefore grows up fearful of his sexuality and thus, unable to approach the woman without shame.

Why? Because relationship with the father has been broken—even as Adam sinned before his/our Father God, and thereafter felt shame when naked before the woman.

Indeed, turning from the Father breaks not only relationship with Him, but with the woman as well—because the man can no longer see her as the Father's daughter and thus, a sister worthy of love and respect. She is no longer trustworthy. She is unsafe.

The biblical story says that the man cannot reveal himself to the woman when relationship with the Father has been broken. When powers of brokenness have been unleashed, the man's identity must be covered, his masculinity protected. Without the Father to cover him, he must cover himself. Hence, the fig leaves—and a host of other shields we fabricate in order to maintain "safe" distance from the woman.

I was initiated to perhaps the most graphic of these deceptions as a third-grader, on the school playground at recess one day, when a boy several years older approached me holding a strange piece of folded paper in his fingers. Split in four segments each covering one finger, the paper opened like a bird's beak as he pulled me aside and stuck it under my face. "Look at what I've got!" he exclaimed, his fingers pinching and opening the segments.

"What's that?" I asked innocently.

"See this?" he said, squeezing the segments in two pairs and opening them in one direction. "It's clean, right?"

I looked into the open beak of paper—and nodded, puzzled.

"Now watch me," he said. Dropping his hand secretively to his side, he walked over to where several girls were jumping rope. Greeting them, he reached over to one with the paper piece, pecked her shoulder with it, and ran back to me.

"Look at this!" he exclaimed, opening the beak jaws again, this time in the other direction. To my amazement, tiny black dots now filled the inside.

"What's all that?"

"They're cooties!" he declared. "Girls have 'em. All over."

Astounded, I looked back at the rope jumpers. "Really?"

"Sure!" he said, turning to run off. "Just remember not to get too close to girls, or you'll get 'em too!"

Disturbed by this new knowledge, I stood there thinking—and suddenly wanted to ask him, "What about my sister and my mother?" But he was already across the playground, evangelizing other classmates of mine to this gospel of saving power for frightened boys.

Soon, however, I had discovered such cultural reinforcements as Little Lulu's comic book friend Tubby in his "No Girls Allowed" treehouse. Indeed, by the fourth grade, I had learned to make and "use" my own "cootie catcher."

Even though living with a mother and two sisters offered ample evidence for me that "cooties" do not exist, nevertheless I remained strangely seized by the whole exercise—and became quite proficient at drawing large, ugly bugs on the proper segments of paper.

Why?

Because to move close to the girl is for the boy to enter "the forest"— that is, to engage spiritual powers far beyond his ability to discern or negotiate. Untutored, he feels inadequate, and therefore, afraid.

The cootie premise—that a boy *should* not approach girls because they carry contagious bugs—saves him from having to face not only his inadequacy, but the fearful spiritual reality which proclaims it.

Without the father to accept, initiate, and guide him in this essential process of male growth, a boy not only withdraws from himself and his true feelings, but also sacrifices the female's integrity—for the "cootie

—59—

premise" wounds the feminine soul in little girls by rejecting them as inferior.

Boys who lack godly fathers to guide them in the forest grow up feeling inadequate and afraid before the woman. They therefore perpetuate this puerile charade later. In some Spanish-speaking cultures, a woman is referred to as "enfermada"—literally, "sick"—during her monthly period. Some Middle-Eastern men demand "chador" cloaks cover the woman's body totally, and thus feel safe from the mysterious power she evokes. Men in some African tribes cut off a woman's clitoris to deprive her of sexual satisfaction, ensuring her fidelity.

Closer to home, as a teenager I recall hearing many derogatory jokes among men about "women drivers." On turning sixteen and getting my driver's license, I naively assumed my auto insurance premium would be much cheaper than any woman's. Imagine my shock at discovering I would have to pay almost twice as much, because young men cause auto accidents twice as often as women!

Any man who cannot remember fear in the presence of a woman is, by definition, too old. A helpful memory tool is Elvis's 1958 hit, "All Shook Up." It tells the story of a young man who gets tongue-tied around his girlfriend and begins to shake and have heart palpatations. He thinks the answer is the hobnail boot approach—he'll "have" her.

The unspiritual man can only perceive the awesome power generated in the woman's presence as coming from her. Hence, he fears and resents her for holding such literally body-shaking power over him. He reasons, "She has what I need, but won't just hand it over; how am I going to get it from her?"

The man who lacks a father to confirm his manhood doubts anyone so insecure as himself will ever "get it" from the woman. He may lash out violently and seize her in rape.

A more socially adept man realizes he has only two choices: He can either charge ahead with sports car, sexy clothes, and other accoutrements to seduce the woman and "score," or he can run from her like a coward.

The awesome power which seizes a man in the woman's presence, meanwhile, does not come from her, but rather, from the realm of the spirit. Neither he nor she generates it. Fear in the woman's presence, therefore, is not overcome or "cured" by seizing control—an impossible fantasy for mere human beings—but only by surrendering to the Father who rules that realm.

All too often, men run from this power by committing adultery, chasing another woman, or entertaining such fantasies—and thus short-circuit the intimacy which beckons the power and fear. In order to run but not appear cowardly—to establish a "safe" distance from the woman and even appear righteous for doing so, a man often simply criticizes her.

When moving close to the woman a man may, for example, suddenly begin thinking that she is "too quiet" or "too loud," her legs are "not that good after all," she put "too much/not enough" salt in the dinner, has "weird friends," etc.

Such barbs hurt, causing the woman to get angry and withdraw. Then, the man feels safe—justified in his critical opinions, and not responsible for the distance now between them.

Nancy, who at thirty had been married to Mark for five years, called me early one evening in tears. At her regular physical exam, she said, the doctor had found a lump in her breast and ordered a biopsy. When she told Mark, he hesitated, then burst out, "Well, you always were too fat, anyhow!"

I had played basketball and prayed with Mark several times, and found him to be a decent man. Why in the world, I wondered, would he lash out at Nancy so viciously?

"My educated guess as a man," I told her, "is that Mark's afraid of getting close, and doesn't want to tell you that directly. If you want to get through this, you're probably going to have to push him to speak the full truth. I know you're deeply hurt, and I wouldn't blame you for keeping your distance. But of course, that would play right into his game. If you want, I'll pray that you'll have the courage to talk to him and push through this."

Through her sobs, Nancy hesitated, thanked me, and said simply, "Okay." I prayed, then said I'd continue to pray later, and we hung up.

The next morning she called back, her voice calm and confident. "You were right," she said. "I went back to Mark and said, 'What are you afraid of, that you'd rather push me away than deal with?' He kept balking and saying 'Nothing!' But I kept insisting until finally, he said, 'Okay, I'll tell you. I'm afraid you'll have cancer and die, and I'll be left alone.'"

Instead of surrendering to the Father, Mark—who had been raised by his mother after his parents' divorce—had surrendered to the fear, and bailed out on the woman. Lacking an earthly father as a boy, he did not trust the Father God to be with him in uncertainty, much less to use it as an occasion to draw him into deeper relationship with Himself and with Nancy.

As it turned out, Nancy's body was healthy. But the man's wound to her feminine soul took some time to heal. "It's okay to be afraid," she told him. "I'm afraid too. Just don't run away from me when I need you to stand by me and pray for me."

Whenever a man runs from the truth, others pay for it—usually, those closest to him. But when he trusts that his Father is with him—when he trusts in Jesus, who says, "I am the way, the truth, and the life; no one goes to the Father except by me" (John 14:6)—he walks as a man of God, who bears the truth that sets others free (see John 8:32).

In a remarkably apt country-western song, "You're Talkin' to the Wrong Man,"[4] a teenage son turns to his dad for help after his girlfriend seems to invite affection, and then rebuffs him. But the father can't help. He admits that he still doesn't understand the boy's mother.

Rather than list several points of wisdom, the father essentially tells his confused son, "I understand where you are; in fact, I am where you are. I cannot take your pain and confusion away, but I will not leave you alone in it." And that, for the son, is enough. For it mirrors the incarnate Christ, who demonstrates on the Cross that to be one with the father enables the son to walk in victory through the darkest forest, unto death itself.

Certainly, this father and son are both "talkin' to the wrong man" as long as they talk only to each other and not to the Father God who created both them and the "forest" of sexual attraction that awes them. Without Jesus, men can easily bond together as frightened boys to protect themselves against women, rather than bond with the Father as bold men to love His daughters.

Even as he approaches her, therefore, the man in broken relationship with his father must shield himself from the woman, for the spiritual power generated by their closeness threatens to overwhelm him. Cut off from the father, he is alone in the forest with his inadequacies. He lacks grounding in the masculine through his father's call, and thus, he lacks basic trust in himself as a man. Therefore, to give himself to the woman is to lose himself in her—even as he lost himself in his mother when his dad abandoned him.

The man desires the woman physically, needs her emotionally as "a suitable companion to help him," and misses her as a spiritual complement—but he dares not draw close to her. Only his physical desire seems objective enough for him to control, so he forfeits emotional, spiritual intimacy with the woman, supplanting and thus confusing it with sexual acts.

This pervasive fear of the woman in men is therefore not necessarily rooted in any will in the woman to destroy the man, but more likely, in his own sense of sexual shame and inadequacy from broken relationship with Dad.

The biblical faith, meanwhile, proclaims that the woman is fashioned out of the man. In his sexual desire, the man's body feels the longing to rejoin, to reunite with the missing part of himself that the woman literally embodies—and therein, to become wholly human and completely himself again at last. If, indeed, the Father has come in Jesus to restore relationship with His sons—broken by Adam's sin at the Fall—then as a man surrenders his sexual impulses to Jesus, he allows the Father to reopen the gates to genuine intimacy with the woman, even the missing part of himself.

A simple prayer might be, "Father, I give up—not to my sexual impulses, but to You. Take over my heart and body, Lord Jesus, and give me the strength to cooperate with Your righteous purposes in me."

The boy whose father talks to him openly and compassionately about the mystery of sexuality, however, need not protect himself behind harmful practices that enforce distance from the female. Indeed, such a father can affirm the wonder and mystery of his son's sexual energies, even as he holds the son accountable for expressing them in a godly way.

The father of a sixteen-year-old told me he came home from work late one evening, and his wife greeted him with, "Steve just got back from a date with Sally Smith, and you'd better go talk to him about what he did to her!" Fuming, she turned to leave. "He's in his room."

Startled, the man was left standing alone in the living room. He had heard his son talk disparagingly about Sally Smith, and was as surprised to learn about such a date as to be greeted thusly by his wife.

Sighing uneasily, he went to his son's bedroom, knocked and waited. After no answer, he entered—and found the boy in bed, covers pulled to his head.

Clearing his throat, he approached the bed. "Steve?"

"Huh?"

"Your mom tells me you went out with Sally Smith tonight."

"Yeah."

"She said you . . . did something to Sally—is that right?"

"No—I didn't do that much."

"Your mom seemed pretty upset. What did you do to Sally?"

Steve sat up. "Aw, Mom always gets upset about everything you tell her—it's no big deal."

Uncertain, the father hesitated. "Did you . . . kiss her?"

"Yeah, I kissed her."

"Did you . . . feel her up?"

"Yeah, some."

"Anything else?"

"Just a little. I mean, we didn't . . . go all the way or anything."

Oh, Lord! the father thought; *what do I do now?* After some thought, he said, "It felt good, didn't it?"—surprising even himself.

"Huh? Uh, yeah. Yeah, it did."

The man paused. "Son . . . I know you've talked about Sally before, how she's always chasing after you and you wish she'd go away. You don't like her much, do you?"

"No."

"Was she coming after you again?"

"Yeah."

"So you took advantage of her then, didn't you?"

Hesitating, Steve nodded.

"Do you really want to be a person who goes through life taking advantage of people?"

"No," said Steve.

After talking it over, the father invited the son to pray and ask God's forgiveness for taking advantage of Sally. Then, he told his son to call Sally and ask her forgiveness.

"Do you think I handled that situation okay?" the father asked.

"Definitely," I said, amazed.

Indeed, the father had respected his son, affirmed his sexual energies, and still held him accountable. Sexual contact with a woman does feel good, and no honest man, whether sixteen or sixty, can be convinced otherwise.

Indeed, if sinful acts themselves felt so terrible, we would never have needed Jesus to save us from them; we'd avoid them by ourselves. A father must stand with his son in the truth closest to the son's experience if he is to lead the son to any deeper truth.

In acknowledging matter-of-factly, "It felt good, didn't it?" the father taught the son to distinguish real guilt from learned shame. That is, when he as a man thereby said, "Your feelings are understandable," the son did not need to defend himself. In that security of being accepted by the father, the son could begin to recognize his sin, and take it to the Father God for cleansing.

If the father had stormed into the son's room, condemned his behavior, and punished him severely, he would have broken relationship with the son, who thereafter would surely have shared nothing more about his sexuality. He would have taken off by himself into the "forest" to save face—and ultimately, become dangerously lost.

The Father God convicts of sin in order to transform and heal the sinner; the Enemy, in order to condemn and destroy him. The father must at times declare his son guilty of wrongdoing, but must never condemn his son to the shame of "wrongbeing."[5]

Without such fatherly guidance, men grow up substituting physical sexual expression for emotional/spiritual intimacy with the woman.

The biblical faith, therefore, points to a wholly different basis for intimacy with the woman. Significantly, the Father God who cuts His son Adam to draw forth the woman is the only one who knows where the grooves have been made in the man, and therefore, is the only one who can fit the two pieces together properly. The man and the woman, that is, are designed to unite only under the authority of the Father God.

Failure to respect this reality bears quite practical consequences, in spite of the seductive humanistic view that "sex is okay outside of marriage as long as the two love each other." For example, most men who marry today, including Christian men who became believers later in life and those divorced, have had sexual relations with other women previously. The world, which can recognize only human powers, holds that all bonds cease when the partners decide to break them.

Thus, if the humanly endowed powers of the State comprise all contracts in the relationship, then a court-certified divorce sets the man and woman "free," both emotionally as well as physically, to pursue new partners as if the previous one never existed. But any man who has had intercourse with a woman knows that forgetting her is not that easy. Dreams and fantasies persist long after he has stopped seeing her. For indeed, human governments can break only those bonds which human governments make. Only God can break bonds made in the spiritual realm.

And a bond is formed in the spirit through sexual intercourse.

As Paul declared in dismay when the early Church had apparently forgotten this truth,

> Or perhaps you don't know that the man who joins his body to a prostitute becomes physically one with her? The scripture says quite plainly, "The two will become one body." (1 Cor. 6:16)

As Eve was taken from Adam, only God can separate two who have become one body.

John Sandford explains it well:

God has so built us in our spirits that whatever woman a man enters, their spirits are united to each other from that moment on. Each person's spirit seeks, from the moment of union, to find, fulfill, nurture, and cherish the one who entered into that union with him/her. . . .

[O]nce a wrong union has been entered, our spirit still remembers that union and seeks to fulfill the other. If there have been many immoral unions with many partners, our spirit becomes like an overloaded transformer, trying to send its current in too many directions. Having been delivered by confession, absolution, and prayer for separation, counselees have often cried out, "I have never felt so free. I didn't realize how scattered I felt. I feel together again." Of course! Their spirits were no longer having to search heaven and earth to find and fulfill dozens of forgotten partners![6]

Therefore, when I minister to a Christian man who wants to be fully cleansed and ready for a new union under the Father God's blessing and authority, I lead him in a prayer such as this:

Father, I confess the sin of fornication with (names of women), and I ask Your forgiveness. In the name of Jesus, I now renounce all bonds of the flesh with (women's names, including ex-wife), and take the sword of the Spirit and cut all remaining spiritual ties between us. I ask for Your blood, Jesus, to cover and cleanse me from all attraction and wounds there, and I release those women to You for Your purposes in their lives apart from me. And I put myself in Your hands, Jesus, to bond me to my wife alone.

Other emotional and spiritual healing may be required to sever fully some past sexual relationships, but this prayer facilitates that process by cutting the major spiritual taproot which has nurtured those relationships and the ongoing fantasies.

Clearly, the man who respects this mystery and its power can offer such wisdom to his son.

Les, thirty-four and a believer, was divorced for eight years and living several hundred miles from his ex-wife and fourteen-year-old son. During a visit, Les encouraged the boy in his many activities—friends, schoolwork, baseball, horseback riding, camping—and noticed him glancing often at girls.

"Before I left," Les said, "I sat down with him and told him I noticed he was looking at the girls, and that was good. I encouraged him to date around when he felt ready. But I told him not to have sex, that if he did at his age, all his energies would go into the girl, and all the good activities he now enjoys so much would take a back seat to her. I told him that when he grows up he will become secure enough in himself that he can get married, and his sexual attraction to the woman won't push him off balance like now. He seemed to understand that, and thanked me for saying it."

Thus, bonding to the woman requires first breaking from the mother, bonding to the father/company of men, and then bonding to the Father God.

At forty, Ted had been divorced for several years and during that time had become a Christian. When he began dating again, he experienced so much anxiety over "how far to go" with a date that he resolved not even to kiss a woman. When he came to see me, he had just met Grace, who seemed especially well-suited for him.

As we talked, Ted demonstrated a good relationship with the Father God and was in regular prayer fellowship with other men, so I encouraged him simply to ask for His Father's word as he walked Grace up to her apartment door next time.

"I asked the Lord if I could kiss her," he reported after their second date, "and I sensed a hug was okay."

After the next date, Ted reported much good sharing between them— and another hug.

The following week, Ted was smiling broadly. "When I asked the Father if I could kiss her, I didn't feel any check like the times before, just kind of open and happy. I waited a minute, asked again, and felt the same—so I kissed her! It was great!"

Some months later, when the two realized God was knitting them together for marriage, and they had talked openly about boundaries on their sexual expression, Ted told me he mentioned those first dates and his prayers at the doorstep. Grace laughed good-naturedly and told him, "You weren't the only one praying! By that third date, I was beginning to pray, 'Come on, Father—make him kiss me!'"

Both Ted and Grace had had sexual relations with other partners previously, but had been celibate for years since becoming Christians. I led them in prayers to cut all past bonds of the flesh. Still, fears and confusions arose soon after their marriage, which drove them to their knees.

"We naively assumed we'd just pick up sexually where we left off with the other partners years before," Ted said, shaking his head and smiling. "But it wasn't long before we were wearing knee-holes in the carpet by our bed, confessing together that we'd bought into the world's approach to sex, and had never been taught differently by our parents. We begged the Father to clean that out of us and teach us what making love really is—and we discovered the Father had a closeness to give us that we'd never before experienced."

In my own marriage, I have learned to go to the Father God readily when differences arise. Once, for example, we had discussed, debated, and argued a point to no agreement or resolution. In frustration I huffed, "Okay, then, I'm going to the Father!"

I took Mary's hand and we knelt. "Father," I prayed, "I've told Mary my opinion on this and she's told me hers; we've gone over and over this and neither of us wants to give up to the other. So we both give up to You. Speak to us, show us how You see all this."

I waited, and sensed the Father's saying simply, "Listen to her."

"But Father," I protested, "I really feel like I'm right this time!"

"I didn't say you were wrong," I sensed the reply; "I said 'Listen to her.'"

Puzzled, but at my wit's end, I sighed, turned to Mary, and told her what the Lord had said. "Maybe I've been so anxious to make my point that I haven't really listened to you. Would you tell me once more how you feel about all this, and I'll try my best to listen?" *Okay, Father, I prayed quietly, I give up to You all my right to win this argument. Now help me listen to her and hear what You want me to.*

Mary hesitated as a flicker of distrust was swept away by love, and then told me again how she was feeling. As she talked, I sensed her pain and began to see why this issue was particularly upsetting to her. Many tears and hugs later, we could only wonder together at the Father's love for us both.

"I don't always trust you in the moment," Mary said, "but I trust your relationship with the Father. Also, I know He loves me, and that gives me all the confidence I need that we'll work things out."

I realized that I feel the same way about Mary.

As a husband, at times I overreact, miss the point, or just plain shut down. Sometimes, I handle things very honestly, openly, and maturely, and still worry that I've done it wrong. But when I remember my Father God and surrender it all to Him, I know that we're on the same side—bonded in the Spirit, and ready to celebrate that in the flesh.

CHAPTER FIVE

The Wolf Loves The Lone Sheep

Our Father . . .

(Matt. 6:9)

And he called to him the twelve, and began to send them out two by two.

(Mark 6:7 RSV)

The host congregation of several hundred had listened intently to my Sunday evening message, and as they stood and began chatting with one another after the benediction, I moved off to the side to gather my materials.

"Excuse me, but I need you to pray for me," a man's uneasy voice broke in from behind me. I turned to see a clean-cut man, perhaps thirty, in a sport shirt. "Would you pray for me?" he asked. "All that you were saying about men, I mean, it's true for me. I'd really like you to pray for me. It's like all my life, I've wanted my father to . . ."

Strangely, his voice trailed off in my mind as I sensed something amiss. Naturally, I was inclined to listen to this sincere young man's story and to pray for him. But even as he continued his sad tale, I balked.

"I think it started when I was a boy," he was saying, when I interrupted. "I . . . would like to pray for you," I began, hesitating as I prayed under my breath, *Why am I so resistant, Lord?* Then it struck me. "No, I won't pray for you," I said, matter-of-factly.

Surprised, the man drew up.

"Are you a member of this church?" I asked.

He nodded. "I've been coming about two years."

"Look around you," I invited, gesturing toward the crowd. "How many men do you see out there in your church?"

Turning, he paused. "Oh, maybe a hundred or so."

"And you're asking me to pray for you? Tell me: Have you ever asked one of your hundred brothers here to pray for you?"

Knitting his brow, he stood quietly and shook his head slowly, from side to side.

"My brother," I said, "I respect you for asking me to pray for you. I know that took courage. But I don't want to short-circuit the amazing gift your Father God has for you right here in your own church, with the men you see all the time. I leave tonight and you'll never see me again. These men are your brothers in the Body, where God has called you to root and grow. They'll be here to stand with you long after I'm gone.

"If I pray for you, you'll go out of here thinking your problem has been solved or, at least, taken care of enough for you to manage a little bit longer by yourself. And you won't experience what your Father God wants to give you in the fellowship of men.

"I could never do for you just myself what any two or three other men out there could do, not just once tonight, but for the rest of your life here."

Hesitantly, like a boy standing for the first time on a high diving board, he bit his lower lip.

"How does that sound to you?" I asked.

"Well . . . you really seem to understand, and you've got a lot more expertise in praying."

"Is it a little scary to think about asking another guy to pray for you?" I asked.

"Well . . . yes," he replied.

"You probably haven't talked much with other guys about your dad and other tough things in your life, have you?"

He shook his head, dropping it slightly. At once, I thought of the rich young man whose face fell when Jesus told him to give all that he had to the poor. Asking this young man to be vulnerable before another man was like asking him to give away everything he had.

"One thing you don't have to worry about here," I said, sighing, "is being alone. Every one of these hundred other guys here, like you, is hurting from his father. They just haven't had the courage to talk to any other guy about it, like you've shown in coming up to talk to me now.

"You may need to talk first with your pastor, and ask him if he could suggest a couple of other guys to get together with—and even a Christian counselor to help you sort things out. But if it's that scary, then it takes courage—and that's what God wants to give His men today. That's what I'll be praying for you as I drive home." Excusing myself to talk with others, I put a hand on his shoulder. "Your Father God's with you in this," I said. "Trust Him."

Even as I shook hands and chatted with many others, I glanced out over the "hundred or so" men there—and winced as a wave of fear swept over me. So many men, Father . . . so alone!

Later, on the freeway driving home, I prayed for godly courage in the man who had approached me—and remembered years earlier when, as a pastor, trouble seemed to swarm about me both at home and at church. I had regularly attended several monthly ecumenical and denominational clergy meetings, and I began asking the group at each if anyone else there might want just to "get together sometime, you know, and maybe get to know each other a little better . . . ?"

To my dismay, my invitation drew no takers. Soon, in my private conversations, I began berating clergy for being so "insulated." As my life grew more tumultuous, I continued my offer at various meetings, but to no avail. Finally, as I prayed desperately one day at home, a question arose within me: *Have you told any other man that you really need him?*

I gulped. Sure, I'd told plenty of ministers that it might be good to get together in a small group . . . but, after all, God is big and powerful enough to help me by Himself. I mean, why bother other guys and . . .

Have you ever told another man "I need you"? No still, small voice, the question seemed to leap out at me, braking my thoughts.

I sighed.

No, I hadn't. Never.

In the utter silence wrought by such conviction, the thought came to me: The wolf loves the lone sheep.

At once, it made sense. The lone sheep are easier to catch, fatter because they're not keeping up with the herd.

I remembered talking with a former ministry associate of a well-known Christian leader who fell to sexual immorality. "He [the leader] was so afraid of looking bad that he just wouldn't open himself up to any other man," the associate had said. And so, instead of risking looking bad to one or two Christian brothers—who presumably could minister mercy and healing—he fell to temptation and looked disgraceful before the merciless millions of men in the world who were grateful for yet another "hypocrisy-in-the-Church" excuse to avoid meeting Jesus.

Again, I sighed.

Knowing what I had to do, I ran down a mental list of friends, selecting the four with whom I felt most comfortable. I called each and said matter-of-factly, "I'm dealing with some tough things in my life right now, and I need you. Will you come meet with me and two or three

—71—

other guys at 7:00 A.M. in my office next Friday, to talk and pray for me, say 'til 8:00?"

Every man agreed.

Nervously, I greeted each at my office that Friday morning. After we'd all settled in, I said again, "I need you to support and pray for me." I then shared what was happening in my life.

The prayers and support that followed buoyed my spirits, even as the others sat glowing themselves.

"It's not eight o'clock yet," one remarked finally, after all had prayed for me. "As long as we're here, I've got a few things I'd like you to pray for me about, too, if you don't mind."

"You bet!" the rest of us chorused.

By 8:30, each of the other four men had asked for prayer, and we parted with hugs, agreeing to meet again the following week. Soon, one man became uncomfortable with the depth of sharing and dropped out. But our group of four met for the next three years, while I pastored my church, and has been meeting now for five years with several replacement members since my leaving.

Not only did my humility before other men open the door in my own heart to receive from them, but it also provided the occasion for us all to experience strength in helping each other. As Los Angeles Dodgers manager Tommy Lasorda declared in a *Sports Illustrated* interview,

> It's my job to get [the team] to put forth all the effort they have. To do that, you have to let them know they're appreciated. They want to know that. When I took over with four games left in the '76 season, I called [outfielder] Reggie Smith in my office and told him, "I just got this job as manager. It's a dream come true for me. I want to do good. I need your help." He looked at me and said, "No one ever told me that before, that they needed me." The next year, he hit 32 homers.[1]

Since 1985, in addition to several occasional groups, I have prayed on the phone with a prayer partner every weekday morning at 6:30 for half an hour—and at other times as the need arises. For several of those years, we lived a toll call's distance apart, but we knew our fellowship in the Lord was utterly essential and thus, priceless. Periodically, we've paused to wonder aloud, "How in the world did we ever survive before, without praying for each other like this?" Our joy of thanksgiving for each other, however, is always tempered when we think of the millions of men, even churchgoing Christian men, who are struggling by themselves.

While the wolf drools.

Authentic men's groups can only be formed out of genuine need. As

Dr. Bruce Larson, author of *No Longer Strangers* and *The Relational Revolution,* declares, "There is only one infallible way . . . to get small groups going in a church. You start one group because you need it. You don't whip up a program. You don't say, 'This will be good for our church.' You say, 'I have said Yes to Jesus and Yes to the family of God. Therefore I need to be in a group.'"[2]

As I have prayed about my original experience in asking four other men for help, I sense that someone has to blaze the trail with his own vulnerability before other men can overcome their fear and follow the Father's call into fellowship with Himself and other men. Indeed, Jesus did that on the Cross. He could do it because He trusted His Father, knowing that no matter what the risk, He and the Father were one.

Because the essential bond with the father has not been forged among men today, however, the prospect of bonding with other men becomes fearful—and at best, tentative. His experience of being physically and/or emotionally abandoned by the father has led the average man to distrust other men.

A boy who grows up with an abusive or absent father can become as anti-male as the most strident feminist—who often was "fathered" similarly. Often, for sympathy, the man may bond with women, who have themselves learned that "you can't depend on the man to be there when you need him." Ultimately, this hiding from men among women is a sham, reflecting the man's own self-denigration.

With no hope of healing his father-wound, a man can only distrust and reject his own masculinity, as if to say, "If being a man means being like my father and abandoning people who love and need you—I don't want any part of it." To mask this fear of his father—and thus, of his own masculinity—he may seek respectability as a "feminist male," righteously committing his energies to the women's movement—as if God has no agenda for healing men themselves.

The "movement" women who "affirm" and thus harbor him, not only enable such a man to avoid the tough inner work requisite to his manhood, but ultimately, they deprive themselves of the masculine character they need in him to complement and call forth their femininity.

Still, a growing number of women today are realizing that their husbands need something from other men which they as women cannot provide. Because she holds such a high stake in the man's healing, the woman may even push to involve him in men's programs.

At one conference of about four hundred men, I asked, tongue-in-cheek, "How many of you are here by 'domestic invitation'?" One third to half of the hands went up. Another time, the pastor of a church where

I led a packed-out men's retreat told me that several wives in the congregation had called to register their husbands for the retreat. To his credit, he refused.

"A few of those wives got pretty upset," he said, "but I just told them if he's going to get on this retreat what we feel God wants to give him, the man must want to grow for himself, not for the woman."

Meanwhile, the lone sheep get picked off, as men prefer the arms of death to those of the Father. Drugs, fear of women, job confusion, sexual immorality, suicide at a rate three times that of women, heart attacks—these and many other "wolves" are devouring men today who are running from the father-wound.

One by one, like hors d'oeuvres. Easy.

During the Persian Gulf War of 1991, a *Los Angeles Times* feature headline asked, "In Face of Death—What Makes Soldiers Disregard Instinct?" If we translate the secular term "instinct" to the biblical "human nature," or "desires of the flesh," this becomes the key question for Christian men who would run from the lethal father-wound. What, indeed, enables a man to overcome the powers of death, which routinely intimidate him and fuel his natural human desires to avoid pain—ultimately leading him to retreat from his higher calling?

"Military specialists agree," notes the reporter, that soldiers "will stand and fight more because of loyalty to each other than to their officers or their country." As four Army and Marine servicemen amplify:

> When you get down to the zero hour, and it's you and almost certain death, it is the team [sic], the immediate family members, that send you over the ridgeline.

> The short answer is to be found in the small group that forms within the unit—the squad, the tank crew, the artillery crew—a small group that controls the day-to-day behavior of the soldiers.

> My personal goal is to get home alive and get seven of them soldiers (in my squad) home alive, too.

> They're there for me, and I'm there for them—it's a big family-type thing.[3]

In contrast, a sociologist who "analyzed Egypt's defeat in the 1967 Six-Day War" concluded that "Arab fighting forces lack cohesion—a reflection of a culture in which Arab men are divided from one another by suspicion and hostility. Because of this defect in the social fabric, each Arab soldier, in the critical moments of combat, finds himself fighting not as a member of a team, but an abandoned individual. Consequently, each individual tends primarily to look after himself, and the unit disintegrates."[4]

Ironically, this portrait of the losing Arab soldier closely fits the average American man today in his daily battles on the job and at home. When the boss is on his case, when the woman threatens to leave, when illness strikes, he finds himself divided from other men "by suspicion and hostility." He therefore struggles not hopefully, as part of a team with supportive, caring brothers, but desperately, as "an abandoned individual"—the boy without his daddy forever.

Compare this "squad," or group, orientation among real-life warriors with the traditional "macho" model of manhood proclaimed by the media—the alienated, violent male.

In fact, these two character traits are companions. The more a man is cut off from other men, the easier for him to objectify and strike them; a man bonded to other men recognizes himself in the others, and cannot readily destroy them.

The Lone Ranger offers the quintessential example. Wearing a mask, not only is he alienated from other men, but he is alienated from himself as well, for he has no name. He even calls his closest companion "Tonto," Spanish for "stupid." Other boyhood models, from Superman to Rambo, are all loners—more bonded to their horses or guns than to other men.

From silver bullets to a body of steel, the macho man is by definition invulnerable, that is, he cannot be affected by anyone else. The Marlboro Man, the motorcycle gang leader, Rambo—they always seem mysteriously aloof.

Certainly, the military experience bonds men by circumstance, and may not include any deeper sharing of the self beyond accomplishing the immediate task. Nevertheless, the above testimonies of real-life soldiers clearly expose the lone sheep model of manhood as a lethal fraud, wrought by "the wolf" to lure men out from the fold into destruction. The Enemy also calls men out; discerning the true Father is essential to manhood.

The honest man today, meanwhile, has seen his awful wound and his inability to save himself from its effects. He wants to be affected by others—to be comforted, supported, encouraged, challenged, held accountable. After years of eating the new grain of independence, however, remembering your own needs and reconnecting to others—the life condition into which every man is born—is like shifting gears from overdrive to reverse.

It's so hard, in fact, that often a man simply must sink deeply enough into his loneliness to experience a pain unto death before seeking help.

Thus, instead of pasting on smiles and pretending we're just fine by ourselves, we must recognize, as Bruce Larson declares, that "loneliness is really a gift." He says, "It's like pain . . . the psychic pain that drives us to do something about our isolation."

God made us to need intimacy and He put in us a desire to belong to others. We find in Jesus Christ the way to fulfill these needs. Thus, as Larson says, "Loneliness becomes the very ground of intimacy,"[5] and this bonding requires trust.

Larson identifies three questions he believes God asks us when we try to become intimate with Him:

1. Will you trust Me with your life?
2. Will you entrust yourself to a part of My family?
3. Will you get out and be involved someplace in the world? Will you try to walk My love, My Word, My character to somebody? Will you lose your life?[6]

Thus, godly masculine energy in our society today—as the final question—is missing, because men have not trusted the Father and each other. At the same time, as Larson notes, our cultural heritage fosters alienation:

We are a nation built by people who kept moving on. They started on the East coast and kept heading westward whenever a problem arose. Ellen Goodman, the columnist, says that now, with no more geographical frontiers to move to, we've begun moving away from each other. The frontier is within, and we move away from our spouse or our family whenever we don't know how to solve something.[7]

In fact, the macho alienation in men merely covers up the fear of being close to other men, learned as boys by being naturally close to the father and suffering his abandonment. Overcoming alienation from other men and its accompanying defeat in life's struggles, therefore, requires healing the father-wound by knowing the true Father God. Even Larson's cultural explanation above might be viewed from this perspective, since America was settled by men who left their fathers and cut their roots in the "fatherland."

I believe a man can experience healing for the father-wound most readily, and most authentically, in a small group with other men covenanted in that goal.

One man in his mid-thirties, whose father died when he was a boy, explained to me what his men's support group meant to him.

"The group started out with all of us sharing problems in our jobs, relationships with women, and such," he said. "But before long, we were talking about good things going on in our lives, too. Then once in awhile we felt we had to warn a guy about where he was heading with some bad decisions. The whole thing kind of took off and got to be more than we'd planned."

He paused, and knit his brow. "Actually, I guess you could say the group has become like a father to me."

It makes sense, both theologically and practically. The Spirit of the Father, His Person and Presence in this present age revealed in the historical Jesus, has been poured out today on the Body of believers. We therefore meet Him wherever "two or three are gathered" (Matt. 18:20 NKJV) in His name.

Indeed, what does a boy need from his father?

If he falls off his bike, he needs a father to pick him up and comfort him. Later, as an adult, if a man loses his job or girlfriend, for example, he comes to his men's group for comfort and support.

If a boy gets a home run at recess, or makes an *A* on his book report, he needs a father to pat him on the back, and maybe reward him with an ice cream. So, if a man wins a promotion at work or finally learns to curb his temper at home, he goes to his men's group for affirmation: "Good going, Bill! Hey, guys, let's take Bill out to a ball game and celebrate!"

If a boy has been hanging around with guys who think it's fun to steal from other kids' desks, he needs a father to say, "Son, what you're doing is not good for you, and let me tell you why."

So, if a married man in the group begins regularly taking out a woman coworker to lunch or another man plans to save money by cheating, he needs the other men in his group to call him into account and say, "Jim, we're really concerned about what you're doing, and here's why."

Thus the father-wound becomes the catalyst for fellowship; when a man realizes what his father didn't give him, he can seek it among fellow men. Therein, he encounters the Father God. Larson describes his first experience of entrusting his inner self to another man as "like Pentecost for me. The power of God was suddenly released when I gave up being invulnerable."[8]

Bret, for example, at thirty-one was engaged to a Christian woman who seemed just right for him, but he was feeling afraid of the marriage commitment. As we talked, he mentioned several long-distance phone calls to his parents. "Mom's been all excited and talks a lot," he said, "but Dad hardly says a word."

"What do you wish your dad would say?" I asked him.

Bret sighed, sadly. "I wish he would just say something like, 'You're okay; I understand how you feel. I felt scared with your mother too. All guys do. It takes a little time to adjust to each other, but it's going to be all right.'" Dismayed, he shook his head. "Obviously, a part of me knows that's all true, but . . ."

"But you need another man to know it with you, don't you?"

Tight-lipped, Bret nodded, dropping his eyes.

For several minutes, I grieved with Bret. Finally I said, "If the Father God uses men's groups to give men what they didn't get from their dads, what could you do now with your sadness and need?"

Bret knit his brow. "Maybe I could make an announcement at church to see if any other guys want to get together who are engaged, or recently married?"

"Go for it," I encouraged.

Obviously, a man could seek the Father's presence through other men at church for other life circumstances. A man whose wife is pregnant could seek out other men whose wives are pregnant and those who have recently become fathers. A man recently divorced, or retired, or who lost his job—all could seek out men with similar experiences. The list of possibilities is as long as men's genuine needs.

By ministering the presence of the Father, the men's group overcomes the most essential root of the problem.

For if the pathology of mother-son bonding lies in the possessive, clinging presence of the mother, then healing requires the boy's breaking away from the mother, through the father's call. But in our society, the father has not called. The boy is ready to be born again as a son of the father, but no man stands ready to receive him from the womb-like emotional bond to his mother.

The pathology of father-son bonding therefore lies in the emotional or physical absence of the father. Healing requires first not a cut, but bonding at last to other men in godly masculine fellowship.

Most heroes offered to men in our society are aimed at younger males and emphasize the physical prowess that is more accessible to youth. Such models clearly cannot lead males into mature manhood, which requires facing one's need for and responsibility to community. Most often, this maturing process is precipitated by the decline of physical power, the end of one's own strength—as indeed, the death of the flesh.

"What an unhappy man I am!" as Paul declared. "Who will rescue me from this body that is taking me to death?" (Rom. 7:24). Who, indeed? Certainly, no muscle-bound, wrinkle-less young "hero," but only one who has himself dared face head-on the powers of death, unto his very body itself. "Thanks be to God," he therefore concludes, "who does this through our Lord Jesus Christ" (7:25).

To die to the flesh today means for a man to reach out to other men, confessing his weakness and fear, and trusting the Father God to meet him there among two or three other men.

Robert Bly, a central figure in the secular men's movement today,[9] notes that most of the men drawn to his gatherings are over thirty-five.

> I think that's because the images of manhood we're given in high school—Gen. [William] Westmoreland or John Wayne or some fool like Clint Eastwood—may last us through our 20s to some extent. But by the time you're 35, it's clear that those models are not working. The myths and ancient stories we tell provide models of masculinity with more soul, more range and a greater integration of the feminine.[10]

Bly also says that usually by the time a man is thirty-five he has begun to realize that his "job life and relationships . . . are not working." He has begun to accept "a little sense of failure." Bly therefore looks to a form of male fellowship much different from older models like the Moose Lodge or Masonic Temple.

> Unlike those lodges, our gatherings are not meant to be comfortable. We're not asking for a conventional life. We're asking men to get in touch with their souls. To do that, they must have what D.H. Lawrence called "a purpose."
>
> A purpose is not the same as wanting to be rich. Or wanting to control the junk bond market. Or wanting to be dominant over other men in the business world. Or to have many mistresses. We ask men to become dissatisfied with their own lives. In that way it's almost the polar opposite of the Moose Lodge.[11]

Too often churches have offered men no more opportunity than secular lodges to "get in touch with their souls"—which requires facing the authentic "sense of failure" that drives us, like Paul, to seek saving power from the Father God among other men.

In preparing this chapter, I dusted off an old magazine article which I wrote shortly after my thirtieth birthday—as I entered seminary—to reflect on the changes taking place then within my body and soul. Now, over fifteen years later, I see in it the seeds of a truth that required a decade of considerable pain and struggle to take root. Because of its power as a trail-marker on my journey as a man, I offer a portion of it here.

ON BECOMING THIRTY: THE SEASON FOR LOVE[12]

When the leaves are falling again and you're thirty years old at last, it's hard to realize you're on the East Coast after ten sunny, unseasoned years from Nigeria to California and back again in college. Everything is just like I remembered. The weather in the East still turns hot and cold at the same particular times of the year; where Californians embrace and then drive off quickly in different directions, Easterners still crowd together forever without saying Hello.

And yet, everything is different. Ten years later, a young man of twenty seems to me now a world of unlimited possibility, without season or occasion. Twenty has no sense of time or of timeliness. You do what you want to do, when you want to do it, and you don't let even large things like summer's heat and winter's cold get in your way. Twenty is not needs, but desires; no pain is too great to be contained, no thrill too slight to be overlooked.

Life is a straight line ahead when you're twenty, and you carry your own energy with you, like the yolk in an egg. Youth, in fact, is all the self-contained energy necessary to sustain the fantasy of self-sufficiency. With the currency of its own boundless vitality, youth can buy its way out of the pains of intimacy and into the more elevated concerns of "universal brotherhood."

And so, at twenty, I left my home on the East Coast, after graduating early from college, and headed west to the Canadian Rockies, San Francisco, Tijuana.

Some thirteen thousand miles later, I joined the Peace Corps, flew to Nigeria, and later traveled throughout West Africa and Europe. Afterward, I moved not only far from my white, middle-class heritage, to work in San Jose, California's Chicano community, but far as well from my love of writing to teach math. At twenty-six, I quit teaching, and determined to move on. Santa Fe, New Mexico, sounded good.

Just before leaving San Francisco that warm October of 1970, I quietly decided merely to "check out" Santa Fe, to see if I might like to live there. On a sunny afternoon, I packed my guitar, typewriter, and sleeping bag in my VW Bug, crossed the Sierras, and headed southwest.

I spent the first night alone in the Death Valley campground—deserted after the tourist season. I tossed mightily in my sleeping bag that night, and if, as with Jacob in the dark river gorge, the angel did not put my thigh out of joint during the struggle, he surely lowered my resistance. The next night, I reached Flagstaff, Arizona, and shivered terribly in a stiff, seven-thousand-foot-high wind. Instead of finding a wooded area, building a fire, and cooking my dinner, as I'd often done excitedly while traveling years before, I found myself eating at a heated restaurant and watching television later at the Arizona State College student union lounge.

That night, I slept not under the stars, but in the back seat of my VW—four thousand feet lower and tolerably warmer, just off the highway to Phoenix. The next morning, I knew it was no use, and I turned back to San Francisco.

There, on the high and chilly plateau of Flagstaff, had come the first subliminal if teeth-chattering realization that my time of youth was passing, that the natural "egg yolk" of youth's energy surrounding the core of my vitality was used up. At thirty, I can see that this was the time of my true embryonic, adult awakening—the proverbial breaking of the shell, with all its authentic, life-stirring possibilities.

At twenty-six, however, I saw only a terrifying vision of my vulnerability and need. No longer self-sufficient, I felt suddenly not valiantly alone, but painfully lonely. Indeed, I felt naked and impotent, as if I were a baby once again.

Sputtering in the straight-ahead road I had carved for my life, I knew at last that I would have to go back somewhere for supplies, motivation, and direction. I panicked. Would I have to give up on my own self altogether and be at the mercy of someone more powerful? Would I have to give up all that I had accomplished through my former youthful desires and self-energy?

The adult male culture around me answered, "You'll never regain your natural youth energy, but you can cover up the pain of your exposed needs and hold onto what you have achieved. In fact, you can refabricate the entire youthful fantasy of self-sufficiency, all by simply using the synthetic, man-made potency of money and guns."

Yet, to a young man who had never known material deprivation, who had spent precious years protesting war-making, "money and guns" could only offer a retreat from the lonely straight line ahead into an unending, manifestly vicious circle. In desperation, I had fantasies of returning to Nigeria to help the war-ravaged Biafrans, among whom I had been so enthusiastic years before as a Peace Corps Volunteer. I had visions of myself whimpering "home" to the East Coast.

By no coincidence, I could see no central concern in my life at that time, no compelling cause or focus. I stopped writing and went back to teaching, this time as a substitute. Soon, a sensation strangely akin to the cold winds of Flagstaff overcame me, and I began stoking my inner embers of youth with frantic, quick "highs," exciting one class of students one day and then hurrying on to yet another class the next. In effect, my straight line ahead had become a self-enclosing circle, not unlike that of the traditional male culture I had ostensibly rejected. . . .

When I was twenty-six, someone asked me, "When did you cry last?" and I couldn't answer. [Today, in my late forties, I would respond, "Which part of the day do you mean—morning, afternoon, or evening?" For the Father God has allowed me to be broken enough to see clearly my need for Him and other men.]

In theological language, the human contribution to this "lesson" is repentance—a word which has its roots in "a turning back," that is, the confession in pain and surrendered joy which signals a return to your true self. And God's contribution, the saving grace which gradually woos you out of a self-confined circle into a reaching, growing spiral, is love.

To be sure, love urges us not to mold, but to serve others in their times of need. God, therefore, who is love and who is always present, has several timely voices: the warning rustle of fallen leaves, the peremptory quiet of still snow, the tender beseeching of new seedlings, the full and bursting welcome of sunshine and flowers.

And so at last, when the harvest of youth's season has been drawn and the unproviding coldness beckons—when the leaves are falling—it's a time to begin life anew, to gather and inspect your resources for the journey, and to turn back to your true self in painful need of one another, in joyful gift of love.

Thus, at thirty, a young man peered across the threshold of maturity, into a vision of God's wholeness and healing in authentic fellowship.

Medical professionals today are recognizing our need for one another. Many say that more of their patients would get well if they could spend time "just talking" with them about their jobs, families, and other important issues. We each need contact with people who've had our experiences and survived them. As Larson says, we all need the "touch of an ordinary person in whom the Spirit of God has been loosed. If we would claim our birthright," he says, "we would be that kind of church. The medical world is looking for somewhere to refer people. They think our business is religion, but our business is life."[13] We men today are missing not only the support, encouragement, and accountability of fellowship, but also its joy.

Recently, a friend who has given countless hours helping other men, including myself, called to tell me with great relief and joy that his doctor had told him he might have prostate cancer, but after a week of testing, the diagnosis was only inflammation.

"Oh . . . that's . . . really good," I responded, hesitating strangely—wanting to join in my friend's joy, but feeling nothing. He paused himself, sensing my disengagement, and in that embarrassing moment I prayed, *Father, what's going on in me?* Cautiously subdued, my friend proceeded to tell me about the tests—and then it struck me.

"Listen, I . . . want to be more enthusiastic for you," I said, "but I need to tell you that's really hard, since you didn't call before, when you first heard what looked like bad news from your doctor. I would've wanted to be in touch and praying for you. Since you didn't let me take part when you were afraid and hurting, I haven't been with you in this, and I can't really take part in your joy now."

When men do not struggle together, we cannot celebrate the victories together. We may explain graciously, as my friend, "I just don't want to burden you." But if we are to walk together as brothers, we must confess the painful truth before each other and the Father God: "I don't trust you; I'm afraid you just won't stand by me when I'm broken." Here is where Christian men often confuse the Father God's call to holiness with the conditioned alienation from their dads.

By definition, "holy" means set apart for God's purposes. To make holy is to make sacred, or literally, to "sacri-fy." In the Old Testament, the animal "sacri-ficed" on the altar served not just to feed the priests, but to fulfill God's purpose of requiring that blood be shed for the forgiveness of sins. For a man to become holy, therefore, he must be cleansed of his own purposes and yielded to God's.

No man can do this alone. God cannot use a man for His purposes unless the man is surrendered to Him—which requires confessing his sins to others (see James 5:16) and walking together in accountability.

Holiness means separateness from the world—but not from each other. Indeed, only through intimate sharing with and caring for each other can we overcome the world's self-centered purposes within us and discover God's. Our Christian love for one another is precisely what makes us different from the world. "See those Christians, how they love one another," as one ancient Roman historian remarked.

A man who lacks relationship with the Father, however, will be adulterated with alienation. He will confuse holiness with morality, and define it negatively, as "not doing bad things," or even "not associating with bad people." Thus the Pharisees scorned Jesus for associating with prostitutes and other outcasts.

Such false "holiness" that separates us from others allows the fantasy that we can become without sin—and thereby, becomes self-righteousness. A truly holy man, that is, one set aside for God's purposes, is accountable to other men, confessing to them and offering up his brokenness to the Father God, allowing Him to crucify his pride. He is not afraid of other men's sin, because he has learned the Father God's mercy for his own sin—by experiencing it among brothers.

And so today, daydreaming in the Spirit, I wonder: What would happen if all the men at a church were gathered in one place, and on the count of three, all shouted together, "I'm hurting and I need you!"

I know only this: the Father would be freed to act, and the Wolf would flee.

CHAPTER SIX

Making a Living or Making a Life: The Father and The Job

Whatever you do, work at it with all your heart, as though you were working for the Lord and not for men.

(Col. 3:23)

When we first meet another man, one particular question identifies him: Where do you work?

Our primary concern, the most important fact to help us know the other man most quickly, is rarely How many children do you have? or Are you married? or even Where are you from?

It's the job that tells other men who we are.

This paramount value among men is taught very early, for men commonly ask boys the same, though slightly adapted, question. I can recall my father's taking me at three or four to visit his office at Philadelphia Naval Shipyard and lifting me proudly up onto the desk of one Chief Petty Officer—who patted a well-rounded waist and boomed, "Well, son, what do you want to be when you grow up?"

Even at that tender age, I knew it would not suffice for me to answer that I aspired to be "a good man," or "a man of God," or "a father," or even "happy." I might just as well have said I wanted to be an Army officer.

I knew that the men's question of my future "being" could be answered properly only with my "doing," that is, a job title. And indeed, I had been fascinated one day to see some men building a house; "I want to be a bricklayer," I answered thereafter, and the men would nod approvingly.

The message to the boy was clear and fundamental: For men, to *be* is to *do*. What a man does, defines who he is; a man's job is his existence, his life.

The most immediate—and devastating—consequence of this worldview grows out of its logical conclusion that if a man *does* not, he *is* not. That is, if a man has no job, he does not exist, is not a man.

We see this cruel judgment passed upon "retired" men, who are essentially told by the world, "You are used up, finished, nonproductive, and thus, worthless." Small wonder that such a high percentage of us die so soon after retiring.

The first Monday morning after I left the parish ministry to write full-time—after much prayer and numerous confirmations of that leading from God—I sat down at my desk, looked at my calendar . . . and froze unto death. One blank page after another stared at me, mocking my self-esteem and drawing me into a deep void of nothingness where I, Gordon Dalbey, would drown and disappear forever.

I had eaten the world's "new grain" and bought its assessment of my situation: Without a paying job, I was not a man, not even a person.

I was terrified, and only by grace did it occur to me to cry out to my Father God, "Oh, Lord, lead me on, lead me out of here, and somehow get me going!" I travailed for at least two weeks in that pit of despair before beginning my own writing schedule.

A recent university study notes that cultural "differences in basic attitudes toward life, work and leisure" result in a wide variation in retirement ages around the world. For example, "nearly 60 percent of Japanese men over 60 years old are still in the work force, compared with 33 percent in the U.S., 13 percent in the United Kingdom and 8 percent in France."[1]

Could this indicate how much different cultures value the gifts of older men? In any case, Christian men must note that Hebrew has no word for "retire"—suggesting that a man is never so old that he cannot contribute to God's work in this world. The apostle Paul, in the Colossians text, does not speak of paying jobs, but says only, "whatever you do," when referring to working for the Lord. Sometimes—most often in a man's younger years—God's work includes producing some product which others pay to buy. But these jobs in no way comprise all that God needs men to do in this world.

Men's very names reflect graphically this belief among us that we are what we do. If, indeed, a man's name tells others who he is, consider the vast number of surnames which are simply job titles, such as Smith, Carpenter, Taylor, Miller, or Fowler. One man named Wolcott told me his English ancestors were wool-cutters. Examples in German include Schneider (tailor), Fleishmann (flesh-man, or butcher), and Bauer (farmer). I do not know how commonly other societies do this; a study of men's surnames in different cultures, comparing the percentages of job titles among them, might reveal in each the deeper cultural link between working and masculine identity.

In any case, the man receives his surname from his father; in his work, therefore, a man historically became one with his father, taking the father's name and job title as his own. In earlier generations, a boy was commonly apprenticed to follow in the father's work. So Jesus, "the carpenter" (see Mark 6:3 NKJV), was known in Nazareth as "the carpenter's son" (see Matt. 13:55 NKJV).

Indeed, insofar as the man's very surname carries his job title, passed on to him from the father, not working means you are not your father's son. Suppose you work with wood alongside your father, named John Carpenter. If you lose your job, you no longer work with wood, and thus, are no longer a "Carpenter." Not working has cut you off from your masculine heritage.

Every boy's longing to be one with his father, therefore, takes shape in his early desire to grow up and do Daddy's job. Certainly, it did not take long for me to switch my boyhood professional aspirations from bricklayer to "Navy man"; by the age of five or six, I was proudly wearing my father's Navy hat. I very likely would have pursued a Navy career myself, had I not discovered when candidating for NROTC in college that I am color-blind, and thus ineligible—a crushing blow.

A recent *Los Angeles Times Magazine* feature titled "Like Father, Like Son" answers the subtitle question, "How Did Milt McColl, NFL Player and Orthopedic Surgeon, Come to Mirror His Dad's Life So Precisely?"

> For Milt McColl, explanations for having produced a virtual carbon copy of his father's life don't come easily. Milt pursued the legacy not at his father's urging, nor even upon great reflection, but instead almost instinctively, as though guided by providence. He never observed his father in surgery or accompanied him on hospital rounds. Milt simply gravitated toward his father's achievements like water seeking equilibrium. "Sometimes I think I didn't think about it as much as I could have," he says. "It just seemed natural."[2]

Clearly, even the world's vocabulary—as in "instinctively" and "as though guided by divine providence"—reaches after, but cannot communicate the spiritual longing in the male child to be one with the father, like Jesus. Indeed, with so little interpersonal bonding to the father today, a man may turn to his job for surrogate bonding in a desperate attempt to be—that is, to work—at last like Dad and/or the other men.

The Catch-22—the mutation on the masculine gene which ensures generations of insecurity in men—is simply that every boy grows up seeing his father as a god, and thus, one who embodies a standard forever the focus of his reach. One mother told me how at the dinner table her husband had asked their eight-year-old boy, "Who do you want most to grow up and be like—President Bush? Joe Montana? The Hulk?" Without missing a beat the boy replied, "I want to grow up and be just like you, Daddy!"

Certainly, a man can set out in his own work and have more education, make more money, rise higher in the company, gain more esteem than his father. But no man, in his own mind, can ever be as good a carpenter, businessman, truck driver, or President as his father was.

No matter how old a man becomes, he remains the son of the man who came before him and, in that natural sense at least, the lesser. The father's footsteps are always larger than the son's, and the man who seeks to match them must overcome a deep fear of falling short, of feeling inadequate, and thus, unsuccessful as a man.

At twenty-six, St. Louis Blues' hockey star Brett Hull set an NHL scoring record in 1990, and by '91 had become "the premier right wing in the world."[3] Son of hockey great Bobby Hull, Brett quit hockey in his late teens after becoming "unsure of his future" when "father and son were separated and had little contact" following his parents' "bitter divorce."

After several years of struggling, Brett's 1991 record included the first father-son pair to score 50 goals in a season, and his father was there to see number 50: "To have my father there [in the stands] . . . was very exciting. And to emerge as a hockey player from that kind of shadow is really satisfying. To know for myself that I can score and play the game is a great feeling. Because in my mind, Dad is the greatest left winger ever."

The bond with the father implied in a man's job places tremendous pressure upon him to succeed. Often at men's retreats, during a time of inviting men to surrender their lives anew to Jesus for reordering, I hear painful testimonies from men who have allowed their jobs to consume their entire energy—to the severe detriment of themselves and their families.

The man who does that is the one who doesn't have time for his children while they're growing up—he is always too busy at work. He is the same man who, when the children are grown and he is ready finally to slow down and enjoy his family, finds the children are too busy. They've become like him and he is left alone.

I do not disparage hard work. In fact, I believe it's part of shaping true manhood. But a job does not and cannot tell a man who he is. Manhood is defined by the Father God, who will instruct His son where, how long, and how hard to work. Thus, the biblical faith urges men to work "as though you were working for the Lord." Certainly, a boy receives from his father's working a sense of security and worth in the world and a model of strength and provision. But these values are not specific to any particular job or intensity of work required.

The late Richard Feynman, Nobel-Prize-winning physicist and chairman of the committee which investigated the 1986 Challenger shuttle disaster, titled the first chapter of his autobiography "The Making of a Scientist," and speaks immediately about the influence of his father, a uniform salesman:

> When I was just a little kid, very small in a highchair, my father brought home a lot of little bathroom tiles—seconds—of different colors. We played with them, my father setting them up vertically on my highchair like dominoes, and I would push one end so they would all go down.
>
> Then after awhile, I'd help set them up. Pretty soon, we're setting them up in a more complicated way: two white tiles and a blue tile, two white tiles and a blue tile, and so on. When my mother saw that she said, "Leave the poor child alone. If he wants to put a blue tile, let him put a blue tile."
>
> But my father said, "No, I want to show him what patterns are like and how interesting they are. It's a kind of elementary mathematics." So he started very early to tell me about the world and how interesting it is.[4]

With poignant simplicity, Feynman recalls a further example from his later boyhood:

> My father taught me to notice things. One day, I was playing with an "express wagon," a little wagon with a railing around it. It had a ball in it, and when I pulled the wagon, I noticed something about the way the ball moved. I went to my father and said, "Say, Pop, I noticed something. When I pull the wagon, the ball rolls to the back. And when I'm pulling it along and I suddenly stop, the ball rolls to the front. Why is that?"
>
> "That, nobody knows," he said. "The general principle is that things which are moving tend to keep on moving, and things which are standing still tend to stand still, unless you push them hard. This tendency is called 'inertia,' but nobody knows why it's true." Now, that's a deep understanding. He didn't just give me the name . . .
>
> That's the way I was educated by my father . . .: no pressure—just

lovely, interesting discussions. It has motivated me for the rest of my life, and makes me interested in all the sciences. (It just happens I do physics better.)

I've been caught, so to speak—like someone who was given something wonderful when he was a child, and he's always looking for it again. I'm always looking, like a child, for the wonders I know I'm going to find—maybe not every time, but every once in awhile.[5]

Unlike Richard Feynman, the average man today has not been initiated to the "wonders" of life by his father. Thus, he sees life's mysteries not as a promising invitation to the humble, but as a fearful threat to the inadequate.

Instead of seeing relationship with the father as an enhancement to their work, most men today have not had relationship with the father precisely because of work. That is, the boy who sees his father so busy working that they have no time together can grow up to despise working itself as something that breaks relationship with the father.

The Father God, meanwhile, has gifted each man with certain talents and abilities, and then called him forth into the world to serve Him accordingly. The secularized term, "vocation," carries the meaning well, for it bears the same root as "vocal," or "voice"—hence, it implies "calling." The job is therefore very much a part of the man, for it properly reflects his Creator's voice—but it does not comprise or define him.

The question, "What is my calling?" might more aptly be put, "What would I do even if I weren't paid?" Mary once noted that I spend a lot of my spare time writing letters to friends, unlike most people. "That's because you're a writer," she added.

Certainly, when you're out of work, the job looms high above all other needs. But very often, I find that men who are unsettled in their jobs, who cannot seem to find "the right place" to work, have forgotten their true and prior identity in the Father God—who does indeed have a vocational calling for each man, but it can be identified and fulfilled only out of the bedrock knowledge that "I am a beloved son of the Father."

The biblical notion of "working for the Lord" contrasts the worldly notion of "making work your Lord." That is, you lose your manhood to whatever you sacrifice yourself. The man who sacrifices himself to his job, therefore, loses his manhood in the job—just as truly as the one who sacrifices himself to the woman loses his manhood to her. For his identity is no longer in Christ, as a son of the Father/Creator God, who alone defines a man. Thus Jesus demonstrates, unto the Cross and resurrection, that the man who sacrifices himself to God loses himself to the

Father, and in this way alone, he finds his true self at last (see Matt. 16:25).

In fact, this loss of true identity in the job is the direct and primary consequence of the Fall—of broken relationship with the Father—in the lives of men. For when Adam has sinned by disobeying, God pronounces a very specific punishment:

> And he said to the man, "You listened to your wife and ate the fruit which I told you not to eat. Because of what you have done, the ground will be under a curse. You will have to work hard all your life to make it produce enough food for you. It will produce weeds and thorns, and you will have to eat wild plants. You will have to work hard and sweat to make the soil produce anything." (Gen. 3:17–19)

The curse of Original Sin on the man therefore manifests in workaholism and burnout, which reflect a broken relationship with the Father. Indeed, such a man is pushing himself to do more than he has been called and empowered by God to do. Not knowing he is a beloved son of the Father, he works out of his own energies, burning himself out instead of waiting upon and moving in the Father's direction and strength.

God has promised that those who trust in Him for help

> will find their strength renewed.
> They will rise on wings like eagles;
> they will run and not get weary;
> they will walk and not grow weak.
> (Isa. 40:31)

Episcopal priest Terry Fullam has noted that you never see an eagle flapping its wings furiously, like a hummingbird or a sparrow. Rather, the eagle waits on its perch for the wind current to rise, steps off and spreads its wings, and lets the current carry it aloft.

God may call a man to difficult work at times. But often men who complain chronically of overwork are simply being unfaithful. As others have noted, the man who proclaims how he has worked for weeks without a day off, needs to be reminded that even God took off one day out of seven. A man trying to work harder than God walks in the very pride of Original Sin. Others have also noted that the Sabbath is the Manufacturer's warning that this machine will not function properly without one day of rest per week.

The man who "complains" most about working so hard, is often the most resistant to retiring. His work has become an addiction. He's like the enabling, co-dependent spouse of an alcoholic, who complains about "my wife's drinking," but does not call her into account for her behavior for fear she will leave him, and thereby, expose his deep emptiness and alienation.

The truth that sets a workaholic free can only emerge from the question: What pain in your life does your constant working attempt to mask? Whatever circumstance that appears to prompt it—whether arguments with the wife at home or a desire for affluence—the pain is rooted in being cut off from the Father God, from not knowing yourself as a cherished son.

Jesus came to redeem the effects of the Fall, to break its curse by showing us we cannot work for the Father's approval, but must—and can—rely on His mercy and grace. Surrender to Jesus therefore enables you to draw close to the Father once again and hear His "call"—that is, to allow the Father to direct and empower your "vocation" as you work "for the Lord."

What, indeed, would it mean for you to know on the job that you are working "for the Lord and not for men"? What if the Father God has given you all your talents and gifts, and called you to your job—assuming you have sought His will in your job search? In that case, you do not answer to your boss on the job, nor even to the person who signs your paycheck, but to the Father God.

What if you then went to your men's prayer group, got down on your knees, offered your job up to Jesus, and asked Him to evaluate your work on the job?

To sense how God might respond, think of your own son. What if you told him to mow the lawn, and he came to you while doing it to ask, "Dad, how am I doing?" Whatever your thoughts about his work, your first feeling would be appreciation and respect for the boy's coming to seek your guidance. Certainly, you know the lawn will get mowed better.

So is God pleased when we go to Him.

If, however, the boy didn't bother to ask your opinion, but just mowed the lawn, put the mower back in the garage, and took off, you would have an entirely different attitude toward his work. His actions say he doesn't respect your providing a home for him or value relationship with you. Such a son will require your constant vigilance to make sure the lawn gets mowed well.

So does God wish we would come directly to Him.

When you do, like a good Father He is prepared to respond in whatever way that will fulfill His calling upon you and make you into the man He created you to become. Where you are doing well, He can encourage and reward you; where you are falling short and need help, He can redirect, empower, and support you. He may show you where you need to work harder, but He may just as readily show you where you are working too hard, expending too much energy in the wrong direction. The Father who calls you to a job has far broader vision and far greater intention for you there than you know.

One man with whom I prayed about his job got no word about his own performance—but clearly sensed the Lord was telling him to pay more attention to a fellow worker who recently had been dragging around the office. "Everyone else just backs off from that guy, since he seems so preoccupied," he said, "but I think he's hurting about something and needs another man to reach out to him. I'll invite him to lunch on Monday."

The Father may say, perhaps through others in your men's group, "You need to do some more to improve that last job," or "Pack it up, leave it until tomorrow, and get on home at five o'clock. You've done fine for today, and I have greater purpose for your life besides just working here."

Jason, a forty-one-year-old professional, came to me after being treated unfairly in front of other workers by his boss, who had a habit of treating employees disrespectfully. No one else in the office had ever dared speak to the boss about this. As we prayed about it, Jason and I both felt the Father God was telling him to talk with his boss the next day and explain matter-of-factly why he felt treated unfairly. "I'm teaching you more than how to do a job," the Lord seemed to be saying; "I'm making you into a man, so you can show others how to be a man."

Jason's father had never affirmed his needs and feelings as a boy, and had punished him harshly. He was therefore plagued with fears and self-doubts, such as "Maybe I'm just overreacting, and the boss wasn't that out of line" and "What if I get fired?" We prayed for healing from his father-wound, and that, regardless of his boss's response, through this encounter he would know himself more deeply as a son of the Father God, and thus, worthy of respect.

We also sensed that the boss himself was disrespectful of others because he had never been treated with respect growing up, and that he needed Jason to model self-respecting manhood for him.

We prayed for healing and receptivity in the boss as the Spirit led. We asked the Lord to go ahead of Jason to fill the office with His Spirit and ensure that His will be carried out. Finally, we prayed for courage in Jason to speak the truth with love.

The next evening, he called excitedly. "I told the boss how I felt, as honestly and directly as I could, without putting him down—and he listened to me!" he said. "I mean, he didn't get down on his knees or anything, but he did say he didn't realize how he was coming across and would think about what I said."

Several weeks later, Jason mentioned that his boss "is treating me with more respect these days." And Jason himself enjoys his work more now, because he can focus his energies on doing a good job instead of worrying that the boss will crush him.

This story is not an example of how to confront your boss, but of how a man's recognizing the Father God as his boss enabled him to gain a deeper sense of his manhood at work. The Father may not indicate such confrontation in every case. Jason's story here does not offer a technique for problem-solving on the job, but rather, invites relationship with the Father, lived out in fellowship with other men—even with an intimidating boss.

Is your job an extension of the real you, or a diversion from it? The answer can come only insofar as you surrender your job to the Father, and allow Him to show you who He's made you to be and draw forth what He has seeded within you. The Father God not only has a greater vision of any particular job than the man has, but He also orchestrates job changes appropriately for sons who have surrendered their work to Him.

Years ago, after pastoring a church for eight years through considerable upset to a new plateau of harmony, I realized I had given all the church could receive—and began to listen more closely to my longtime desire to write full-time.

While this was urgently on my mind, I came home one Sunday evening around ten o'clock, after an evening meeting with the church leaders. Before I walked through the door, I realized I had left my guitar in my office, which had been burglarized some months earlier. Sighing in dismay, I drove back to the church. Later, guitar in hand at last, I closed my office door behind me, reached to flick out the hall light . . . and paused.

Quiet, still, and peaceful, the church waited.

I stood there a minute, hesitating.

And then, I set down my guitar, and walked into the darkened sanctuary, stopping at the altar steps and turning. Again I hesitated.

Far, far away, a car horn sounded faintly, a dog barked.

Slowly, in the hush of silence, I stepped up to the altar and knelt down.

"Father," I said, sighing, "You know what's been on my mind these weeks." I waited—and felt simply the Lord's gentle and affirming Presence. "I . . . I've made my share of mistakes here at the church . . . but it's been a good battle, and I thank You for all You've used me to do and taught me through it."

I paused, then realized it was no use mincing words. "Father, I don't want to be here any more."

Waiting, I sensed no immediate response, so I plunged ahead. "I know I've said that before, when the flak was thick, but this time, things seem different. We're at a good place; I've done my best, and don't think I'm trying to run away."

I listened, but felt only His continuing Presence.

"What I really want to do is write. I've got so many ideas in my mind and stories to tell, I can hardly look ahead to tomorrow until I get them all written down.

"Now . . . You know I'll stay at the church if You want me to. I'm Your man, no matter what. But I want to hear from You on this, Lord. If You want me to stay, or to leave, let me know."

Kneeling, waiting in that most gentle of silences, I heard no words, saw no pictures, felt no urging—just the Presence of God.

After a few moments, I got up and left.

The next morning, I received a delightful phone call from Bert Bochove. A furniture upholsterer in his late seventies, Bert had been honored during the previous Thanksgiving Eve community service at the local synagogue for saving many Jews in his native Holland from the Nazis during World War II. I had participated in the service, and spent some time talking with Bert afterward. In fact, I had been so moved that I wrote a short essay on the evening[6], and gave a copy to the rabbi, who had shown it to a Dutch member of his congregation. The latter had made a copy and sent it to Bert, who was calling to say how much he appreciated my writing.

Several moments into our conversation, it occurred to me how good it would be to talk in person. I mentioned that I would be driving out near his home late that afternoon, and perhaps I might stop by to visit? With warm enthusiasm and gracious hospitality, Bert insisted.

At about five o'clock, Bert and his charming wife, Betty, welcomed me into their living room. For the next several hours we enjoyed chatting over a wide range of subjects, from European culture to healing prayer. Around 7:00 P.M., Bert asked if I would stay and share a Dutch cheese which he had saved for such a special occasion.

Politely, I said I really should be going and did not want to wear out my welcome. But my hosts were clearly genuine in their desire for me to stay. As we chatted further, I realized I wanted to stay—so why not?

The cheese was delicious, and the fellowship heartwarming. By ten o'clock, we capped the evening by praying for one another, and I left feeling thankful for such people as Betty and Bert, and for my gift of writing, which had opened the door to our friendship.

Uplifted and pleasantly tired from a fulfilling day, I entered my apartment and saw that my phone answering machine message light was blinking. Casually, I flipped the knob to "playback" and began unbuttoning my shirt.

"Gordon?" the tape voice began hesitantly. At once I recognized the church Moderator, or lay leader. I decided that a sandwich might taste good before bed, and turned toward the refrigerator. But the words I heard stopped me cold.

"We're here at the Church Council meeting . . . and wondering where you are. Give us a call as soon as you can."

Oh, no! Not Council meeting! Tonight?

I stared ahead in disbelief. In eight years, I had never missed a Council meeting. The pastor does not miss a Council meeting. Second Monday of the month, every month, for eight years—announced the day before in worship, written in blood on my calendar.

How could I have forgotten the Council meeting?

Mentally, I kicked myself. Just when things were going so well at the church, I had to go and forget the most important meeting of all with the leaders!

Glancing at the clock, I realized I had better make as many phone calls as possible to Council members before bedtime. As I dialed the Moderator's number, it struck me: What was I going to say? Fortunately, perhaps, I had no time to formulate an excuse.

"You mean you just 'forgot' it?" he exclaimed, in genuine surprise.

Apologizing profusely, I told him about being with Bert Bochove, who had been the subject of my sermon some weeks earlier. Nervously, I noted that it was getting late, and I needed to call the other Council members.

"Well . . . I guess we all forget things once in awhile," the Moderator offered, puzzled nonetheless.

"Uh . . . yeah, I . . . guess so," I said.

Several embarrassing calls later, I sighed and flopped onto my bed, now quite unpleasantly exhausted. "Father!" I cried out, "What's going on here? How in the world could I miss the Council meeting like that?"

Disgusted with myself, I was about to throw my shirt into the closet when . . . suddenly it struck me: *Could this be the answer to my prayer at the altar last night?*

Clearly, my heart just wasn't in pastoring any more. Was I just being lazy, or . . . could it be?

For some time, I lay quietly on the bed, and a gentle sense of peace and strength settled over me.

It made sense. I had told the Lord I wanted to write full-time and no longer be a pastor. And then, the very next morning, someone calls to say how much he appreciates my writing, and that night I'm enjoying myself with him instead of pastoring.

Could it be?

An exhilarating mixture of fear and excitement rose within me. Would my detractors at the church claim the victory, and say they had successfully driven me out? No. In fact, I had stayed and worked things through as faithfully as I could. Indeed, as long as I knew that God Himself was calling me away from the church into writing, I needn't worry.

Of course, I was not about to make so important a decision as leaving my job simply on the basis of one evening's experience, no matter how dramatic. Rather, I saw the experience as a likely word from God, and hence, an invitation to seek further confirmation from other witnesses (see 1 Cor. 14:29). In the next few weeks, I visited five fellow pastors and asked them to pray with me; after much prayer, all agreed that, indeed, God was calling me into a new ministry of writing.

Still, questions swirled within me. *Would my loyal supporters at the church feel abandoned? How would I support myself? Would everything I had worked to build at the church die?* Rationally, I knew that if indeed the Lord were calling me away, He would take care of those and any other concerns. But still I worried.

A month earlier, I had signed up for a conference on healing in San Diego with John Wimber of the Anaheim Vineyard Christian Fellowship. Then, it had seemed simply a chance to learn more about the healing ministry. Now, I began to anticipate it as an opportunity to receive a more clear word from God about leaving my pastorate.

Strangely, as I joined the crowd chattering excitedly around the registration table that Friday afternoon, I found myself nervously going through the motions and withdrawing. In fact, after paying my money, I hung out awhile, and then got in my car intending to leave the conference and go home. At the freeway on-ramp, I pulled over, prayed . . . and turned back.

During that evening's worship, Wimber called for silence and waiting upon the Lord for any word. Moments later, a voice spoke up from the crowd of perhaps four hundred: "My children, come to Me and open your hearts, for the desire of your heart has been placed there by Me."

I sat forward. Could that be for me? Could the desire in my heart to leave my pastorate have been placed there by the Lord Himself, and not by my own selfish nature?

After worship, I caught sight of a man I had seen occasionally at a pastors' fellowship in Los Angeles. We were not well acquainted, but in that moment of the Lord's encouragement, I went over to him, introduced myself to him and his wife, and asked if they would pray for me.

"Is there anything in particular you want us to pray for?" he asked.

About to tell them my entire story, I hesitated. "Actually, it's about a situation at my church. Could we just see if the Lord will show you anything about that?"

They agreed, and as I sat down, they laid hands on my shoulder and prayed quietly. In a moment, I had a distinct sense of a voice within me saying, "Through you, I will touch thousands." Puzzled, I "answered" in my mind, "But I don't want to be pastor of a church with thousands of members!" Then it occurred to me that I might "touch thousands" with my writing.

I realized that my friend and his wife were still praying quietly for me. I waited, and then spoke. "Are you sensing anything as you pray?"

"Well, I've been getting this picture," the man said, "but it doesn't seem to have anything to do with your church."

"What's that?" I asked.

"I just see you sitting at a desk, and there's fire and power, like explosions coming out of the desk, and people running, big crowds of people moving around." He paused as I sat there, awestruck. "Does that mean anything to you?"

"Incredible!" I burst out at last, shaking my head in amazement. I then shared my own "words," which seemed a perfect caption for his picture—the "thousands" of people and the desk image for my writing.

"Now that's really something," he said, knitting his brow. "I have to tell you that actually I saw the word 'writing' across my picture, but it seemed so specific that I was a little hesitant to mention it."

I sat quietly and basked in this dramatic work of the Holy Spirit. The Father was genuinely orchestrating my professional life. A freedom, a release welled up within me, and in that moment, I realized why I had been so withdrawn up until then. I had come to the conference hoping to hear the Lord's final word on whether I was to leave my pastorate and write, and I had simply been afraid He would say no. I trusted Him enough to speak, but was afraid He might deny me my desire—never allowing that in fact, He had placed the desire in me.

Shortly thereafter, I resigned my pastorate. For the next two years, I lived in a spare room at a pastor friend's parsonage, making about five hundred dollars a month doing an occasional wedding and substitute preaching. I wrote one book the first year, and a major publisher debated over my manuscript for six months—and finally rejected it. The next year, another book—and no sale.

I knew both books were significant to the Lord's work in these times; confused and angry, I spent much time on my knees, crying out to the Father. It took over three years before I wrote my third and first-published book, *Healing the Masculine Soul* (Word, 1988).

Thus the Father God began to reverse in my life the effects of the curse in Genesis on men. That is, I began to shift my sense of self away from what I do, to the Father God, who calls me to do it.

I began regularly to pray for release from my compulsive workaholism—not so I could be lazy and not work, but so my gifts and talents would serve the Father and not rule me. I prayed to understand in my heart and soul what the Sabbath of rest in the Father God meant for me. I began, that is, to let Jesus do at last what He died to do: to save me from the effects of the Fall.

And so I prayed, "In the name of Jesus, I set the Cross between me and my father, between him and his father, and down the generations of men unto Adam. I take the sword of the Spirit and break the generational curse of working to achieve my identity, and I ask that the blood of Jesus would cover me from all the effects of that in my manhood.

"In place of that, Father, restore me to my true and original identity as Your beloved son. I ask for the blessing of discerning the talents and gifts You have given me, where You have designed me to focus them, and for how long."

Every so often, my peace in working is overtaken by a frenzy of "jangled nerves," as I find myself fearful of not getting everything done and pushing ahead on raw energy. At other times, when my writing and speaking engagements are going especially well, I feel guilty and worry that I should be working harder, suffering more. When by grace I eventually realize what's happening, I stop and pray again to break the curse and to ask for the blessing Jesus died to give me.

In that process, I have discovered that the curse robs a man of renewal in play. Granted, life is serious, but the man who recognizes and responds to that needs at times to be renewed, restored, even re-created— hence the term recreation. Under the curse, true play is lost in a striving after release rather than simply enjoying it; a man goes not "to play ball," but essentially "to work ball"—desperate to win rather than simply enjoying doing his best.

In your job, are you laboring under the curse of sin, or rejoicing in the blessing of Jesus? A good test is this: How much do you enjoy playing, and thereby let the Father recreate you? If you're not sure, ask those who are closest to you. They'll be quite sure. A man who labors under the Law cannot know the joy in relationships; he's not much fun.

And so, in my prayer to supplant the curse, I often ask for another blessing: "Father, free me from my fear of not working enough, and help me just to have fun sometimes."

As the father's appreciation for a son's job well done gives the boy joy, so joy is not generated from work itself, but rather, from the heart of the Father who has ordained the task and empowered the worker. A worker who has forgotten the Father God has cut himself off from the source and vitality of his task. He therefore labors without joy—much like the Pharisaic moralist, who coldly performs the "work" of righteousness without relationship with the Father.

As Jews for Jesus Director Moishe Rosen has declared,

> Jewish people concern themselves as much with worldly pleasure as any other people, but I think we also differentiate between hedonistic enjoyment and *simcha,* the higher joy that comes from appreciating what God has provided.
> One Jewish writer [Jacob Klatzkin] put it this way: There is a moral duty which your [Christian] moralists underrate criminally—the duty to enjoy the world which God has created.[7]

After one teaching program, a man brought me an old letter written by his great grandfather, which included a word of thanksgiving that "God has neither oppressed us with poverty nor burdened us with riches." I like that: We have a Father who simply meets our needs—and in faithfully doing so, delivers us from greed as well.

A man's work, therefore, is not an effort to please the earthly father by following in his footsteps, but to respond to the heavenly Father's call. To find peace in his job, a man must walk in freedom from the curse of Original Sin. He must appropriate the blessing of Jesus in restoring living relationship with the Father, who both calls us to a job and equips us to do it.

A major thrust of the women's movement has focused—however unwittingly—on breaking the specific curse of Original Sin upon the woman, namely, that she will lose herself in the man instead of drawing her identity from the Father God:

> You will . . . have desire for your husband, yet you will be subject to him. (Gen. 3:16b)

Insofar as the women have not surrendered to Jesus, they have not been able to appropriate true freedom from this curse and respond freely to the Father's calling—whether in the home or marketplace. Indeed, they have simply exchanged their curse for the man's by charging headlong into the job market and getting burned out.

Even as the women, we men are responsible for our own choices. May we choose to surrender to Jesus, who alone empowers us to proclaim, "Who I am is a son of the Father God. What I do is what He has called me to do. What I become is what I allow Him to make me."

CHAPTER SEVEN

The Procrastinator, The Rebel, and the True Son of the Father

[And Jesus said to them] "Now, what do you think? There was once a man who had two sons. He went to the older one and said, 'Son, go and work in the vineyard today.' 'I don't want to,' he answered, but later he changed his mind and went. Then the father went to the other son and said the same thing. 'Yes, sir,' he answered, but he did not go. Which one of the two did what his father wanted?"

"The older one," they answered.

So Jesus said to them, "I tell you: the tax collectors and the prostitutes are going into the Kingdom of God ahead of you. For John the Baptist came to you showing you the right path to take, and you would not believe him; but the tax collectors and the prostitutes believed him. Even when you saw this, you did not later change your minds and believe him." (Matt. 21:28–32)

"The road to hell is paved with good intentions," as the saying goes.[1] If the essence of hell is separation from the Father God, the second son's good intentions in Jesus' parable confirm that adage. His knee-jerk "Yes, Sir" sounds good. But the father tells his son to go and work today—and in the face of deadline reality, the son backs out of his commitment.

Consider the parable with God as the Father who calls us out as His sons to do His work in this world. Then translate: "Sure, Father God, I'll go right out there and love my enemies like you say. I'll forgive the one who hurt me—seven times, even! Uh . . . what's that, Father? 'Seventy times seven'? Well . . ., how about tomorrow?"

Or, we might say, "Okay, Father, I'll call a few guys and ask them to pray for me about my problem, even if they might think I'm a wimp and . . . well, on second thought, they've all got their own stuff to worry about, and I've survived this long on my own. . . . So maybe later, okay?"

Or, "Yes, Father, I'll talk to my wife, lovingly but honestly, about how what she's doing hurts me. I hope she won't make life miserable for me if I do but . . . well, actually, it won't matter that much if I give it a few more days."

Or again, "Okay, Father, I know what I'm doing hurts me and others who love me, so I'll quit—this week, for sure. Still . . . it can't hurt that bad, really, if I wait a bit. . . ."

How much easier to say, "Yes, Father," to appear obedient and please Him than to roll up your sleeves and actually do what God commands. Even when we know what the Father wants us to do, often we don't want to do it; it seems easier to get off the hook by saying, "Yes, Father," and then just put off doing it.

The second son in Jesus' story reflects this common malady among us men, namely, procrastination. The man is agreeable, but not active. Like the first son, he wants to avoid his father's disapproval and judgment, so he verbally commits to the responsibility asked of him. But he doesn't follow through.

Psychiatrist Hugh Missledine, in his classic book *Your Inner Child of the Past,* titles a chapter, "Overcoercion," and says, "If you can't stop procrastinating, you should consider the possibility that your 'inner child of the past' is continuing the pattern with which he reacted to the coercive directions of your parents. Overcoercion is the most common pathogenic parental attitude in our culture."[2]

For example, when a father commands his son outside playing, "Come in right now for dinner!" the boy may likely not feel free to yell back, "I don't want to come inside! I'm having too much fun playing!" Instead, the boy learns to procrastinate: "Yes, Sir, I'll be right there!" he says, to please his father. Yet ten minutes later, the boy is still outside playing.

Delaying and dawdling, that is, become the only weapons behind which a boy can safely assert his own desire against the father's demands. This pattern of behavior, learned in childhood, takes root when you continue "as an adult to press parent-like directions on yourself— 'Do this! Do that!'—and then resist your own directions, stalling and daydreaming. This is how your inability to act develops. You paralyze yourself, using the same kind of slyly concealed passive resistance and distractions to your own directions—just as you once resisted the coercive demands of your parents."[3]

Certainly, a father must from time to time make demands upon a son. But the procrastination response begins to suggest itself when the boy finds that he is not permitted to question those demands openly, that his own feelings and desires are not honored—and thus, he can not trust his true self to the father.

By no means does honoring a son's feelings and desires require the father to "give in" and indulge the boy's laziness.

Significantly, God often commands His people to do something, but does not command us—and very likely, does not expect us—to agree with Him or enjoy doing it. His bottom line, as with the father in Jesus' parable, is simply, who "did what the father wanted"? No commandment says, "Thou shalt enjoy having no gods before me."

The psalmist declares, "As a father is kind to his children, so the Lord . . . knows what we are made of" (Ps. 103:13–14). God knows our childish, self-centered human nature and, therefore, knows we'll dislike any command that requires danger or sacrifice, regardless of its ultimate benefit to us. The most significant men of the Bible, including Jesus, were human enough to balk and trusting enough to express their reluctance to God—but faithful enough to obey. Indeed, their willingness to express their dislikes openly to the Father—and thereby, to trust their relationship with Him—virtually ensured their faithfulness. Without such freedom, a son may obey the rules, but he cannot have relationship with the father.

Moses—on the lam when his picture was in every Egyptian post office for killing one of the king's men—was called back to Egypt, not to confess his own sin, but to proclaim the Pharaoh's sin to his face. Not surprisingly, he begged off: "You know that I am such a poor speaker; why should the king listen to me?" (Ex. 6:30).

Called to a similarly dangerous task, Jeremiah protested, "Sovereign LORD, I don't know how to speak; I am too young" (Jer. 1:6). Job challenged God's intentions (see Job 3:1–26).

The night before He was crucified, Jesus begged, "My Father, if it is possible, take this cup of suffering from me!" (Matt. 26:39). The author of Hebrews describes more fully the way Jesus made His feelings known to His Father on this life-or-death matter.

God said to him, "You are my Son; today I have become your Father."
. . . In his life on earth Jesus made his prayers and requests with loud cries and tears to God, who could save him from death. (Heb. 5:5, 7)

We see here that obedience is not simply God's demand and a man's bite-the-bullet giving in, but rather, a process of relationship with the

Father, of engaging Him honestly and openly—even loudly at times:

> But even though he was God's Son, he learned through his sufferings to be obedient. (Heb. 5:8)

The Father God is secure in His authority. Therefore, He does not see a man's honest protest as a challenge to His rule, but a natural balking at discomfort, to be expected of any human child. The Father is not threatened by you, not even by your worst anger, and will not zap you for protesting His demands. In fact, He much prefers you to raise your fist at Him than to run away from Him.

The biblical faith understands that the opposite of love is not hate, but forgetting. For God, to forget is to forsake. Lovers know this: It's better to quarrel than to forget about each other.

The longing to be one with his daddy is deeply rooted in every boy's masculine soul. The father thereby wields overwhelming authority in his son's life. As a reflection of the Father God's call to and authority over us His sons, this inborn authority of fatherhood is a holy mantle to be taken up both humbly and deliberately.

Like all spiritual truth, this fact is borne out in the natural realm. As one father interviewed in *The Father's Almanac* put it:

> From the viewpoint of kids, all adults just have a real natural authority, and especially the parents. And you really don't have to exert that. Simply by being big and being competent and being able to do things that they want to do, we just have an incredible amount of authority. And you can just let it flow naturally.[4]

The man who has dared to understand this—by facing his own father's authority in shaping his manhood—is not threatened by his own son's protests. Indeed, he can understand and accept the boy's reluctance to do the task—even as he insists it be done.

Consider, for example, a boy's household chore like taking out the trash. The father who has not accepted his true and given authority over his son may fear looking weak and thereby losing authority unless he commands, "Take out that trash right now—or else!"

Fearing his father's punishment, the boy may stuff his natural desire to resist, and take out the trash now. Later, however, in the freedom of adulthood, that desire to resist will resurface at the demands of daily life. His boss gives him an order, the government tells him to pay taxes by April 15—and procrastination offers the only way to honor his own feelings.

The father who knows his authority, however, can approach his son in an entirely different spirit, as if to say, "It's okay, son—you don't have to like doing it. In fact, I'd worry about you if you smiled and danced taking out the trash!"

A healthy exchange, therefore, might look like this:

Father: "How about taking the trash out, Billy?"

Son: "Aw, do I have to, Dad? I don't want to—I'm just getting into this Nintendo game!"

Father: (goes to boy and puts arm around him) "I know—it's not a lot of fun, and it interrupts things sometimes, doesn't it? (pats Billy on the back) I wasn't too excited when your grandfather told me to do it, either. But yeah, it's got to be done, so go ahead and get on it now. The sooner you do it, the sooner it's done, and you can get back to your game."

This kind of family focuses not on establishing Dad's authority, but in building father-son relationship. Billy is therefore free to grumble as he heads out to the garbage cans. His grumbling is no threat to Dad's authority, which is secure—not because Dad demands it, but because the Father God has ordained it in the male child.

Indeed, whether Billy grumbles or not, Dad should say clearly he's pleased once the son has put out the trash cans, even say, "Have a good Nintendo game!" Thus, the son learns a precious lesson: As I set out to accomplish my life's tasks, no matter how difficult, my Father knows how I feel, and in that critical sense, is with me. As Jesus put it, "I and the Father are one."

As an adult, he can be gentle with his natural resistance to tasks—neither coddling nor coercing himself, but allowing his human feelings even as he gets on with the job.

Again, consider the common case of a father's company's transferring him, requiring the family to move. Simply to announce the move to the child and tell him how great it will be in the new neighborhood, translates as a command, since the boy's feelings have not been honored: "We're moving, whether you like it or not!" Very likely, the boy will procrastinate or put off enjoying the new place, by criticizing it often when he gets there, resisting new friendships, and scoffing at new activities. This can consume much family energy and spark considerable anger.

The upset could be avoided simply by sitting down with the boy and asking him how he feels about moving. This is not to kow-tow to the child, for clearly the family must and will move regardless of his feelings. IBM or the Army is not about to say to the father, "Well, since your son Bobby doesn't want to leave his playground here, we won't transfer you."

The father's authority, that is, has already been established, and he need not feel threatened by Bobby's protests. Let the boy say out loud, "But I don't want to move! I'll miss Jimmy and all my friends." Then say, "You've had some really good times here with Jimmy and all your friends, haven't you? I can tell you there are other boys you can be friends with where we're going, but for now, I'll only say, it's sad to say good-bye, isn't it?" Let the boy grieve—openly, in front of the father. Indeed, let the father lead the boy by example and say, "I know how you feel. I'll miss my friends here, too." Knowing he is thus one with the father frees the boy to be open to the new life ahead with his father.

Unfortunately, the average man today has not had this kind of open, trusting relationship with his father, so he cannot readily offer it to his own son. He has been so wounded by his own father's coercive, fearful misuse of authority that he cannot recognize, trust in, and uphold the father's authority over the son—even in himself as a father. And so, too often, he resorts to the same threats and coercion toward his own son, repeating the generational wound and ensuring the same pattern of procrastination in his son.

If every time the boy tries to express his own feelings, the father represses him with, "Don't talk back to me! You'll do what I say or else!" then the boy must find some way to maintain the integrity of his feelings without provoking his father's anger. So he simply says, "Yes, Sir," right away, but then does nothing.

Certainly, such dawdling is frustrating to a parent. As child psychologist Dr. Benjamin Spock has noted:

> (W)hen a child dawdles, an impatient parent feels like pushing. The more the child feels pushed, the more he slows down. It's a neat way for him to fight back. He's asserting his right to resist domination. At the same time, he gets back at his parents in a way which is particularly irritating to them. Yet he doesn't have to take the dangerous course of openly defying the parent (the way a less strictly controlled child might). It's as if he and his parent were both afraid of open hostility, the parent because of conscientiousness and self-control, the child because of fear of losing the parent's love. Instead, they all tacitly agree on a restricted sort of combat which never becomes lethal but which never ends.[5]

Procrastination therefore falls under the psychological category of "passive-aggressive" behavior, which on the surface seems quite nice and agreeable, but underneath is fueled by resentment and aimed at revenge. In men, this childhood pattern becomes, "Yes, honey, I'll get to fixing that faucet soon . . ." Translation: "You really made me mad the other day when you pulled away from me, but I'm afraid to say that directly, so see if I ever do anything for you!"

Or this: "Yes, boss, I'll be getting that contract on your desk before long." Translation: "I hate the way you push me around, but I can't say that to your face, so I'll get back at you by making you wait for the contract."

Clearly, such dawdling responses are ultimately self-defeating; the wife only gets less affectionate, the boss less respectful.

As Missledine notes, "People whose work—and through it their self-esteem—depends primarily on their own inner organization are particularly vulnerable to the demands of an overly coerced 'child of the past.' Among those are salesmen, housewives, composers, executives, scientists, businessmen, ministers, artists and writers."[6]

The self-defeating pattern of procrastinators, he says, is completed when they wait until the last minute to do the job—when "the pressures on them to produce have reached a maximum, threatening level"—and "thus, instead of being able to do an outstanding or even satisfactory piece of work, they barely manage to get along."

To the extent that authentic, mature manhood requires taking initiative based upon an "inner organization," and not simply reacting to external demands, procrastination is a major deterrent to manhood. Furthermore, if procrastination stems from harsh or coercive fathering, then recognizing and overcoming it becomes an essential focus in healing the father-wound and restoring men to relationship with the Father God.

The second son in Jesus' story models the classic procrastinator caught in the "command-resistance cycle," and is therefore not the model Jesus holds up for us to emulate. Yet even the first son does not seem to be one whose behavior Jesus would want us to copy. Indeed, does the Father God want us to say, "No, I don't want to go!" when He calls us to a task?

To understand what Jesus is saying in this story, we must remember the larger book in which it appears.

The Bible itself is a story about an often rebellious people, who hear God's command and promptly turn away. The loving Father God calls His children to a task, and they rebel—from the very beginning when Adam and Eve eat the forbidden fruit, to the disciples who leave Jesus in the lurch on the Cross, to our own selves today. When we turn away from God's commands, we are squarely in God's story, not outside it.

This rebellious nature of biblical folk is not simply a literary counterpoint to create action and suspense. In fact, it reflects the life-truth that often the rebel shows greater knowledge and understanding of God's ways than the quick-and-ready "yes man."

When I perform weddings, for example, the groom waits nervously with his best man in a side room. Inevitably, the best man turns to his groom friend just as the wedding march begins and —perhaps with the best intentions—says, "Are you nervous?" Often, the best man is simply nervous himself, and instead of admitting that, he projects his apparent weakness onto the easy target at hand. Nevertheless, with the grooms- men gathered there, this question puts the groom on the spot before his closest male allies just when he's struggling to remain calm before the crowd that awaits him.

As the groom struggles to decide whether to admit he's nervous, I interrupt. "I hope you are nervous! I'd be worried if you weren't. This is a pretty big event in your life, after all, and not something you do every day!"

It's true: If the groom is calm and cool, clearly the powerful mystery of God's covenant ceremony is not touching him deeply—and likely his faith and his feelings for his bride do not touch him deeply, either. Mar- riage is a major life event, fraught with all the pains and fears and dan- gers of any faith journey. It is therefore to be approached with genuine nervousness and even some reluctance.

Even though God has called this man and woman together, the one who sometimes feels, "No, Lord, I don't want to go," has a deeper and more realistic grasp of what marriage entails than the one who jumps in blindly with, "Yes, of course, why not get married?" The man who real- istically anticipates some pain and struggle in his marriage, knows he will need his Father God with him in it.

Ultimately, the man who trusts the Father God enough to pour out honest feelings of reluctance to Him, can trust that the security of such freedom and acceptance will allow him to move through the fear into true commitment—born out of deep and genuine love for the woman, not mere "doing what's right."

When the Father God calls us out as men to work with Him in the vineyard of this broken world, it is entirely appropriate to balk at first. If we burst out, "Oh yes, Lord, please send me right away!" Jesus likely wonders, "Does this man really understand what I'm asking him to do? Does he realize the terrible danger in trying to love others in a world paralyzed by fear and sold out to selfishness?"

Indeed, when the wife of Zebedee came to Jesus and asked Him to promise that her two sons would sit at His right hand in heaven, He replied in amazement—not to the mother, but man-to-man, to the sons themselves:

"You don't know what you are asking for," Jesus answered the sons. "Can you drink the cup of suffering that I am about to drink?" (Matt. 20:22)

The man who is honestly reluctant to follow Jesus at first, sees Jesus realistically—and thereby, is closer to Him and more open to true and lasting conversion. Too often today, young men either drop out of church altogether or say, "Oh, yes, I guess I'm a Christian. I mean, I'm not Jewish, or Buddhist, or Muslim, or anything else."

I'd much rather hear a young man burst out angrily, "No way am I going to be a Christian! Following Jesus is just too hard for me. It causes too much sacrifice, pain, and upset in my life. I'm going to be happy doing things my way, and not by letting God tell me what to do!" Here is someone who at least knows not only that Jesus is real, but what relationship with the Father requires.

When pain and adversity strike—as they must in this broken world— whose faith will be most open to the saving, outstretched arm of the Father God? The bored, go-with-the-Christian-crowd youth will abandon his "faith" for any cult or fad that promises his fantasy of an easier life. But the ex-rebel, who has wandered enough to discover the limits of his own human self-sufficiency, will be ready for a true surrender to the Father.

Thus Jesus warned the Pharisees, as religious yes men, that the prostitutes and pimps would meet the Father before they would. It's harder to convince a squeaky-clean "religious leader" that he needs help, than a street person.

The fullness of God's power and grace can be experienced only by those who have experienced the fullness of their own weakness and sin. It is the prodigal son returned whom the father celebrates, and the lost sheep whom the Good Shepherd seeks. "I tell you," Jesus declares, "there will be more joy in heaven over one sinner who repents than over ninety-nine respectable people who do not need to repent" (Luke 15:7). No man is so sick as the one who thinks he's healthy, none so far from the Father as one who doesn't need Him.

A man therefore doesn't need to scorn, curse, reject, or coerce the resistant child—whether his own son or the boy within himself. The Father God has another way, preferring to see greater potential for engagement, interaction, and thus, relationship with such a child. In this Spirit, Jesus introduces His parable to His listeners saying, "Now what do you think?" The Father revealed in Jesus respects His sons, wants to engage them in dialogue.

Some years ago, I began school teaching with an unruly class of ninth-graders. Within the first week the students had thoroughly intimidated me. Between barked orders I sent students to the principal's office two and three at a time. Eventually, a wiser, more experienced teacher took me aside. "The students have a right to complain," she advised, "and you have the right to insist. Try to maintain a balance."

She was right. In my compulsion to gain complete control and obedience, I had cut off the students' own feelings, creating frustration and disobedience in the class. When I could begin to tell the class, in effect, "I know this work isn't fun a lot of the time, but we need to do it. What can we do to have some fun when we're finished?" both the class and I relaxed considerably, and in fact more work was done.

The conversion of William Penn to Quakerism also illustrates the point. Born in England the son of an admiral of the Royal Fleet, young William at first fit the role of arrogant gentry. Accustomed to swaggering with a long sword at his side, he once visited a Quaker meeting on impulse and was strangely seized by the power there. When he returned to that pacifist fellowship, sword and all, members complained to George Fox, founder and then leader of the Quaker movement in England: How were they supposed to tolerate this haughty military son with his sword in their meetings, as they proclaimed the gospel of peace?

Fox met the young Penn and explained the Quaker position of pacifism. Indignantly—still operating out of the rigid legalism of his military father—Penn demanded to know if this meant he must take off his sword or be expelled from the Quaker meeting?

Fox replied No, he didn't have to take it off. He was invited to worship with the Quakers and wear his sword as long as he could.

If Fox had affirmed in that encounter his members' fear instead of God's power—if he had taken refuge in the Law from dependence upon God's Spirit—and cast young William from his church, the young swashbuckler would almost surely have stood his ground and left, to preserve his dignity. A young man's fragile opportunity for relationship with the Father God would have been destroyed or painfully delayed, and the later American Quaker witness to peace, which young William grew to establish, might have been lost or considerably postponed.

George Fox honored Penn's dignity. He could do that because he trusted ultimately in God and not some fabricated authority of his own, which would be valid only within the narrow confines of his church and not for an outsider like Penn. He spoke to a rebellious young man with the authority of a son whose Father both respects and holds him accountable. A dedicated pacifist, he eschewed the language of violence and refused to engage in a power play of coercion and punishment with Penn. He trusted the Father God to win the young man to Himself through the faithful witness of his congregation.

The father, that is, need not react harshly to his son's wrongdoing, or wrong attitude. The biblical faith understands that relationship with the Father requires first that the man be a sinner—the easiest requirement for us to fulfill, albeit the hardest to proclaim, because we fear the Father's rejection. God knows we cannot change our inborn self-centeredness (see Rom. 7:18); indeed, that is precisely why He sent Jesus.

The Father God does not demand we change in order for Him to accept and love us; rather, He invites us to let Him accept and love us in order that we might be open at last to His changing us.

Clearly, if procrastination is rooted in our reaction to overcoercion, then it can't be overcome simply by pushing ourselves harder. Satan cannot cast out Satan.

How then, a man might ask, can I acknowledge I don't want to do something, and still be motivated to go ahead and do it? Doesn't it make more sense just to stuff your feelings and get the job done?

The answer is clear: You can't—unless you have a Father who respects you, who wants you to tell Him how you feel and thus surrender yourself to Him, who you can trust will then give you what you need to get the job done, and bless you for doing it.

To live in the awful tension of knowing what you'd rather do and having to do something else, requires trust in the Father that He knows best, no matter how much inconvenience and pain is necessary for you to obey Him.

To tell God you don't like what He's doing in your life is not to "delete" your feelings, but to file them in a holy "glossary"; not to give your money away, but to invest it in a trust fund; not to lose your personality, but to commit it to relationship with the Father.

Sure, it seems more efficient just to discount your feelings, coerce yourself, and do what you have to do. But as this becomes a habit, you will begin to discount others' feelings as well, and begin trying to coerce them as you do yourself. Like the Pharisees, you will begin to wonder how you work so righteously hard, while everyone else is a slouch.

The process is deadly: You sacrifice relationship with the Father by distrusting Him and stuffing your feelings. This leads to losing relationship with yourself as you forget what you really feel and need, and then you become cut off from others. Eventually, you become angry, and with no sense of the Father who honors you as His son, you begin the procrastination game, resisting your own commands to yourself.

I am not promoting laziness, but rather, respect for your feelings that leads you into relationship with the Father—who calls men to tasks and empowers you to get the job done as the full person you are, not a zombie-robot. In this way, He preserves you for His lifelong purposes.

For example, one often extremely difficult "command" of the Father to His sons, is to reserve sexual intercourse for marriage. Any man today who pretends this is easy has either been given the rare spiritual gift of celibacy, or has fooled himself dangerously, inviting procrastination in sexual fidelity.

According to Jesus' parable, the disagreeable but honest son is ultimately more likely to obey than the quick-to-please yes man. Therefore, if we want to avoid sexual disobedience and falling, we had better be fighting with God over this command regularly. Better to fight with God than with your flesh; you're going to lose in either case (see Rom. 7:24), and God is far kinder than the flesh to those who surrender.

"Ron" is a composite example of the many men I've ministered to in this struggle. As a young man, Ron had slept with many women. Converted in his early thirties, he resolved to wait for "the right woman God would send." To his surprise, thereafter he battled fiercely with sexual desire. Ashamed to tell any other Christians about it—convinced that surely God hated him for it—he went along with the "Christian program" and quietly bit the bullet.

Soon, he began seeing "good-looking women everywhere." Even some of the old girlfriends called him and "wanted to get it together again." Overwhelmed with desire, eventually he could see just two possibilities: Say No to God and fall, or say Yes to God and lose his sex drive altogether.

That's not much of a choice for a healthy young man, who'd rather be a pagan than a eunuch any day. Soon the procrastination option entered his prayers: "Yes, God, I hear Your command to stay celibate, and I'll definitely do that . . . when the right woman comes along."

The almost-fatal flaw in Ron's faith, as in so many men, was that, in turning his life over to Jesus, he learned the rules of the religion, but not the joy of the relationship. He had never allowed Jesus to introduce him to the Father, because pain from his demanding earthly father blocked the way.

Fortunately, Ron was intelligent enough to know that God must have another way, and finally, he had the courage to go to another Christian man and talk about his problem.

First, I reassured Ron that his sexual desire for a woman was entirely normal—even something God had created in him as a man and, therefore, nothing he needed to be ashamed of in itself. As for occasional lustful thoughts, I reminded him that we live in a broken world where such thoughts are as common as any other germ. It's no sin to have a germ on your hand. But if you cut your hand and don't take care of it, the infection is your own fault. As Martin Luther put it, "You can't stop the birds from flying overhead, but you can keep them from making a nest in your hair."

If the "lust germs" get imbedded and infect his mind, a man needs to take responsibility for himself and go to a doctor. That is, he needs to see a Christian counselor and get healing for the inner, emotional wound that is allowing the "germs" to enter his mind.

Next, I encouraged Ron: "Tell me honestly, now. If your Father God has given you sexual desire, and at the same time has said you can't use it fully right now, how does that make you feel?"

"Pretty angry!" Ron declared. "I mean, that doesn't seem fair!"

"I can't blame you one bit," I said. "But don't tell me. Tell your Father." Ron hesitated.

"Go ahead," I urged. "Tell God how you feel about not having a woman."

Shifting uneasily, Ron sighed. Then he prayed, "God . . . Father, I don't like having to sleep alone. I want a woman."

Again, he paused.

"That's great," I said. "Keep telling your Father how it feels."

This process continued until Ron finally raised his fist and shouted at God how much he hated not having sex. Such trust led him eventually into talking to the Father about his feelings for women in general—an experience his earthly father had never afforded him.

Surprised that no lightning bolt came from heaven to destroy him, Ron felt encouraged—even refreshed. I invited him to offer this time of sexual fasting to the Father and to ask God "What do you want to do to make me ready for the woman You have for me?"

Now God had a free hand at last to deal with the inner healing Ron needed, which included deliverance from lust, breaking bonds of the flesh from past relationships, and reconciliation with his father and mother. Some time has passed, and God's woman has not yet appeared. Ron still gets angry at times about this. But instead of stuffing his anger and letting it lead him to "command-resistance" temptations, he talks about it openly in his men's support group. Periodically, he takes it in prayer to the Father, and they have it out together, sometimes—like Jesus—loudly.

As for temptations, Ron has had some difficult moments. Once, he became so angry at being celibate that he told God, "I've had it with Your commands and promises! I want a woman, and I'm going to get one!" That weekend, he called an old girlfriend to his apartment, and before long, they were beginning to undress. She was willing, even eager. And then, something strange happened.

"Somehow . . . I just stopped," Ron said, shaking his head with a mixture of dismay and wonder. "Right there in the middle of everything, I just stopped . . . and realized, 'This isn't what I really want.' Oh, I was physically ready all right. But it was just no good."

Ron sighed deeply. "It was pretty awkward. I apologized, mumbled something about God, and took her back to her place." Genuinely puzzled, he hesitated. "I guess . . . it was just too late. Like it or not, something's happened in me . . . with the Lord. I hadn't realized how much of me had changed until then. I guess . . . there's just no turning back anymore. I've really got nothing left but the unknown ahead—nothing to hope in but Jesus, that someday, when the time is right, He'll bring the woman."

In that holy moment of realization, we sat quietly. When eventually we prayed, Ron could only be as honest with his Father as he had already become. "Come on, Father! I don't like this. I'm Your man, You know that, and I'll hang in with You forever. But I want a woman, and I'm coming for her to You, my Father. I'm not going to go to old girlfriends, to bars, or any places like that again.

"But You've given me this sexual desire, so You've got to take care of it in me. If I need more healing to prepare me, let's get on with it. If not, bring her to me.

"Maybe . . . You don't have a woman for me, and I'll never get married. If that's true, I'll keep on with my job and friends and regular life anyhow. But You're going to have one angry son on Your hands, Father, because I'm going to have it out with You for a long time on this!"

I encouraged Ron to channel his energies toward faith and begin praying for the woman—not just "Lord, bring me a woman," but, trusting the Father to be preparing a particular woman even as himself, interceding: "Lord, show me any needs this woman has that I can be praying about in her behalf." That's good practice for when you eventually do meet.

Obedience has become for Ron a process of relationship, not a resentful burden, or fearful denial. Certainly, this kind of relationship with the

Father takes time. But it is so much more real, so much more promising than gritting your teeth in the Law or losing yourself in the flesh. As Jesus' parable suggests, the older son, who has known the father longer—and presumably, more accurately—trusts the father more. He is therefore more free to express himself openly as a son and thereby, to grow as a man.

I hasten to add that Ron's story is not a prescriptive technique, but rather, an invitation to relationship with the Father yourself. I wrestled awhile before including it in this book, and decided at last to trust my reader-brothers—namely, that you will not rush out now and call up an old girlfriend and put yourself in Ron's compromising situation. Yes, the Father dealt with Ron—a particular son—in this particular way. But He has another, particular way of dealing with you. Talk to Him, listen to Him, shout, cry, pray, wrestle it out with the Father for yourself.

When a man finds himself faced with a task and tempted to procrastinate, he can talk to his Father. He can say, "Father, I don't want to do this!" and add whatever else of his feelings is necessary to bring him to the point of saying, "But I'll trust You and do it. Father, give me what I need to do it well, to Your glory." In such trust, he can even add, like a beloved son, "And then, Father . . . show me what would be fun to do as a reward."

The energy expended in gritting your teeth at the Father's command just grinds you down, and becomes distorted in passive-aggressive procrastination. Better to invest it in relationship with the Father, pouring out your heart to Him. For this is how God makes men.

If a man is to honor his own son's feelings and respect the boy's integrity as a person, he must first learn that the Father honors him. While this learning process requires time spent alone engaging the Father in prayer, it becomes confirmed most securely through relationship with other men.

With this understanding, we are ready to see how relationship with the Father God sustains a man through special times of trial and uncertainty.

CHAPTER EIGHT

Seeking God's Will, Trusting His Love

> The new covenant that I will make with the people of Israel will be this: I
> will put my law within them and write it on their hearts. I will be their
> God, and they will be my people. None of them will have to teach his
> fellow countryman to know the LORD, because all will know me, from the
> least to the greatest. I will forgive their sins and I will no longer remem-
> ber their wrongs. I, the Lord, have spoken. (Jer. 31:33–34)

The fellow pastor's prayer request seemed so routine at first, but all of
us at the clergy prayer group meeting found ourselves strangely reluctant to proceed. Facing an important decision in his life, he asked us to
pray for him "to be sure and see God's will clearly." Wringing his hands,
he declared, "I've prayed and prayed about this many times, and have
asked many others to pray for me, too. I want to be sure and do only
what the Lord wants me to."

Leaning forward to pray as the young man so fervently asked, I hesitated. Apparently, everyone sensed something was amiss, as a strange
silence settled over the group. His request was so normal, so
understandable—hadn't all of us gathered there felt such an urgency to
know God's will for us at times? And yet . . .

The silence was broken appropriately by a middle-aged pastor widely
recognized for his wisdom. "You know," he began gently, "when I was a
lot younger, I always used to be searching and asking for 'God's will'
before I ever did anything at all. Over the years, though, as I've grown
closer to the Lord, I don't find myself doing that anymore.

"Sure, we all want to know the Lord's will in any situation, and we
ought to ask for His guidance. But most of the time, you just don't get
anything as clear as handwriting on the wall, and you can waste a lot of

good time and energy forever 'seeking God's will.' Instead, most of the time the best thing to do after you've prayed is just to give yourself and the situation to the Lord, then go ahead and act on your best judgment at the time."

Matter-of-factly, he shrugged his shoulders. "You'll make some mistakes, of course—even the apostle Paul knew we only 'see through a glass darkly' (see 1 Cor. 13:12 KJV). But you've got to trust that He'll keep on loving you and put you back on the track—and even teach you important lessons through those mistakes."

A wry grin spread among us all as we recognized that this was a true word spoken not just to the young man who had asked for prayer, but to all of us there.

In my own case, this lesson had cost considerable pain.

Some years earlier, my life seemed to overflow with turmoil. As a pastor, my church was beset by in-fighting and upset; my family faced several painful situations; as a writer, I had not been able to write anything for months. I was in uncharted waters and the storms raged mercilessly around me. Daily I cried out, "Lord, help me! What am I supposed to do now? Give me a word! Speak to me and show me Your will!"

I learned then that when you cry out so desperately in the apparent void, the Lord is not the only one who hears. For the Enemy roams about like a hungry lion (see 1 Peter 5:8) and, not unlike the wolf to Little Red Riding Hood, he may appear disguised as Grandma.

In my quest after "God's will for my life," I visited a wide variety of prayer groups. And then one Sunday, an older lady about sixty, from one of those groups, came to my morning worship and told me afterward that the Lord had shown her my anguish and sent her to pray for me.

At once, my heart leapt with hope. I remembered that this lady was particularly decisive in her prayers, which often flowed from phrases like, "The Lord would have you do (such and such)." To my pleasant surprise, she rose at prayer time during worship and told the congregation that they should be thankful for their fine pastor, who was such an able spiritual leader. Still, her tendency to be pushy made me cautious, and I decided I would not seek her prayers unless she first asked me to pray for her as a pastor.

Sure enough, she stayed for prayer group after worship and asked people to pray for her overweight condition. As we left, she took me aside and asked if I would counsel her regularly.

At several weekly sessions, I prayed for her in my office. As the storms about my own life worsened, however, I became more fearful and desperate to "know God's will." Finally, I asked her to pray for me.

For two or three weeks, she offered "words from the Lord" which assured that I was right and my critics wrong. Then, abruptly, she announced that the Lord was telling me to sever all close personal ties and relationships, and that I was her "spiritual son."

In shock and dismay, I sought out other pastors and discovered that this lady had visited other churches over the years and had been unmasked as a false prophet. With some effort, I confronted her with this and she left our church—along with several families who were angry that I had "kicked out this kind old woman." Shaken, I nevertheless learned that a major danger in seeking God's will so compulsively is that it leaves you especially vulnerable to ungodly sources of knowledge.

John and Paula Sandford of Elijah House Ministries, for example, tell of a friend who was "trying to do everything by listening to God," and ended up being misguided by what he thought was God's will.

On the surface, it seems like trying to listen to God about all things is good. But God does not want to reduce us to slaves or robots. He has given us good minds and He expects us to use them. Moreover, questioning soon revealed that our friend had been fearful of failure. He would use "listening to God" to be overly certain. That became the sin of divination. Had God wanted to steer him away from one (way) to another, the Lord would have taken the initiative to speak, and would have confirmed by at least two witnesses. But our friend's fearful heart sought to turn God into his diviner. The Lord let him listen to a wrong voice, as both discipline and teaching. That was a rough way to learn, but it was certainly written on our friend's heart to listen when God wants to speak, but not to push God to be his diviner.[1]

Like the Sandfords' friend, I, too, had been "fearful of failure," in my family and church. Indeed, my fears kept me so busy crying out for the Lord's direction that I could not hear His still, small voice. I was so desperately "seeking God's will" that I did not trust Him and wait faithfully on His timing.

After talking and praying with many men, I now believe that such a fear stems from an image of God as the demanding, punishing Father. In a man's fearful, childish heart, that is, he feels that the terrible upsets in his life must be God's punishment for his somehow having disobeyed Him. "If I could only know the Father's will with absolute certainty, I'd do it," he reasons, "and then all would be well, because He would love me again."

The biblical faith understands that this fear is rooted in a sense of not being loved. As John declares, "There is no fear in love; perfect love drives out all fear. So then, love has not been made perfect in anyone who is afraid, because fear has to do with punishment" (1 John 4:18).

During this upsetting period, I went on a two-day retreat with four other pastors, and one of them told me that I was "trying too hard to find God's will." The very next morning—June 3—I turned to the daily devotion in Oswald Chambers' *My Utmost for His Highest* and read:

> At the beginning of our Christian life, we are full of requests to God, then we find that God wants to get us into relationship with Himself, to get us in touch with His purposes. . . . At first we want the consciousness of being guided by God, then as we go on we live so much in the consciousness of God that we do not need to ask what His will is, because the thought of choosing any other will never occur to us. If we are saved and sanctified God guides us in our ordinary choices, and if we are going to choose what He does not want, He will check, and we must heed. . . . God instructs us in what we choose, that is, He guides our common sense, and we no longer hinder His Spirit by continually saying—"Now, Lord, what is Thy will?"[2]

Here, I believe, the Lord was bringing my condition into the light through His initiative and confirmation by witnesses. Indeed, I had been so concerned with my "requests to God," that I had not been able to hear God's calling me into "relationship with Himself" in order to get me "in touch with His purposes." I simply did not trust that God had indeed "saved and sanctified me," and made me His own son; therefore, I could not trust my "ordinary choices" or "common sense" to reflect His will.

Shortly after the retreat, my pastor friend sent me an excerpt from Robert Raines' *To Kiss the Joy,* in which Raines characterizes his own maturing faith.

> I used to labor under a particular kind of burden . . . that in any given context and among all the options available, one of them was God's will. And, by God, I had to find it so I wouldn't make an awful mistake and have the terrible guilt of having missed it. Well, I don't feel that way anymore. In any given context, among the options available, I believe that we are responsible to try to seek what love would indicate with the persons and groups involved. We are responsible to weigh consequences, to assess probabilities, to take what seems to be the most loving and wise course of action. And then, as always, to trust that whatever we decide, however we choose, even if it is wrong, even if the consequences are disastrous, even if the choice is foolish or malicious—even so, God stays with us to forgive us and help us pick up the pieces, build another bridge, try all over again. Martin Luther's comment is comforting to me, "Trust God and sin on bravely."[3]

The good news, therefore, is not that we are perfect, but that God is perfect, that His perfect mercy in Jesus breaks the bonds of our self-centered human nature and allows His nature to enter and grow within us. As the apostle Paul declared, "Everyone has sinned and is far away from God's saving presence. But by the free gift of God's grace all are put right with him through Christ Jesus, who sets them free" (Rom. 3:23–24).

Thus Raines notes, "We cannot avoid participating in evil insofar as evil consists of making decisions that either hurt, in part, or fail to help, in part, some other person or persons. We cannot be perfect." We are therefore called "to be responsible, to make the best choice we can in a given circumstance, and to trust that God will bring something creative out of what happens. We no longer need the security of our beliefs or the security of being right when we are able to trust in God. Our search for security, our making of a golden calf, is our way of asking God and each other, 'Do you love me?'"[4]

One way to fabricate security—and escape from the fearful business of trusting relationship both with each other and with the Father God— is to surrender to some self-styled "prophet," as I did, or perhaps some strong "godly" authority figure. Most cults, I suspect, prey upon this longing for father-love in our society; Jim Jones, of the 1971 Jonestown mass suicide, instructed his followers to call him "Dad." When out of pride and fear we resist relationship with God, the longing within us for the true Father becomes dangerously open to distorted, false substitutes.

An easier way to conjure false security—so common in churches to-day that it is rarely recognized as such—is the time-honored manner of the Pharisees, namely, to seize upon "my beliefs" or written creeds as absolute, and thus, safe. It's quick; it's easy; I say the "right" things, and the Father loves me.

The terrible price for such "safety," ironically, is precisely the constant fear we've been trying to avoid—the fear which "has to do with punishment," and prompts vigilance of ourselves and others. What happens when I discover, like the apostle Paul that I "am not able" (see Rom. 7:18) to do what the Law requires, and face "this body that is taking me to death" (see Rom. 7:24)? I lose my already flimsy chance to win the harsh Father's love. My beliefs must then be absolutely correct, and I must judge and reject others who do not share them precisely. If you differ with me and retain any integrity, my beliefs must be flawed—I must be wrong, and therefore must lose the Father's love.

The man who clings to such false security is therefore marked by alienation from others and loneliness. Together, such men foster division.

When we dare not face our own sin for fear of losing the Father's love, that is, we project it onto others and judge them. Ultimately, as the old saying goes, it comes down to "just me and thee, and I ain't so sure about thee."

In families, the fear of losing the father's love prompts sibling rivalry; brothers kill brothers, as Absalom killed Amnon (see 2 Sam. 13) when their father David showed partiality. In society, it manifests in cliques and prejudices. Mercy is forgotten, personhood is lost, and love is remaindered—because relationship with the Father has been pre-empted by fear of punishment.

In surrendering to the Father God, however, a man can trust that the measure of God's truth in his beliefs is not lost, but indeed, is properly readied to be written at last on his heart, as Jeremiah prophesied of the New Covenant. The essence of this prophecy, central to the biblical faith, is that in the New Covenant, through Jesus, we shall be one with the Father. We shall know His mind (see Jer. 31:31–34), and no longer need to beg for His will.

Knowing "my Father God loves me" frees a man from his fearful compulsion to know God's will perfectly in every situation. He no longer needs to hide his fear of not being loved behind the Law or "my beliefs." Instead, he can walk freely in the Spirit—Who is the sure sign that we are united with God and loved by Him. As John emphasizes,

> No one has ever seen God, but if we love one another, God lives in union with us, and his love is made perfect in us. We are sure that we live in union with God and that he lives in union with us, because he has given us his Spirit. (1 John 4:12–13)

Burt, a thirty-six-year-old architect, had gone through a painful divorce several years earlier and had been dating Teresa seriously for a year. He sought Christian counseling to work through the pain and lessons of his first marriage, and in his words, Teresa was "everything I want in a woman." He came to me in a panic, asking, "But is she the one God has for me?"

Together, we reviewed his relationship with Teresa. She was a faithful believer, similar to him in education, outlook, and hobbies. She was well able to encourage and support Burt in his faith and calling. He had prayed with several other godly men and each sensed no reservation on God's part in the relationship.

"I made such a mistake in my first marriage," Burt said anxiously. "I want to be sure and get the right woman this time."

"Is Teresa the woman you want?" I asked.

"Yes," Burt said, still anxious. "But is she the one God wants for me?"

"I don't know if your first marriage was God's will or not," I said. "I can only say that it didn't work, that you were hurt badly, and that your Father God has done some great healing in you and will continue to heal you. I don't blame you now for wanting ironclad reassurance that it won't happen again as before.

"But until the Lord returns, we still 'see through a glass darkly' in this world, and no other man can give you that reassurance with Teresa. What I can say without reservation is that your Father God loves you as a son, and will walk with you and Teresa as long as you both let Him.

"You've considered the facts about her and sought your witnesses; that's all a man can do. The real question is not whether Teresa is the woman God has picked for you, but rather, even if she's not God's choice, is she the one you've picked, and can you trust your Father God to honor and bless you as a beloved son with the woman of your choosing?"

Burt shifted uneasily.

"Did your dad respect your own choices when you were growing up?" I asked.

Burt dropped his head. "I was always afraid I'd do something wrong and Dad would disapprove and punish me."

"And now you're afraid your Father God will disapprove, and punish you with another bad marriage?"

"Yeah . . ." Burt sighed. "I guess that's it."

"The Father God I know in Jesus wouldn't punish you for marrying 'the wrong woman,' but instead, would do everything the two of you would let Him do to make it a good marriage. He was just as hurt when the first marriage broke up as you were. But now, you've allowed Him to heal you and He wants to bless you."

Burt looked up. "I really do want Teresa. In fact, I just can't believe how good she is."

"No," I said. "Your problem is that you just can't believe how good your Father God is."

Certainly, obedience to God is central to our salvation; the writer of Hebrews proclaims Jesus as "the source of eternal salvation for all those who obey him" (see Heb. 5:9). But the New Covenant proclaims the Father's Spirit, not His Law.

Does a man obey God as his earthly father, because he fears the punishment for disobedience? Or does he obey because he is so overwhelmed by the Father God's loving mercy in the face of his own inability to keep the Law, that his thankful heart seeks to please Him? For this is the process by which the Father God woos us unto Himself: He calls each man to surrender his father-wound to Him, thereby allowing Him at last to replace the man's self-centered human spirit with the Father's Holy Spirit.

Suppose your wife asks you to take her to breakfast at a restaurant you don't particularly like. You might take her out of fear she'll get angry if you don't, or even because she went to your restaurant last time, so it's only "fair."

But what if you just love her, if her delight makes you feel good—and you take her to her restaurant thankful for the opportunity to show love to her. You may not enjoy the food, but when she says, "Thanks, Honey, for taking me," you feel better—more loved?—than any other restaurant's food could have made you feel.

Obedience requires knowing the Father's Law; that is the function of the Old Covenant. Relationship with the Father requires not only knowing His Law, but knowing His character as well. In particular, to move beyond Law to Spirit, from slave to son (see Rom. 8:14–16), a man must know the Father's mercy—that is, that relationship with the Father/ Lawmaker is sustained even when we in our human weakness inevitably break the Law.

Far too many boys have experienced rules and punishment with their earthly fathers, but have not experienced deeper knowledge of the man behind the rules, which only mercy can beckon. The father who wants his son to know him and invites the son to ask questions —who can offer his own shortcomings as opportunities for the son to see an example of humility in a man and mercy in the Father God —gives his son a precious gift.

In his book, *Just between Father and Son: A Weekend Adventure Prepares a Boy for Adolescence,* Dr. James Wilder offers his son—and all men—an excellent model of this fatherly strength through vulnerability. During a week's camping trip with his twelve-year-old son, Wilder invites the boy's unlimited questions about sex and talks openly with his son about his own sexuality as a man.

In the preface, he states:

> What you can hope to find in these pages is one father's attempt to lead his sons into Christian manhood without blinders or pretenses. You will not find the ideal life or the ideal way to tell your children about growing up to be men or women. Those who wish will find flaws in my character, theology, judgment, knowledge, and methods. It isn't hard to do, I see several myself. I open my struggle into Christian manhood and male sexuality to encourage others in their growth.[5]

A marvelous journey follows, in which rules and laws are subordinated to relationship between the father and son. Any fear in the reader that "has to do with punishment," has by the end evaporated. Indeed, the reader feels confident that the boy has internalized a right and godly sense of his male sexuality in the very process of entering into the world of a father who knows the merciful character of his Father God. The father has not condescended to enter into the boy's world. Rather, he has by example invited the boy to enter into the Father God's world, that is, into the place of authentic manhood, where all men are humbled by His mercy, uplifted by His grace, and guided by His living Holy Spirit.

Only through such intimacy with the Father—even at His initiative in Jesus to take on our flesh and thus be utterly vulnerable to us—can we become like Him. Just as being physically close to the father lets his "brown ooze" rub off and bonds a boy to manhood, so being close to Jesus—and the covering of His blood?— bonds us to the Father God and our true purposes as men.

Hence, the New Covenant, which Jeremiah proclaimed, declares that the Law—read, "will of God"—is no longer something out there to grasp after desperately, but written on our hearts. Therefore, as Chambers put it, we can "live so much in the consciousness of God that we do not need to ask what His will is." This Covenant is sealed by the Father's heart of mercy: "I will forgive their sins, and I will no longer remember their wrongs." Thus, we are set free from any panicky desperation to know the Father's will, as Raines says, for fear of making "an awful mistake" and bearing "the terrible guilt" for it.

The man of the Law pleads, "God, please show me Your will so I can do it and not be punished!" The son of the Spirit, who knows he is loved by the Father, is free during times of uncertainty to pray, "I praise You, my Father God of mercy! Thank You for Your steadfast love, that You came and died for me even when I was still a sinner and didn't care about Your will. I offer my present situation to You and ask You to guide me with Your wisdom in my decision, trusting in Your word that promises, 'If any of you lacks wisdom, he should pray to God, who will give it to him; because God gives generously and graciously to all' (James 1:5).

"And when my imperfect human nature leads me astray from Your will, use that as an occasion to learn Your mercy and newer ways to get close to You. When I am in Your will, use me to serve others as You have served me so fully in Jesus."

The key to praying this way simply lies in knowing that the Father loves you. Unfortunately, most men agree that God loves "everyone," but really mean "everyone else but me."

While praying with Sean, a thirty-five-year-old engineer, I encouraged him to ask God to open his heart to know and feel the Father's love for him. In that process, Sean saw how as a boy he had sought love from his demanding father by striving to be perfect. Since we can never be perfect, he always fell short, and never felt loved by his father. Indeed, he began to realize that his father had demanded perfection, but needed him to fail, in order to divert attention away from the father's own inadequacies and inability to give approval. Finally, Sean saw that he had projected his brokenness onto others, criticizing and judging them as his striving failed to bring forth the love he sought from them. He had become just like his father.

Eventually, Sean had to bring his pride to the Cross, kneel and pray, "Lord, I need Your love. Forgive me for striving to get it from other people. I stand on faith that You do love me, and I ask You now to pour out Your love on me." Much pain was released through this simple prayer.

As he renounced his striving and its accompanying judgment of others, asking instead for God's love, Sean became less compulsive in seeking God's will. The more he trusted in God's love for him, the more he began to make decisions without fear. He's still learning to trust the Father's love; it's fearful for him, because his earthly father's love was always conditional.

Once you leave slavery to the Enemy and follow God's lead into the desert, you realize that either way is fearful—whether back to slavery or ahead through the desert.

Thus, you might as well renounce slavery and struggle toward the Promised Land, where your identity in the Father is secured and you become "a light to the nations" serving Him.

"One day I was unsure of the will of God in my life," writes Lloyd Ogilvie. "When I prayed, all that came to me were the words, 'The restless search for the will of God is a sure sign you are out of it!' You can imagine that this was not a very comforting answer to my prayer for an undeniable word from the Lord for the decisions I had to make. I mulled the words over for weeks. They led me to a confession that my walk with the Lord had become dull and perfunctory. Several areas of my life were not in good order. I had moved from trusting to strenuous effort to do God's work. My life was more self-effort than a flow of God's grace."[6]

Ogilvie was learning first-hand what Paul said long ago. "But God's mercy is so abundant," he said, "and his love for us is so great, that while we were spiritually dead in our disobedience he brought us to life with Christ. . . . For it is by God's grace that you have been saved through faith. It is not the result of your own efforts, but God's gift, so that no one can boast about it" (Eph. 2:4–5, 8–9).

Our self-striving, fear of punishment, and inability to believe in God's love invites desperation into our otherwise faithful desire to know and do God's will. If a man is truly to walk in the will of God, it will happen not by his keeping the Law, holding to the right doctrine, or accomplishing enough good deeds— but only as he confesses humbly and hopelessly before the Father that "he is controlled by his human nature; for he does not obey God's Law, and in fact *he cannot obey it*" (Rom. 8:7, italics added).

If we are literally unable to obey the Law—if we are incapable of doing God's will even when we know it as clearly as reading it on a page of the Bible—then a desperate seeking after His will can reflect pride and presumption.

The Law, as evangelist Dudley Hall has noted,[7] "did not come to produce righteousness, but to reveal wickedness" (see Rom. 3:19–20), that is, "not to make you holy, but to expose your sin." Without God's Law, we set our own standards, and quite naturally fancy that we meet them, and feel thereby righteous and saved. But God's Law is so beyond our capacity to fulfill, that it forces us to our knees in confession—into a posture to know the Father's character of mercy.

We grow up, as Hall notes, in a world which tells us "Who you are is what you do," and if you perform well, you are good; if you fail, you are bad. Yet God has come in Jesus to show us that "Who you are is what I've made you," namely, a loved, forgiven, empowered son of the Father. In bondage to the world's definitions, often enforced by the earthly father's model, we begin to believe wrongly that "God is keeping score."

The biblical faith, however, declares that "love does not keep a record of wrongs" (1 Cor. 13:5). Yet all too often, we men labor under an abiding fear of making a mistake—as if, indeed, we had never experienced the Father God's love and mercy.

Hall notes three major misconceptions basic to this "legalism":

1. You fear darkness more than you trust the light, being more oriented to punishment than mercy,
2. You focus on the faults of people, not the glory that is in them. That is, you miss their value and identity in Christ, because you do not know your own value and identity as a son of the Father, and
3. You presume upon the predictability of God's response, reducing faith and relationship with the Father to a forumla: "If I do A and B right, then God will bless me with C and D."

Clearly, Hall adds, a lethal effect of legalism is "withdrawal from the world," out of a fear that "I'll get overcome, defiled." Hence, a man isolates himself, fearing that to relate to others will contaminate him. The masculine presence, so desperately needed in our broken world today, is thereby lost.

How much better for a man to confess he's already hopelessly contaminated by his very human nature, to surrender to Jesus, and to seek the Father's mercy. In this way, a man can know the Father God's Spirit and, as a redeemed son in the fellowship of God's men, can move ahead and exercise His saving power in this needy world.

The Holy Spirit, as Hall concludes, "takes the legalism out of man" by drawing him into relationship with the Father according to Paul's declaration:

> Those who are led by God's Spirit are God's sons. For the Spirit that God has given you does not make you slaves and cause you to be afraid; instead, the Spirit makes you God's children, and by the Spirit's power we cry out to God, "Father! My Father!" God's Spirit joins himself to our spirits to declare that we are God's children. (Rom. 8:14–16)

For example, Hall takes the commonly quoted text, "If we confess our sins to God . . . he will forgive us our sins and purify us from all our wrongdoing" (1 John 1:9), and declares, "This is a wonderful promise. [But] don't let that be a formula for your life . . . so you run through your list of confessions and say, 'I must be forgiven, because the formula says so.' Let it be an invitation of a Heavenly Father for you to come in, sit in His lap, let Him talk to you and straighten things out."

A man can be that humble, honest, and vulnerable before the Father God only insofar as he knows the Father loves him and will not destroy him for his sin, but in fact, wants to save him from its effects.

Sadly, the average man today has learned legalism instead of mercy from his earthly father. "Do what I say and I will love you," he has essentially heard growing up; "disobey or make a mistake, and I will not love you." He has not seen his father model mercy either by forgiving the son's mistakes, or by asking the son to forgive him for his own mistakes. Thus the son grows up fearing failure, equating it with losing relationship with the father.

This is how the powers of the world deceive us. For it is precisely a man's inability to keep the Law—his certain "failure" and need for a Savior—which ensures relationship with the Father God through Jesus. If, indeed, we could keep the Law on our own, we would never need Jesus.

The New Covenant therefore frees us from the fear of making a mistake to the joy of serving a loving Father:

And if under the old system the blood of bulls and goats and the ashes of young cows could cleanse men's bodies from sin, just think how much more surely the blood of Christ will transform our lives and hearts. His sacrifice frees us from the worry of having to obey the old rules, and makes us want to serve the living God. (Heb. 9:13–14 TLB)

The animal sacrifices, as noted by Pastor Sam Thompson of Christian Life Fellowship in Orange, California, represent our dead works, the things we do "in order to be okay with the Father." But this striving only keeps us from trusting Him and humbly confessing, like the apostle Paul, there is "nothing in us that allows us to claim that we are capable of doing this work" (2 Cor. 3:5).

Since the longing to be one with the father is basic to the male child, the fear of losing the father's love can govern a boy's life—and obsess him as a man. In fact, a boy who has experienced only rules instead of love and mercy from his father, can only believe, albeit falsely, that rules define relationship with the father.

To fill the empty longing from his boyhood, as a man he will seek rigid rules, clearly defined structures, and legal systems as a surrogate "father"—to communicate clear and measurable approval, acceptance, and bonding insofar as he abides by their dictates. The father-longing is so painful, and ignorance of the Father God's merciful character so widespread, that most men today prefer the cold dictates of the Law to the terrifying insecurity with their earthly fathers. They would rather say, "At least, I know whether I'm right or wrong" than wonder, "Does Dad love me or not?"

Jesus came precisely because men, like the Pharisees, had begun to grasp after the Law as a replacement for the Father, who seemed distant. When the Temple fell twice in six hundred years, God made it clear that He was fully prepared to destroy the religion in order to preserve relationship with the Father. But the Father seems distant only when we do not trust His love and mercy, and humbly surrender our brokenness to Him.

Thus God proclaims, "Let my people return to me. Remove every obstacle from their path! Build the road and make it ready! I am the high and holy God, who lives forever. I live in a high and holy place, but I also live with people who are humble and repentant, so that I can restore their confidence and hope" (Isa. 57:14–15).

In the humble process of repentance, of offering ourselves to God, we allow God an avenue for His Holy Spirit to enter and take over our lives. We become merciful ourselves as we receive His mercy. That is, we draw close to the Father, and his character rubs off on us like "brown ooze."

The way to know God's will, therefore, is not by fearing His judgment and striving to be perfect, but rather, by proclaiming His mercy and humbly surrendering yourself to Him, in all your brokenness and sin—just as Paul instructs.

> So then, my brothers, because of God's great mercy to us I appeal to you: Offer yourselves as a living sacrifice to God, dedicated to his service and pleasing to him. This is the true worship that you should offer. Do not conform yourselves to the standards of this world, but let God transform you inwardly by a complete change of your mind. *Then you will be able to know the will of God*—what is good and is pleasing to him and is perfect. (Rom. 12:1–2, italics added)

In contrast to this word of God, our human nature makes us desperate to know the will of God insofar as we have not trusted the Father and offered ourselves wholly to Him. It makes us prefer, as Ogilvie notes, to strive after our own salvation by "knowing the Father's will and not making any mistakes."

When a man offers himself to God like Jesus, as a living sacrifice, he is in a position to let God's Spirit "join himself to our spirits to declare that we are God's children" (see Rom. 8:16). And "that same glory, coming from the Lord, who is the Spirit, transforms us into his likeness in an ever greater degree of glory" (2 Cor. 3:18).

In offering his wounds to the Father God—as he may never have dared with his earthly father—a man begins to know the Father's mercy and receives His love. Furthermore, in receiving the Father's love, the man becomes like the Father, for He is love (see 1 John 4:8). The more Father-love we take in, the more we have to give out. Thus Paul prayed for the believers, "Yes, may you come to know (Christ's) love . . . and so be completely filled with the very nature of God" (Eph. 3:19).

This biblical pattern for a maturing faith can be seen clearly by comparing a boy's relationship to his father with a man's relationship to God. Suppose your son comes to you asking, "What do you want me to do, Dad?" At first, you might be pleased that he recognizes your wisdom and authority. But if he persists in asking you this question constantly, at every turn, you would certainly worry that he was not growing properly.

Such a child can never grow up, because he can never develop any trust in his own sense of inner strength and direction. As a father, your goal is to instill your example and standards into the child—to write the law upon his heart—so the boy may become as you, a man himself, and not need always to turn and ask your will.

Otherwise, you must ask, "Why is my boy afraid to step out on his own? Is he afraid to make a mistake? Why? Could it be for fear I would punish him harshly for it?" You would be grieved to think you had been so harsh that your son was afraid to step out and live life on his own, for fear of your punishment. You would want to correct this fear by saying to the boy, "Take what I have given you and go out into the world, knowing that I love you and am here when you need me."

Our relationship with the Father God parallels this description, both individually and in biblical history. We begin our faith journey as infants, seeking the Father's will, and the Father provides rules for our guidance and protection. God gave Moses the Law as His first example of care for us, and we first establish relationship with Him through it. But even Moses, after receiving the Father's Law, wanted the deeper intimacy of seeing the Father's face (see Ex. 33:20).

As a boy grows, he begins to want not just external rules and laws, but relationship with the father. "Show us the Father," as Philip asked Jesus; "that is all we need" (John 14:8). For a teenager, on the threshold of manhood, this translates, "Dad, I do appreciate the ways you've taught me right from wrong. But now, I want to see you, the person: What was it like for you growing up? Did you get scared around girls? How do you like your job now? How do you and Mom get along?"

And so, when in our fear of punishment we had allowed the Law to replace relationship with the Father, God revealed Himself personally in Jesus—who answers Philip, "Whoever has seen me has seen the Father" (see John 14:9).

The earthly father's willingness to draw the boy into relationship is crucial to the boy's ability to pass into the company of men, and thus see himself as a valued member of adult society. Similarly, the Father God "is faithful, by whom you were called into the fellowship of His Son, Jesus Christ our Lord" (1 Cor. 1:9 NKJV).

God, that is, calls the infant believer into the Church, the Body and fellowship of Jesus, and there, in the sanctuary of fellow believers, he confesses his brokenness. As together in the Church we accept and experience and share the Father's merciful love, we begin to discover that His Law has been internalized in our hearts as the New Covenant, and we may walk faithfully with Him without nagging fears of making a mistake.

It's right to seek God's will.

But it's good, so good, to trust His love.

CHAPTER NINE

A Man of Principle
Or a Faithful Son?

This is the story of the birth of the Messiah. Mary his mother was be-
trothed to Joseph; before their marriage she found that she was with
child by the Holy Spirit. Being a man of principle, and at the same time
wanting to save her from exposure, Joseph desired to have the marriage
contract set aside quietly. (Matt. 1:18–19 NEB)

Recently I was given a series of teaching tapes aimed at men, and was
deeply moved as the speaker told in the first tape of being abused by a
father who constantly berated him. Eagerly anticipating the second
tape, I was dismayed to hear the speaker promise at once to share the
"biblical principles" he had learned, which now enable him to overcome
his childhood wounds. Men willing to uphold these principles themselves, he declared, could avoid similar pain in their own lives and in the
lives of their children.

As he proceeded to declare that a father's primary job is to "teach
biblical truth" to his children, I turned the tape off in frustration. For all
his efforts to avoid his father's harsh, judgmental spirit, the speaker had
fallen headlong into the same trap himself, albeit disguised as religion.

"You foolish Galatians!" I heard the apostle Paul shouting. "Who put a
spell on you? Before your very eyes you had a clear description of the
death of Jesus Christ on the cross! Tell me this one thing: did you receive
God's Spirit by doing what the Law requires or by hearing the gospel
and believing it? How can you be so foolish! You began by God's Spirit;
do you now want to finish by your own power? Did all your experience
mean nothing at all?" (Gal. 3:1–4).

Sadly—tragically—such teaching of "principles" has largely characterized men's ministry since the days of the Pharisees. "Men want struc-

ture, guidelines, plans," Christian leaders in our consumer-oriented society have declared—without ever asking if that desire in men is prompted not by the Father God's call, but indeed, by a lack of authentic relationship with the earthly father, and consequent fear of punishment.

In the absence of fathering, traditional Christian men's programming has borne a false gospel, namely, "Here's what the Bible says to do; now be a man and do it." It's false because if we could do it, we wouldn't need Jesus. The Bible is not a how-to rule book of game plans, but a love story. Jesus came not in response to a how? question, but rather, who? God's Good News is not a technique, but a Person. Jesus, that is, reminds men that their true Father is calling them to Himself with a love that "endures forever" (Ps. 118:2 NKJV). As another has said, "Religion is people reaching to God; Jesus is God reaching to people."

The Father God will not allow relationship with Him to be reduced to a set of principles.[1] Men who live by principles therefore cannot know God, for He is approached and known not by striving after righteousness, but only by confessing brokenness.

"You do not want sacrifices"—that is, efforts to win His favor—as the psalmist declared, "or I would offer them; you are not pleased with burnt offerings. My sacrifice is a humble spirit, O God; you will not reject a humble and repentant heart" (Ps. 51:16–17).

The most graphic biblical example of a man whose life of principles God upended in order to draw him into living relationship, was none other than Joseph, husband of Mary.[2] The Bible introduces Joseph as "a man of principle" (NEB), or, "a man who always did what was right." Undoubtedly, this means that he was a Law-abiding, Bible-reading, synagogue-going man. And we may certainly assume that, like all good, principled, mainstream Jews of his day, Joseph was a Pharisee. Beyond his moral principles, he was a carpenter, and a good carpenter knows that, if you cut the angle right and fit it to the rule, the cabinet comes out smooth and straight.

So this upstanding, principled man becomes engaged to a young woman named Mary. Certainly, getting married makes a man pull himself together and become even more responsible. Joseph knew the right way to do things, whether in angling off the edge of a wooden drawer just right, or in marrying the right woman.

But then, something catastrophic happens to this "righteous man" (NIV). Before Joseph has touched her, Mary finds that she is pregnant. We can imagine the bewildering scene that follows, as she tries to explain to her "man of principle" what happened:

"I know it sounds unbelieveable, and I know it doesn't fit 'the right way' of doing things, but all this was done by the Holy Spirit, Joseph. This is God's work. I can only ask you to trust me and . . . please . . . stand by me, Joseph. . . . Joseph?"

Poor Mary! What a fearful task, to tell her fiance something like this. But Matthew goes right ahead, in a tone so matter-of-fact that the words cut severely, ominously, through the emotional turmoil: "Being a man of principle . . ."

We hardly have to read further to know what's coming. Joseph presumably liked Mary; he may even have loved her. But the man of principle has begun to shake the stars of romance from his eyes. Certainly, Joseph was man enough to chalk it all up as a lesson—albeit a tough one—and he could be thankful to have discovered Mary's true character before it was too late.

And so, we can imagine Joseph's pulling himself together to do what a man must do, and saying with his deepest, most principled voice, "I'm sorry, Mary, but being a man who always does the right thing, of course I have to break things off between us. But I do want to save you from any disgrace (TEV), so let's just forget the whole thing quietly and go our separate ways. Okay, Mary?"

Funny thing. If Joseph really wanted to save Mary from exposure or disgrace, wouldn't he go ahead and marry her, even with his painful reservations? He certainly wouldn't bail out on her when she needs him most. Suddenly, something deceptive, even a hint of dishonesty, hovers about this moralistic fellow Joseph.

What is this "story of the birth of the Messiah" telling us?

Could God be saying here that He has been born in Jesus to upend all human pretense to righteousness—that when the chips are down, a man can't hide the fact that his rigid principles are not moral absolutes, but weapons to shield his own fearful weaknesses? Tongues wag when you marry a pregnant woman. Could Joseph himself be the real one he wants to save from exposure and disgrace?

And what if Joseph really did love Mary? Then the story says that the man of principle is a frightened, lonely, pathetic man indeed. For, as a principled man who knows his moral obligations, Joseph says to the woman he loves, "Forget you, Mary. I have to remain upright, so I certainly can't associate with you!" Even if Joseph is not denying God's work here, in rejecting Mary he is saying, "And forget this so-called Holy Spirit of yours, who does nothing but mess up my life!"

We can almost hear Joseph pleading, "I mean, I've got plans, Mary—do you know that? Do you know how hard I've worked in that woodshop to get where I'd be ready to take a wife and be seen as a righteous man among men? At long last, I'm my own man, and I know what I want out of life. I wouldn't have asked you to marry me if that weren't true. I know what kind of wife I want and what kind of relationship I want with her, and I know the right way to get just that: by sticking to my principles!"

Isn't this precisely the heroic model we offer young men even today? A man's "principles," we believe, are his power, if not his very instrument of virility. Another way of saying "Stick to your principles," is to say, "Stick to your guns."

A very genuine part of every man who reads this story wants terribly to say, "Yes, Joseph, I'm with you. It's a tough choice, but leave Mary behind. Forget the woman you love. If a man doesn't have his principles, he's no man at all!"

Listen to the story: It is not the prostitute or thief who scorns God's Word made flesh. It is not primarily the con-man or the alcoholic who denies and rejects the marvelous gift of God's Self. It is the "man of principle" who first dismisses the Lord's coming into this world.

Listen to the story: The man who "always does what is right" is the most dangerous threat to God's purposes in this world. When we try to follow abstract principles in order to uphold a self-image of righteousness, we are most likely to dismiss God's miracles, unable to recognize God's work among us, and most closed to our own feelings and the feelings of those we love. We are most ready to hurt, even destroy others—and reject what God has ordained for us in relationship with them.

Religious men of principle killed Jesus—because Jesus is the Truth that destroys our cherished fantasy of being in control, of working our way into God's favor, of saving ourselves.

Listen to the story: Right-ness is not righteousness. The man of principle says, "There is no living God, no acting love; there is only right and wrong." And certainly, in such a worldview, there is no mercy, much less grace.

In a video teaching on healing the wounds of divorce,[3] Baptist clergyman Clyde Besson, himself divorced and re-married, notes that "mercy" is God's forgetting your sin altogether, as if it had never happened (see Ps. 103:8–12). That—as any divorced man can attest—is hard enough to receive, and a man may respond, "Thank you, God. And don't worry, I sure won't trouble you for anything else!"

But the Father God says, "Wait, son—there's more: I want to bless you with a new life that's even better than you've ever known." That's "grace," His essential characteristic—inaccessible to the man who lives by the Law.

The man of principle is busy looking high into the clouds for abstract Laws and "shoulds," as a way of avoiding facing his own brokenness. And so he does not face the Father God in Jesus. He dares not recognize the wonder and pain and glory of Jesus' disgrace before the world upon the Cross.

The story says that if you're not ready to be exposed and disgraced by the world, you're not ready for the Father's Good News in Jesus—because you can't welcome God's mercy until you can recognize your own sin. That is, if you're not willing to risk losing your principles in order to gain relationship with the Father God, you're not ready to know Him.

For the angel of the Lord appears to Joseph in a dream and—appealing to his heritage in the bold and faithful King David—says, "Joseph, descendant of David, do not be afraid to take Mary to be your wife" (Matt. 1:20).

And lo, the man of principle becomes a man of faith! Rising from his sleep, Joseph does not do what is "right" according to his religious, Pharisaic principles, but what his living Father God tells him: "So when Joseph woke up, he married Mary, as the angel of the Lord had told him to" (Matt. 1:24).

Very likely, Joseph's heart did not burst at once with new love for Mary. He was probably just as scared to marry her as before his dream. But he could begin now to trust that his Father was with him, that in this refining fire God would burn away all face-saving fantasies of righteousness among men, so he could know a more true and lasting love for his wife.

This "story of the birth of the Messiah" is shocking. For the main character, the man chosen to act as Jesus' earthly father, abandons his principles. What kind of a man would do such an unmanly thing? Clearly, a man who no longer needs to cling desperately to his principles to define himself, because another way—indeed, another man—has been shown him. Joseph trades the worldly security of his abstract principles for relationship with the living Father God—whose uncontrollable mercy and grace alone can empower a man to carry out His purposes in this world.

Men today who dare listen to this story faithfully, must begin to say not, "Yes, Joseph," but "Yes, Father." This cry is most often heard from a man on his knees, saying, "Abba, Father! I don't want to be a man of principle any more. I've tried, but I can't be. It only cuts me off from myself, and from people I love. I just want to be yours.

"Forgive me for thinking I could make myself righteous. I offer myself to You as a living sacrifice. Break me, open my heart, join Your Spirit to mine and draw me close to You, so I can be close to others without being afraid of looking bad."

Every year, we look forward to Christmas, because it means "peace and goodwill." But even as health may require a surgeon's cut, so God's inner peace and good relations with others require a painful surrender. To remember the story, therefore, is to know that the Father came into this world and first shattered not the great sinner safely across the freeway from us, but the man who always did what was right. It was the man of principle—the fine, respectable, dependable person like you and me—whom the Lord's birth first upended and upset.

Sometimes, I wish it were not so. I wish all my principles and morals and high standards would exempt me from God's upsetting, painful birth. I wish I could say, "Lord, I'm okay and you're okay, so just go over there to them. They're the ones who need you. Don't come messing up my life, Lord, not just when I've finally got things going right." In fact, I wish the story were different because, sometimes, I love my principles more than I love God. I love to do what makes me acceptable to others more than confess I cannot make myself acceptable to God.

The pride inherent to such thinking backfires, and buries us in guilt. "If I do everything right, it'll come out right," we fancy. "If it doesn't come out right, that means I did something wrong, and am guilty." But we simply do not have such control over circumstances and other people in this broken world.

If only the story read that Joseph, when he discovered his fiancee was pregnant by someone else, religiously pasted a smile on his face, lifted his arms, and shouted, "Praise the Lord!" Then, I could toss out the whole business as a farce—totally out of reach for me, if not patently unrealistic. I could keep grasping my principles, avoid facing my brokenness, and sustain the fantasy of being in control of my salvation.

Or if only the story read that Jesus was born of Joseph's seed, the right way. Then, the man of principle—like me—could presume to follow this uncontrollable God while sticking securely behind his guns—er, principles.

I do not like this "story of the birth of the Messiah." But I am thankful for it. Because without it, the story of the death of the Messiah would mean nothing to me. For I am not moved by a god who dies for a principle. But I'm humbled unto death—and new life as a son—by the Father God who dies for me.

Jesus, that is, came to restore relationship with the Father. He therefore hates anything that destroys that relationship.[4]

If that sounds like strong language for those who prefer to think of Jesus as a nice-guy milquetoast, consider the volley of anger that he unleashed on the religious leaders of his day: "You snakes and sons of snakes!" . . . "Blind fools" . . . "Hypocrites!" . . . "Blind guides!" . . . "Murderers!" (see Matt. 23:17–34).

Significantly, one major, even dominant population is excluded from Jesus' scathing criticism—here as well as elsewhere in the Gospels.

Remember that as Jesus was lashing out at the Pharisees, the pagan Roman enemy occupied God's entire Promised Land and held His chosen people under its thumb. Yet nowhere does Jesus criticize the pagans. "Pay to the Emperor what belongs to the Emperor" (see Matt. 22:21), Jesus declares when asked if God's people should pay taxes to the pagan enemy. "I have never found anyone in Israel with faith like this" (Matt. 8:10), He remarks about the Roman policeman who asks him to heal a servant.

Even as their swords lay against His beloved people's necks, Jesus did not regard the pagan atheists as God's worst enemy, but rather, men who used their religion to mask their brokenness—and thus cut off themselves and others from relationship with the God of mercy and healing. Indeed, if you wanted to find immorality, from sexual license to idolatry, Rome was the place to look. Yet Jesus never turned His anger against the Romans, not even when they mocked Him and spat upon Him and nailed Him to the Cross!

The atheists do not give God a bad name, since no one would look at atheists to find out what God is like anyhow. The world looks to Christians to know God, the ones to whom God has ostensibly revealed Himself. I am therefore very suspicious of Christians who lash out against the "godless atheists" in our society. Certainly, atheists today may be enemies of God's church, just as the ancient Romans. For Jesus, however, Christian Enemy Number One is the religious man who claims to follow Jesus, but in reality, hides from Him and the Father God behind Law and "principles."

Stephen Arterburn has coined the term "toxic faith" to mean that which "allows the religion, not the relationship with God, to control a person's life. It is . . . a counterfeit of faith . . . manifested in those who try to work their way to heaven. They are on every church committee, they attend every group and are driven to work, work, work for the Lord. In reality they are working for themselves, compensating for emptiness and isolation that will only be filled when they stop working so hard and start developing a growing relationship with God."[5]

Religion is a crutch; Jesus is new legs.

Jesus did not come to bring religion, which could be found aplenty then as now. Rather, he came to bring the Father, who had become so caricatured as a vengeful perfectionist that men had built religious structures to avoid facing Him—only to end up living the caricature themselves.

In contrast, Arterburn portrays a healed, "pure faith":

> What a joy when we watch a person free themselves from the bondage of a man-made religion and find peace with a God of love, a God who is merciful beyond measure, a God who asks us to persevere rather than demand that we be perfect.

Religion comes from the Latin root *ligere,* meaning "to bind or connect," as a ligament connects tendon to muscle. Religion properly reconnects a man to the Living God—as a community of history that preserves the stories which remind men of God's character, and therefore, mark the path to encounter Him anew in their own lives. When disconnected from history, religion becomes false, a hierarchical organization which merely preserves a catalog of moral behavior.

Men avoid and often ridicule church because they want true and not false religion. Men want relationship with the Father, not a list of dos and don'ts among pompous leaders and mindless underlings. Nor do we want thoughtful, tolerant-with-everything people busy shielding themselves from each other and the Father with high-sounding ideas.

Men suspect, often rightly, something dishonest about religion—even as we see the scrupulous, nit-picking perfectionist as unmanly—and are often more delighted than surprised when such "religious leaders" are caught in immoral behavior. The fact that many men who come to church do buy the life of principles which broken church leaders preach, only indicates the terrible depth of the father-wound in men today and the desperation for any kind of approval from a father-figure or father-system.

The Church, meanwhile, invests its energy in avoiding the Father by splitting along political lines. The conservatives say we're saved by right belief; the liberals, by right action. But in his heart and soul, every man knows that he doesn't measure up to what he wants to be—that neither his beliefs nor his actions are ever perfect—and he longs for a father to save him from his brokenness.

Men do not honor "righteousness" in another man, and often mock it, because we somehow know that's impossible in any man, and whoever claims it is a fraud. Instead, we honor integrity—which requires an honest assessment of your own brokenness.

Some years ago when I visited Israel, our tour guide told the story of a Jewish sage who sought an honest man. Going out into the street, he stopped three men and asked each the question, "If you found a wallet with a large amount of money in it and the owner's name and address, what would you do?"

"I'd keep the money," said the first.

"You're a greedy man," the sage said.

"I'd send the money back to the owner immediately," said the second.

"You're a foolish man," said the sage.

The third man hesitated, knit his brow, paced about, and sighed deeply. "I don't know what I'd do," he said finally, "but I hope by the grace of God I'd be able to give the money back."

"You're an honest man," the sage declared at last.

The "man of principle" like Joseph, who "always did what was right," is by definition not a real man. To be real is, like the apostle Paul in Romans 7:14–25, to confess your inability to do what is right and cry out for mercy. That is how a man learns to trust the Father God's mercy and overcome the spirit of religion through relationship—that is, through God's Spirit of sonship.

Being a real man is the difference between knowing "the right way" and knowing the Father. Thus religion-by-rules, whether liberal "political correctness" or conservative "biblical principles," undermines manhood. It allows that, if I do not feel or think "the right way," clearly I am no good, and condemned. Meanwhile, we simply are not able to keep God's Law—if we could, we wouldn't need Jesus.

Too often we men are trying to be good—without ever having dared to confess, like the apostle Paul in Romans 7, that we can't be good. A man cannot know the Father God until he confesses his need for mercy—for only then will he receive mercy, and thereby, know the character of the Father.

Ironically, we embrace religious rules to avoid judgment, to be "good." But in doing so, we only ensure condemnation, as we cannot but fail at some point to measure up. "I can't be real with the father," men today have learned as boys; "if I told him how I really feel, what I really want, he'd condemn me."

Preaching "biblical principles" to men today is like pouring water on a drowning man. Paul's lifestyle of surrender to the Father God, on the other hand, reveals that "there is no condemnation now for those who live in union with Christ Jesus" (Rom. 8:1).

Righteousness is not doing it the right way, knowing the right answer, or supporting the right side in an issue. Rather, rightness with God is a merciful gift to any and all who would surrender their true selves to the Father—trusting that He will meet us where we are in our brokenness and take us where we need to go as we walk in His mercy:

> No one can ever be made right in God's sight by doing what the law commands. For the more we know of God's laws, the clearer it becomes that we aren't obeying them; his laws serve only to make us see that we are sinners.
>
> But now God has shown us a different way to heaven—not by "being good enough" and trying to keep his laws, but by a new way. . . . Now God says he will accept and acquit us—declare us "not guilty"—if we trust Jesus Christ to take away our sins. (Rom. 3:20–22 TLB)

To establish and maintain relationship with the Father, our part is to confess we cannot do in our own power what God requires, and trust His mercy. Recognizing our brokenness, we have to get up on the operating table. His part is then to enter our hearts through this humble opening of brokenness we offer Him, and to transform us, as promised in Romans 12:1–2.

Unlike other compulsions, grasping after righteousness-by-rules and its accompanying condemnation is not overcome by simply renouncing and condemning the compulsion. Satan cannot cast out Satan. A man must focus not on how vicious the compulsion is, but rather, on how merciful the Father is—that is, on knowing and proclaiming himself as a son of the Father.

Certainly, the Accuser will continue to condemn with thoughts — perhaps heard first from the father when a boy—like, "You blew it! You don't deserve to be blessed—you should be cursed forever! Who do you think you are, getting married to such a good woman, taking a job with authority, being a father?" To which the man of God can reply, "You're right about what I deserve, but I'm a son of the Father God—and therefore, I intend to receive the blessings Jesus died to give me."

As Jesus said, it is more blessed to give than to receive. But it is blessed to receive, because only when we receive from the Father God, do we have anything of Him to give. The man who lives by principles can only receive what he has earned—and thus, lives boxed in himself and cannot know the Father God's character.

Early in the spring of 1984, I visited a Christian retreat center in Norway.[6] A woman I met there asked me to pray for her. She, her husband, and I went to their tiny three-room apartment above the meeting hall and prayed for perhaps an hour. To our delight, she received a major healing and was set free from lifelong fears.

As I was about to leave, the woman took from their wall an exquisite hand-painted wooden plate—an ancient Norse art form—which lent beauty to their otherwise Spartan setting. "We want you to have this," she said, handing the plate to me. "It is very special to us."

Surprised, I balked. "Oh, I really don't deserve it," I stammered in disbelief. "It was God who healed you, not me."

A trace of hurt crossed her face, then disappeared behind a gentle determination. "We know," she said simply, "but we want you to have it."

I opened my mouth to protest further, but nothing came out. Awkwardly, I took the plate. "Thank you very, very much," I sighed. "I will always treasure this as a reminder of our friendship and what God has done among us tonight."

Such feelings of unworthiness are a major stumbling block among us men to knowing the Father God's character and receiving from Him what we must have in order to become true men, namely, freedom from shame and fear of punishment.

The world's remedy for unworthiness is to overcompensate in the other direction, to re-program us by telling us over and over again, "You are worthy." Unquestionably, in a do-it-yourself, cash-and-carry world, this secular gospel sells widely. Yet the Pharisees worked hard to keep the Law and believed that they were therefore worthy of God's blessings. Consequently, they believed that those who did not work as hard as they, that is, the less righteous prostitutes, tax collectors, and other sinners, were not worthy.

To live by the Law invites self-righteousness, elitism, and rejection of others. Jesus, therefore, declared that "People who are well do not need a doctor, but only those who are sick . . . I have not come to call respectable people, but outcasts" (Matt. 9:12–13). Only the man who realizes his own human efforts to win God's favor are utterly worthless becomes born again as an eternally worthwhile son of the Father God.

Any belief in human worthiness is patently arrogant, for the man who dares to see himself by the light of God's truth sees a broken, sinful creature. A man who prays, "Lord, give me what I deserve," had better keep his distance from me, because I don't want to be near the lightning bolt!

The gospel is not about the goodness of human beings, but the goodness of the Father God. One man, for example, lamented to our prayer group the "poor treatment" he was receiving from his wife. Another responded, "I get the feeling you don't really think you deserve to be treated any better—and maybe that's why you aren't!"

"It's true," the man said. "I do want more respect from my wife, but deep down I really don't believe that I deserve it. And when I demand she act differently, she just gets angry."

Silence fell over the group. Then another man spoke up.

"I'm uncomfortable with this whole discussion," he began. "In any marriage, each partner bears part of the responsibility for problems. You probably don't deserve to be treated any better, because you've hurt your wife as much as she's hurt you. But I know that God called the two of you together into this marriage, and He wants the two of you to treat each other well. It's not that you deserve it, but that God wants you to have it.

"My suggestion is that you go to the Cross, ask Jesus to show you ways you haven't been the loving husband He's called you to be, and ask Him and your wife to forgive you. Then ask Him to show you events from your past that might be making it hard for you to accept the blessings in your marriage that He wants to give you. We'll help you with that."

At once, the group sensed the "rightness" of this word, and later reports from the husband confirmed that his wife responded to his openness by sharing her own needs and seeking help for her own brokenness.

As the Original Sin, pride is the root of the world's response to our sense of unworthiness. When we proclaim how much we deserve, we demonstrate pride. But even when we balk at blessings because we don't feel worthy, we are proceeding on the assumption that everything depends on our worthiness—that is, on my efforts and achievements. That, too, is pride.

Our pride can be seen readily when we ask the question "Why me?" when bad things happen to us. An equally appropriate time to ask "Why me?" is when good things happen. That is, "Given my long and continuing record of pride and self-centeredness, why would God want to bless me with anything?" Anyone who dares to be so humble will begin to see that God does not bless us because we are good, but because He is good.

Defying all logical principles, Jesus proclaimed that the laborers who came at the eleventh hour received the same pay as those who worked all day (see Matt. 20:1–16). The blessings of this life belong to and therefore come from God, at His determination and not our own. This parable points to the terrible price we pay in relating to God according to the one-for-one principle, "I get what I deserve for my efforts": It robs us of the joy that comes from receiving the unexpected, the undeserved, and keeps us from knowing the merciful, gracious Father God.

The Father God wants us to receive His blessings, because if we refuse Him, we remain in the fantasy of our own principled self-sufficiency. Only when we humbly confess and receive his amazing generosity are we freed from our selfishness to give graciously and generously to others (see 2 Cor. 1:3–5).

Our unworthiness must not keep us from accepting the Father God's good gifts. The Cross itself says that we are free to reject God's most precious gift, Jesus. But when we refuse this, we are saying that Jesus died in vain. How would you feel if you saw your son's excitement around race cars, worked late in your garage to build him a soapbox racer, and when you presented it to him, he said, "No, take it away—I misbehave at times, so I don't deserve it"?

Satan—literally, "The Accuser" in Hebrew—says, "You don't deserve these good things in your life; therefore, you must give them back!"

The man who has surrendered a life of principles for relationship with the Father God can reply, "You're absolutely right that I'm not worthy. But my Father loves me, and has come in Jesus to take the punishment I deserve and bless me as His son. I will walk in every blessing Jesus died to give me, to make me His man and do His work in this world. And because of His great mercy to me, I will forever praise and serve the living God of mercy, my Father God and Savior!"

King David himself humbly received God's blessing in order to further His purposes. When God promised that David's dynasty would last forever, the biblical storyteller reveals that David expressed his unworthiness, then praised God as he received His blessing.

> King David went into the Tent of the Lord's presence, sat down and prayed, "Sovereign Lord, I am not worthy of what you have already done for me, nor is my family. Yet now you are doing even more, Sovereign Lord; you have made promises about my descendants in the years to come. And you let a man see this, Sovereign Lord! What more can I say to you! You know me, your servant. It was your will and purpose to do this; you have done all these things in order to instruct me. How great you are, Sovereign Lord! There is none like you; we have always known that you alone are God." (2 Sam. 7:18–22)

We are not saved by principles, but by the living Father God of love, who in Jesus has broken the bondage of shame, punishment and fear. "Freedom is what we have," the Apostle therefore proclaims:

> Christ has set us free! Stand, then, as free people, and do not allow yourselves to become slaves again. . . . Those of you who try to be put right with God by obeying the Law have cut yourselves off from Christ. You

are outside God's grace. As for us, our hope is that God will put us right with him; and this is what we wait for by the power of God's Spirit working through our faith. For when we are in union with Christ Jesus, neither circumcision nor the lack of it makes any difference at all; what matters is faith that works through love. (Gal. 5:1, 4–6)

The problem in us men today—whether on the job, in fathering, or in sexual relationships with the woman—is not that we lack proper boundaries, but that we lack proper freedom. In Jesus, the Father God has freed us from the bondage of our natural, sinful condition, which keeps us from being able to do His will.

Clearly, this freedom is not "an excuse for letting your physical desires control you" (Gal. 5:13), but rather an assurance that we may walk in this broken world without fear that we will be condemned for our human shortcomings and mistakes. As we surrender to Him in the midst of fear or temptation—as we talk with and listen to our Father—He will uphold us in His will. At last, we can do the right thing, where before, doing the wrong thing was our only option (see Rom. 7:21).

The man who knows his Father God loves him as he is, in all his brokenness, is freed from the shame that compels him to seek perfection through the Law—an impossible task that can only burn him out and exhaust his capacity to fight when the Father calls him to. At its best, the Law protects us by noting boundaries beyond which we get hurt. "Thou shalt have no other gods before me" is as true as the Law of Gravity—which says, in effect, "Don't step off a rooftop or you'll fall and hurt yourself." Other, false gods besides the Father revealed in Jesus, ultimately can only lead men to destruction.

Sadly, however, the average man today does not love himself as much as the Father God does, because he hasn't learned to. He has not been fathered with His mercy and grace. When a man breaks God's Law in rebellion, he only reveals his lack of self-love, because doing so ultimately hurts him.

What then, makes a man do the right thing? Knowing he's loved and accepted, and therefore, that the right thing is best for him. When a man knows his Father God loves him, he loves and values himself. He doesn't want to hurt or destroy himself. He will therefore stay within the protective boundaries of the Father's Law.

Consider, for example, a man struggling to leave the homosexual lifestyle who, after seeking God's healing for some time, asks if it's "right" for him to go to an upcoming "Gay Pride" parade. The Law, or "biblical principle" might say "definitely not." So the man stays away, fearful that if he went, he'd backslide into sin. Thereafter, his fear deepens and he begins to stay away from public restrooms, even male friendships. Where does the bondage of that fear ever end? In suicide?

A "religious solution" to homosexuality—that is, "Don't do it, because it's against God's Law"—allows the man to believe that sexual relationships with other men are the answer to his apparent problem of uncontrollable desire, but a remote and arbitrary God simply won't let him have it. Relationship with the loving Father, on the other hand, reveals that homosexual relationships are the effects of his authentic problem—namely, the father-wound—which keeps him from healing and the fullness of life that God wants him to have.

Consider such a man when he has then faced his wounds, taken them to Jesus, and tasted thereby the freedom in Christ which Paul proclaims, knowing that he's a beloved son of the Father God. While perhaps inappropriate for a man still in the early stages of healing, he may eventually need to go to the parade, see there how sadly deceived and confused its participants are, and say at last, "I don't want this anymore. My Father God loves me and He wants so much more than this for me."

Consider also the man who compulsively seeks sex from women. He may well know that such behavior is "wrong" or "immoral." But he remains in bondage to his physical desires. "Moral principles" alone can only lead a man to bite the bullet and live in fear of falling. But relationship with the Father God allows him to seek healing for the source of his unrighteousness.

Part of that healing for men in bondage to lust is to ask God to show him the woman as He sees her, not as an object of his own lust. One man I encouraged to do this reported that he saw the woman as a wounded, frightened little girl, longing for a man's approval. His lust disappeared as he allowed himself to feel compassion for her. Later, because he had allowed lust to define his sexuality, he began to doubt his manhood when he did not get so sexually aroused as before, in his compulsion. He had to ask the Father God to teach him to love the woman as a person, even as the Father's daughter, and trust that such godly love would manifest physically in the Father's time and way.

Too often, ministries aimed at overcoming compulsive behaviors focus primarily on establishing and maintaining behavior boundaries—a fixation on the Law which by any New Testament standard virtually assures escalating fear and thus, failure. Christianity does not proclaim a moral system, but rather, a loving Father who comes with saving power to His broken children.

Christians who preach "morality" the hardest are therefore often those who fall to immorality—clearly not because they have no standards or principles, but because they don't know the freedom they have in Jesus. They do not trust relationship with the Father enough to know His love, and thereby cannot love themselves enough to seek healing by laying their temptations out in the light before Him among other covenanted brothers. The Enemy loves darkness; hiding evil thoughts down in your mental basement is like throwing Br'er Rabbit into the briar patch. The more of yourself you surrender to Jesus, the less you have left to surrender to any substance or compulsive behavior.

A major root of compulsive-addictive behaviors is self-hatred, for failing to live up to some standard. Exhorting a man to "live by principles," no matter how biblical, only adds kerosene to the condemning emotional fire within that already threatens to consume him.

Jesus' goal of healing for men, therefore, goes beyond merely stopping wrong behavior. It extends to walking in the freedom of knowing I am loved by my Father God no matter what my behavior. For only in that freedom can I love myself enough to recognize what is bad for me, surrender myself to Jesus, and allow Him to save me from it.

God is not, as religion-by-principle allows and the flesh protests, a cosmic killjoy who denies His children pleasure as if it were intrinsically sinful. He is a loving Father, who knows what is ultimately best for His children. He wants relationship with us, not mere legal compliance. That is, He wants to convince us in our hearts who He is, and let that conviction draw us into righteous living.

The Holy Spirit of the living Father God—who conceived Jesus in Mary and directed a confused and frightened Joseph to marry her —is well able to birth the Father's love in a man and guide him through this broken world. For so the apostle Paul proclaims at last, "What I say is this: let the Spirit direct your lives, and you will not satisfy the desires of the human nature" (Gal. 5:16).

May we be so surrendered to the Father that we may walk in His freedom and take pleasure in His goodness.

CHAPTER TEN

God and Flight 191:
A Big Enough Father

Many men and women today are living, often with inner dissatisfaction, without any faith in God at all. This is not because they are particularly wicked or selfish or, as the old-fashioned would say, "godless," but because they have not found with their adult minds a God big enough to command their highest admiration and respect, and consequently, their willing cooperation.[1]

We have noted earlier that a child naturally projects his or her view of the father's character onto God. An unfathered generation, therefore, would hold an unrealistic view of earthly fathers and, consequently, of the Father God.[2] Even as the child of a weak father might draw crayon pictures of the family showing the father smaller than others, we might predict that such a child would view the Father God as small, and incapable of ushering His children out from the home into the larger world.

The child whose father was absent might grow up attempting to fill the awful gap with a fantasized, bigger-than-life Savior Daddy, far beyond any real man's capacity for fathering. Such a child might view the Father God magically, as a supernatural Santa Claus.

Some years ago I taught at a private boys' high school, and one of my students, whose father had died years earlier, told me how badly he wished his father had lived. "We'd have gone fishing and camping together, like the other guys," he declared wistfully, "and when I had problems with schoolwork or girls, he'd have helped me out."

Accepting his assessment at face value, I was surprised when his mother told me at parent conference night that his father had been especially neglectful of the family and had threatened often to leave. When I hinted at her son's quite different view, she sighed in dismay. "We wouldn't have had any more togetherness in the family if he'd lived than we have now. In fact, we're probably closer as a family without him because there's no more fighting around the house."

An unfathered generation grows up without a realistic view of the father's character—and therefore, characterizes the Father God in extremes: either despairing that "God does nothing and we have to do it all," or magically dreaming that "God does everything and all we have to do is sit and have faith." The notion of everyday relationship and interaction with the Father God—encompassing the entire range of emotions and problems in this broken world—becomes as remote as the earthly father himself.

I first recognized such magical "faith" some years ago when a DC-10 passenger jet crashed on takeoff in Chicago, killing 273 people. Soon thereafter, I visited a travel agent to buy my vacation flight tickets. Certainly, I reasoned, people die in car accidents every day; does that stop me from driving?

Then the travel agent mentioned casually that two direct flights to my destination left at about the same time. Would it make any difference, she asked, if I took the 10:00 or the 10:15 flight?

For a strange second I stared at her, pencil poised above her itinerary sheet. "No!" I blurted out much too quickly, as a question from the depths broke its rein and bolted into my consciousness. What if, indeed, it made the difference between life and death? As the agent matter-of-factly put me down for the 10:00 flight, I wavered . . . and wondered.

The next week, as I buckled myself in on that flight, the pilot came right to the point over the intercom: "Of course our first concern is for your safety," he announced, "and we want you to know that your aircraft is a Lockheed 1011."

I don't know what he said after that, because my mind had taken off on its own. *Well, so what? I told myself. Who's worried about safety, anyhow? I mean, I've never been in a plane crash before, and I certainly don't plan on being in one now.* Turning to the window, I watched as several guys tossed suitcases into the cargo bay. *Besides, I'm young and capable and reasonably faithful to God; surely, He wants me around for a good while yet.*

Quickly, I reached for a magazine in the seat-pouch in front of me— and then it struck me: None who buckled themselves into that ill-fated flight a week before had planned on being in a plane crash either. What's more, many of the 273 were likely young and capable and reasonably faithful, too.

Just . . . like . . . me.

Hesitantly, I looked around me at grey-haired ladies smiling, mothers and fathers holding children, businessmen loosening their ties, lovers holding hands, flight personnel reaching to check overhead compartments. *Surely, flight 191 could not have been like this before takeoff. Surely, flight 191 could not have been!*

Not . . . like my flight.

Surely, dear God!

Trembling, I glanced out the window. As the lights of Los Angeles disappeared below the roar of our engines, I heard myself whispering a new prayer: *Please, God, hold this airplane up, and keep us safe!*

In that moment, I saw that faith is not simply assuming that everything will always go just fine for you. Rather, faith is knowing that pain and suffering, however inexplicably, is part of life in this real world, even for productive, reasonably faithful Christians. The bottom line of our faith—as revealed in the life, death, and resurrection of Jesus—is the Father God who stands with us as we suffer in this world, and draws us to Himself fully in the next world.

For men abandoned by their fathers, this is good news indeed. It's the kind of good news God uses to reassure Joshua as he is about to enter the Promised Land. Significantly, Joshua has depended upon Moses, Israel's great spiritual father-figure, to lead him and the others across the desert wilderness. But now, Moses is gone. Joshua must lead the people himself.[3] And in the dark night of fearful aloneness and inadequacy, Joshua hears from his true Father:

> Remember that I have commanded you to be determined and confident! Do not be afraid or discouraged, for I, the Lord your God, am with you wherever you go. (Josh. 1:9)

God did not promise Joshua no casualties in the battles ahead —for many of his men died—but only the ultimate victory of securing the Promised Land as he and the people of God pressed on faithfully. God therefore commands confidence and courage in His sons—not as a distant, arrogant father threatens to come back and evaluate performance, but as a loving father promises to struggle alongside His sons to bring His Kingdom to this broken world.

Jesus has won the war, but many battles remain for us to fight—even as by 1944 an Allied victory was clear, but armistice did not come until 1945, after the fierce Battle of the Bulge.[4]

I therefore began to see that our Christian faith derives from a God who is decidedly larger than life itself—larger even than my life! Indeed,

He is present not only in the bright and blissful Garden of Eden, but in the dark and ominous garden of Gethsemane as well.

And yet, as J. B. Phillips has noted, too often our God is too small. A *Los Angeles Times* reporter interviewed travelers flying on American Airlines flight 191 the day after the crash and found several who had been booked the day before, but changed their plans and thus, unknowingly averted the fatal flight. Among these, only one mentioned God. Instead of inspiring me, however, this person's statement of faith left me dismayed and angry. "I could've left Friday," she said, "which I normally would have done. Then I thought I'd take my time; there'd be less traffic. It made me pretty grateful for the decision I made. It assures me of the presence of God."

Clearly, this person's "God" is too small to encompass and embrace the many who died, for everyone on that filled flight buckled into a seat that she did not take and essentially died in her place. Were they and their relatives "assured of the presence of God" by what happened?

If this person's statement had followed an isolated incident of deliverance when by herself, such as avoiding losing control of her car on an empty road, I confess I would have too easily accepted it as faithful. But its startling self-centeredness reminded me that a god who does not take into account the sufferings of others is not the God revealed in Jesus.

Even an isolated incident of deliverance, if accomplished by that God, is linked to the pain and suffering of others. Consider the commonly accepted but equally self-centered statement, "I used to complain, until I saw someone much worse off than I. Then I just became thankful for what I have."

Another person's suffering does not move a follower of Jesus to feel comfortably thankful, but rather, to "complain" and act to relieve the other's suffering. "O that one might plead for a man with God" (Job 16:21 KJV), Job cries out in anticipation of the Messiah.

A Christian saved from any calamity, as from the power of sin and death by Jesus, must be moved to rededicate his or her life to serve God anew—that is, to serve others in need.

To take a small, personalized god into the big, broken world of human pain and suffering, is to unmask the common myopia: "As long as all goes well with me, I am assured of God's presence." This theology dangerously allows that when all goes ill—as it it does at times for all of us in real life—you are not assured of God's presence, and your faith may very well crumble. Worse, it reflects a near-sighted vision of the Father

God as simply a projection of what seems good for you. That makes Him no more a real God for a real world than your earthly father.

Most pagan religions include a "personal god" to promote the welfare of the particular individual to whom it belongs. The ancient Romans, for example, each had his or her own "lar," or "household god." No pagan, however, would confuse his or her own personal god with the one greatest god who ruled over all the others. Jupiter was not a lar.

The major thrust of Judaism and Christianity was to replace the many personal gods with the one God of the universe, who personally creates, cares for, enlists, gifts, and holds accountable each individual to participate in His cosmic purposes. Such an understanding of God requires the proper bonding between father and child promised in Malachi 4:5–6. For the man who has not been properly fathered will remain within the narrow confines of his own "household," and will grasp after a very parochial deity no bigger than what he sees and wants for himself—even as my former student viewed his deceased father entirely selfishly.

For such a person, Jesus too easily becomes "my lar" who saves me while 273 others die in the plane crash, puts food on my table when half the world is starving, keeps me safe in the suburbs while cities tremble, and fills my car gas tank when others freeze in winter. The irony of such a faith is that this small god cannot go with you when you need it most, namely, when you inevitably encounter life's pain and suffering, if only in death itself.

In contrast to this kind of faith was the statement of another person who was booked on flight 191 as a standby. As his name was called for the last stand-by seat, a woman lower on the stand-by list rushed to the counter and begged to get on the flight. Charitably, he turned over his seat to her.

"My reaction," he said after hearing about the crash, "was that I was thankful I did not get on the plane. I was sitting there trying to rack my brain about why I didn't."

As a Christian, I feel more comfortable with this person than with the one who mentioned God. Both were naturally thankful. The former, however, has made God in her own image, rather than allowing God to shape her in His image. Her own good fortune has assured her of God's presence, and she goes on her way unquestioned and unchanged by a god too small to see the 273 others who died and their loved ones.

Unlike the Father God of Jesus, this god is not one "acquainted with grief" (Isa. 53:3 KJV). This god cannot lead you into a broken world of suffering with power to make a difference. This god and his worshipers, like so many churchgoers, might join the fun at Easter, but cannot be there on Good Friday—and thus, cannot lead us to the Father who suffers with His people.

The man who racked his brain asking why he was delivered, however, is uncertain, seeking. He has been thrust into a mystery so overwhelming, so fraught with the power of life and death itself, that it disturbs his routine assumptions. Struck down by his own limited understanding, he is not assured. He is humbled and broken open.

This is the stuff that Christian faith is made of, the beginnings of relationship with the Father—graphically so in this case, because this man has literally experienced someone else's dying in his place, as Jesus did for him. He is approaching the more valid question of our faith: not, Why do I suffer? but, Why don't I suffer more?

The former is easy to answer: I suffer because I'm hopelessly bound up in the sinful condition of this as-yet-unredeemed world. The harder question is, Why should I, a sinner, be delivered in any degree from pain and death?

To ask this question, a man must have become convinced of his hopelessly sinful nature before the Father God. But the hardest man to convince of his sinful nature is one who was treated unfairly by his earthly father, and thus sees himself as innocent before the Father. Hence, most men today do not ask—like the man who missed the fatal flight—why they are saved, but like boys can only see themselves as victims, and thus, justified in their rebellion.

The opposite of victim is victor—the one in whom the effects of sin have been overcome. Such a man has, like Jesus (see Phil. 2:8–9), humbly gone to the Cross on his own initiative and there surrendered himself wholly to the Father God—regardless of how badly his earthly father hurt him.

No man can avoid the father-wound, because no earthly father is perfect. Those who deny it may seek to be good sons-in-the-flesh, but they cannot become men of God. On the Cross, Jesus demonstrated that the father-wound is not to be avoided—though He naturally balked at first—but must be yielded to, perhaps even embraced, as the doorway to new life.

Jesus' Father wounded Him unto death. And in that willful encounter with death ordained by the Father, Jesus emerged with eternal life, in unbroken relationship with the Father.

The Father God, that is, allows His son to be wounded, even calls him to die—not because He is powerless to save the son from pain, but intentionally, to draw the son to Himself. This is the only way ultimately to overcome the rebellious, self-preserving power of "the flesh" (Rom. 7:18

RSV) or "human nature." A son of the flesh—one still seeking saving power from his earthly father—remains subject to the powers of death in his flesh until he faces death head-on and therein surrenders to the Father God. Thus the writer of Hebrews declares,

> Since the children, as [Jesus] calls them, are people of flesh and blood, Jesus himself became like them and shared their human nature. He did this so that through his death he might destroy the Devil, who has the power over death, and in this way, set free those who were slaves all their lives because of their fear of death. (Heb. 2:14–15)

Richard Rohr hints at the powerful mystery here when teaching about Jesus and his Father God, saying, "Someday I must put together a teaching titled, 'The Father Who Wounds His Son.'"[5]

The question of "why bad things happen to good people," in spite of its being the title of Rabbi Harold Kushner's bestselling book, is invalid from the biblical perspective, because there simply are no good people. Goodness is a character quality of God, not of human beings. Jesus himself, when addressed as "Good Teacher," declared, "Why do you call me good? No one is good except God alone" (see Mark 10:18). Similarly, Paul declares that "there is no difference at all: everyone has sinned and is far away from God's saving presence" (Rom. 3:22b–23).

The mystery, in fact, is "why good things happen to bad people (like us)"—and the answer can only be simply because God is that good. As the Apostle continues, "But by the free gift of God's grace all are put right with him through Christ Jesus, who sets them free" (Rom. 3:24).

Certainly, the very occurrence of such a calamity as a plane crash reminds us that we live in a world broken by the powers of sin and death, where mistakes are made and human lives lost. The question of the flesh is therefore clear and present: How can I avoid such mistakes and not suffer the effects of sin and death?

The biblical faith answers straightforwardly: You can't. At least not entirely, not in this present world until Jesus returns in glory to transform it. You can only trust that whatever your pain and suffering, the Father God will be there with you in it, struggling alongside you. God struggles not to cause a miracle, as if He were otherwise too weak to change things, but to cause you to surrender both yourself and your circumstances to Him so He might be glorified.

The proud question, Why do I suffer? must therefore yield to the ultimate, authentic question—vastly more fearful for an unfathered people: Where—indeed, to whom—do I go with my suffering?

When Job then racks his brain as to why he has been afflicted, he can only end up prostrating himself before the vast and incomprehensible God of the universe—yielding his compulsion to understand the mystery to his deeper need to trust the Father God.

What, indeed, can explain these mysteries of life for the man who missed the fatal plane crash? Certainly not "You were saved as a reward for unselfishly giving your stand-by seat to the woman in need." The woman he "helped," died—even through his kindness.

Nor "This assures me of God's presence." The newspaper article noted that this man was among seventeen Pacific Telephone Company employees on a three-week training course in Chicago, and that seven of them died in the crash. Imagine the outrage if this man had gone to work the next day at the telephone company with its seven empty desks and said, "This has assured me of God's presence."

Any other person in that office "without any faith in God at all" but "living with inner dissatisfaction," as J. B. Phillips posits, could only scoff at such feeble rationalizations: "If that is your Christian God, He is too small for me and my real world."

Precious little commentary from Christian spokespersons followed the DC-10 calamity. Like Job's friends, both liberals and conservatives were confounded. The liberals, like Eliphaz, believe that man brings trouble on himself (see Job 4:7). The conservatives, like Zophar, insist that trouble can be avoided by turning back to God (see Job 11:13). But neither liberal "co-creating with God" nor conservative "getting right with God" clarifies God's ways here. Something bigger than our customary doctrinal disputes is going on.

Are we Christians secretly more embarrassed and defensive than saddened and humbled by tragedy? We easily proclaim our God of love to the world—and then a plane with 273 souls aboard falls out of the heavens. How do we defend God to a world which is already skeptical, disillusioned, and even hostile toward religion?

We don't.

Only a man who has been wounded and confused by the absence of his earthly father feels compelled to defend the Father God.

The Father God is not so weak that He needs us to defend Him. He calls men today not to apologize for Him, but to surrender to Him, proclaiming the awful truth that the God who allows pain and suffering in this world is the only One who can overcome its awful effects among us.

In the absence of such Christian witness, the powers of the world take over. The FAA investigators probe the wreckage in an all-out effort to discover "how" it happened. But long after the engineers have proclaimed their pylons-and-bolts answer to the world's question of how it happened, the question yet lurks in our human spirits. "Why did it happen?"

Why does a loving God allow such pain and suffering? Why didn't this all-powerful God alert a ground crew mechanic to the overstressed bolts that broke? Why didn't God inspire the design experts to avoid all flaws?

"We are supposed to have answers, not just questions," said Rabbi Sanford Ragins at the memorial service for thirty-four unidentified crash victims. "In moments like these we are supposed to defend God and explain His ways. But I find that beyond me today."

Here is a credible statement of faith in a God much, much larger than any one person. That it comes from one whose people have suffered the Holocaust is surely no coincidence. Such calamities as plane crashes remind us that we must admit to our faith vocabulary the fragility of human life in a yet broken world and an inability to understand the very God we worship.

In a world addicted to correctness and control, we Christians must proclaim the Good News that indeed our Father God is far greater than our myopic understanding. But the fearful cost of so great and so real a God is the confession that we do not have all the answers, that indeed, we have no power to save ourselves.

Too often, answers serve only to buttress the lethal fantasy of our own power and control. Jesus did not die to bring us answers, but to bring us the Father. In His death, he demonstrated that the Father is willing to share in our worst suffering in order to restore relationship with Him.

Most men today have never experienced Dad's standing with them in their pain and, therefore, are reluctant to believe the Father God will do that.

Does this mean we should just give up when adversity strikes?
Absolutely.

We must give up not to the adversity, but to the Father, confessing our absolute need for His saving power.

And does this mean we just pray and then pull the covers over our heads, doing nothing?

Certainly not. It means we must trust the Father is present in the midst of our suffering—and therefore, we must engage Him in honest, open relationship as we struggle. We push ahead into and through the pain, trusting that "even though I walk through the valley of the shadow of death, I fear no evil; for thou art with me" (Ps. 23:4 RSV).

In this process, we can see the deception, heard all too often, that encountering problems toward a certain goal means it must not be God's will to continue. Indeed, Jesus had to endure the Cross on the path toward God's will for Him. But He persevered, and fulfilled His destiny in this world, glorifying the Father.

We, too, have our crosses. And we, too, have a trustworthy Father who meets us at them and leads us into His victory—insofar as we surrender and let Him.

At times, we may need to raise our fists and shout at God in anger; we may need to crumple and weep before Him in sadness. But if we are to continue in relationship with the Father God, eventually we must, like Job, confess our smallness and surrender to the omnipotent God whose ways are ultimately too great for us to understand (see Job 42:3).

Certainly, for a man who has been abandoned by his father, this is a tremendous task, if not virtually impossible. That is why faith is a gift of the Spirit, given to those who surrender to Jesus, and not something we manufacture ourselves.

It is one thing to take a chance on a God who promises He will keep you safe from all harm throughout life, but quite another to risk surrendering to the Father who allows His son—even you—to be wounded unto death.

If an unfathered generation is to witness God's saving power in this self-centered world, its men must understand how the Father God overcomes the effects of this sinful world upon His people—from plane crashes to sickness, divorce, and death itself.

The ancient Greeks, in their much-vaunted theater, often employed a *deus ex machina*—literally, "god from machine"—for saving an endangered hero-character. A large bucket on a winch cable, similar to the truck apparatus used by tree-trimmers or telephone line repairmen to lift a man to the job, this device lowered a god-character into the play action, who grabbed the endangered hero and lifted him up and away to safety, out of the audience's view.

Such magical thinking characterizes the immature, Gentile view of God as a Savior-Daddy who airlifts us out of all suffering. Thus the ancient prophet proclaimed to a nation besieged by its mortal enemy:

[People] are always rebelling against God, always lying, always refusing to listen to the Lord's teachings. They tell the prophets to keep quiet. They say, "Don't talk to us about what's right. *Tell us what we want to hear. Let us keep our illusions....* The Sovereign Lord, the Holy One of Israel, says to the people, "Come back and quietly trust in me. Then you will be strong and secure." But you refuse to do it. ...

And yet the Lord is waiting to be merciful to you. He is ready to take pity on you because he always does what is right. Happy are those who put their trust in the Lord.

You people who live in Jerusalem will not weep anymore. The Lord is compassionate, and when you cry to him for help, he will answer you. *The Lord will make you go through hard times, but he himself will be there to teach you, and you will not have to search for him any more.* If you wander off the road to the right or the left, you will hear his voice behind you saying, "Here is the road. Follow it." (Isa. 30:9–10, 15, 18–21, italics added)

The Father God overcomes the effects of sin and brokenness in this world by standing with us in it.

Some years ago, I was initiated to the wondrous workings of the Holy Spirit and at once mistook them for God's *deus ex machina.* A woman came to me with deep wounds from her father's abandonment as a girl, and we prayed for Jesus to show us how He was praying to heal her.

Soon, the woman remembered a childhood scene in which her father and mother had just argued fiercely. The father left the house, and the girl went out to ride her tricycle in the driveway. Preoccupied, she bumped her head painfully on the garage door, which was halfway lowered.

I encouraged her to invite Jesus into that scene, expecting to see Him lift the garage door or somehow deflect the impact. She told me Jesus was there with her on the driveway, watching her. She bumped her head and, to my surprise, He came over to her at once and simply held her close to Him with strong arms as she cried.

That was all. But it was enough to remind this woman that her Father God awaited only her call to come and be with her in her pain. Jesus thus restored relationship with the Father for her, and opened the door for much further healing.

Paul proclaimed Jesus' death on the Cross as the bottom line of preaching (see 1 Cor. 2:2). In Jesus, God did not come to lift us out of the world's brokenness—which infects every human heart—but to stand and fight with us against it, thereby drawing us into relationship with Him and each other.

If in that process we rage against Him or fall weeping at His feet, He is not offended, for He is a Father both secure in His authority and deeply involved with His children. This God is a lover; He rages, He weeps, too.

By all means, Christians are called to battle against the powers of destruction in this fallen world—from working for justice among the poor to praying against cancer to relief efforts after a natural disaster. As in any battle, we are deeply grieved, but not surprised that tragedy and losses occur. And because our Father is with us, we keep on fighting, learning faith in Him whose victory has been established yet beyond our full grasp, and whose "love endures forever" (Ps. 136:1 RSV).

For this, at last, is the journey of victory—not, as the Gentile gods of Hollywood proclaim, that we blast away all enemies by our own power and emerge unscathed, but that our lives witness to the God who calls His people to a glory far beyond our self-centered imaginations:

> But this precious treasure—this light and power that now shine within us—is held in a perishable container, that is, in our weak bodies. Everyone can see that the glorious power within must be from God and is not our own.
>
> We are pressed on every side by troubles, but not crushed and broken. We are perplexed because we don't know why things happen as they do, but we don't give up and quit. We are hunted down, but God never abandons us. We get knocked down, but we get up again and keep going. . . .
>
> Yes, we live under constant danger to our lives because we serve the Lord, but this gives us constant opportunites to show forth the power of Jesus Christ within our dying bodies. . . .
>
> So we do not look at what we can see right now, the troubles all around us, but we look forward to the joys in heaven which we have not yet seen. The troubles will soon be over, but the joys to come will last forever (2 Cor. 4:7–9, 11, 18 TLB).

CHAPTER ELEVEN

Man's Anger and God's Righteous Purpose

Remember this, my dear brothers! Everyone must be quick to listen, but slow to speak and slow to become angry. Man's anger does not achieve God's righteous purpose. (James 1:19–20)

When Saul heard their words, the Spirit of God came upon him in power, and he burned with anger. (1 Sam. 11:6 NIV)

"I really freak out inside when somebody treats me bad." Tim, a thirty-eight-year-old salesman, had recently been lied to by a fellow salesman and cheated out of a sale. "I know I should be able to overlook things like that, as a Christian . . . but I end up just popping Di-Gels and losing sleep, fantasizing how I'd like to beat him to a pulp."

Tim had clearly been treated unfairly and had every right to be angry at his co-worker. But he could only condemn his feelings and not allow himself to have that anger—and therefore, could not move through it to resolution.

"I could sit here and sympathize with you," I said, "but I'd rather find out what's making it so hard for you just to say the truth to yourself and the other guy, namely, 'I'm really angry at you for what you did.'"

Tim made a fist, grit his teeth, and sat quietly.

I hesitated, then decided it was time to open the wound. "What did your father do when he got angry?" I asked.

Startled, Tim drew back. "What do you mean?"

"A boy learns how a man acts by watching his dad. As a man now, you're obviously stuffing all your anger and not letting any of it out. Is that what your father did?"

Tim nodded slowly, understanding. "Dad was a big man, and I was pretty scared of him. It's funny; I don't remember him ever yelling or throwing things, but when he got angry, everybody sure knew it. The tension was awful. All he had to do was look at you, and you'd freeze inside. I was really scared of what he might do."

"Are you scared of what you might do yourself, if you let your anger out?" I asked.

Tim hesitated, then dropped his head. "Yeah, I guess so. Sometimes I think I might hit my wife, maybe tell the boss off and lose my job, or even kill somebody—crazy stuff like that."

"You probably never got angry at your father, did you?"

"Are you kidding?" Tim exclaimed. "Never—no way!"

"A boy learns how to relate to other men by relating to his father," I continued. "What did you learn from your father?"

With a wry grin, Tim nodded. "It's dangerous to express your real feelings to another man." He sighed. "No wonder I'm all freaked out and can't think straight over this guy at work who cheated me!"

Though Tim's father had never sat down and talked to him about anger, the father's model communicated powerfully to the son. Tim was not only afraid of other people's anger, but of his own as well—and therefore found himself virtually paralyzed.

Worse, his "Christian" faith judged his feelings as wrong. Instead of offering him a bold sword of liberating truth, it had become a convenient shield behind which to hide his fears—a spiritual Di-Gel which only temporarily relieved the symptoms and short-circuited genuine resolution for his problem.

Most men today have seen fathers and other men deal with anger in only two ways: either by stuffing it and withdrawing or lashing out violently—as the ineffective wimp or raging monster. Few have seen the father express anger without being destructive—either outwardly, toward others, or inwardly, toward himself. Not wanting to be a wimp, a man is left with violence as his only apparent option when angry; if he renounces violence as well, he has literally no place in the world to go.

No place, that is, except to the Father God, who in Jesus has demonstrated that a man's salvation lies only in another world, another kingdom besides this present one.

Certainly, male violence—from international wars to schoolyard fisticuffs and domestic wife-beating—needs no documentation here. Any man today who has looked honestly in the mirror knows the "monster" capability within himself. The Christian man often feels guilty and confused, believing it's wrong to be angry, while at the same time his body tells him with headaches and ulcers that his anger cannot be simply shoved down and ignored.

—161—

The biblical faith, meanwhile, does not mark anger as a sin, but only a likely avenue to sin, which must be faced readily and resolved deliberately. Thus, the apostle Paul declares, "If you become angry, do not let your anger lead you into sin, and do not stay angry all day. Don't give the Devil a chance" (Eph. 4:26–27).

God does not judge a man for feeling angry, but for how he acts on that feeling. Certainly, a man may acknowledge "a Christian way to act," but any striving under the burden of "a Christian way to feel" only leads to self-condemnation and inaction. A man begins to receive the Father's heart and act like Him precisely insofar as he takes his honest human feelings—no matter how frightening they may be—to Jesus.

Angry feelings are redeemed into godly action—or restraint—only by surrendering them to the Father humbly, at Jesus' feet. Criticizing and judging yourself as "bad" for feeling angry, and then suppressing and denying the feeling, only consume your good energies. The Enemy loves darkness as a fish loves water; he is not overcome by being put out of sight, but only by being brought out into the Light.

Tim, for example, did not sin by feeling angry when his co-worker cheated him, but would have sinned if he had retaliated by hitting the man, as he fantasized. He did, however, "stay angry all day," without facing and dealing with his feelings. In thereby giving "the Devil a chance," he was consumed by resentment and destructive impulses. He did not surrender his anger to Jesus—perhaps by praying with his Christian brothers for wisdom. Therefore, he could not go to his co-worker and talk it out honestly and openly—without violence, but expressing his anger clearly and expecting fair amends.

Others have suggested that anger is not a primary emotion, but a secondary response to feeling hurt. That is, when someone hurts you, your first and most genuine response is to feel pain, perhaps even to cry. But the vulnerability in telling others how badly they have hurt you is frightening—"They'll just hurt me more"—so you protect yourself with anger.

Certainly, anger feels stronger than hurt, and thus, safer. But an honest man soon discovers that the defenses which protected him as a boy only fence him in as an adult, who needs intimacy and fellowship. To resolve the root cause of his anger and be freed to love, a man must face the deeper hurt within which has fueled it.

Most men have so desperately sought to cover pain—so ruthlessly shielded it with anger—that it's hard to set aside the anger long enough to surface the true hurt for healing. Often, in fact, the man has decided as a child to guard himself and not let his hurt surface before another person. After suppressing his pain long enough, a man can no longer surface it even to himself. He "forgets" it, giving it over to the darkness, where it becomes a tool of the Enemy in his subconscious.

When I prayed with Tim, he begged Jesus to come and uproot his fear and set him free from the anger inside him. Eventually, the Holy Spirit led him to a boyhood memory in which he had thoughtlessly over-stepped one of his father's minor rules. Furious, the father had spanked him mercilessly, and sent him to bed early with a harsh tongue-lashing.

When he began to cry, the father came into his room and spanked him harder, saying, "Be quiet, or I'll give you something to cry about!" Terrified, the boy held back his tears—then and forever after.

When Tim recalled that scene and asked Jesus to be with him in its pain, he felt secure in the presence of the Father God. In his mind's eye, he could then safely tell his father he was sorry he disobeyed, but didn't deserve such harsh punishment. And at last, as the Heavenly Father in Jesus stood between him and his earthly father, he tearfully poured out thirty years of anger and pain: "Daddy, don't hit me again! Stop hurting me, Daddy! Please, Daddy, just love me. . . ."

As Tim prayed and cried, he "saw" his father begin to cry, too, and describe how his own father had beaten him as a boy. As pain passed down the generations was thereby extracted in tears from son and father in the presence of Jesus, Tim was able to see with the Father God's eyes of truth and compassion, and forgive his dad.

Out of this prayer experience, Tim learned that his Father God stands with him in his pain. Then he was able to talk straightforwardly to the co-worker who had wronged him, seeking fairness and not vengeance.

A boy with more inner strength before an abusive father often may try to maintain his integrity precisely by not crying when the father punishes him. "I wasn't about to give that man the satisfaction of know-ing he could hurt me," men commonly declare; "and so I decided then and there I'd never cry again." In such cases, I encourage the man to renounce that boyhood vow and call on Jesus to take him through and beyond the pain from his dad, so he no longer cuts himself off from his genuine feelings.

The Father God can and will mediate a man's anger—which, when otherwise left to the man's own devices, becomes a tool of the Enemy. As James declares, simply reacting to unfairness or other hurt by lash-ing out angrily, defines "man's anger," and cannot "achieve God's righ-teous purpose" (James 1:19–20). Indeed, to indulge your anger wholesale, to nurse it and not turn it over to Jesus for the Father God's plan of resolution, is to "give the Devil a chance" to achieve his destruc-tive purposes with it.

In explicitly identifying one kind of anger as "man's," this text allows for another kind as God's. And indeed, God may instill His anger in a man in order to achieve His righteous purpose.

Consider King Saul's response, when told that the Ammonite king had besieged Jabesh and was offering a treaty "on one condition: I will put out everyone's right eye and so bring disgrace on all Israel" (1 Sam. 11:2). It would only be natural for a king to get angry at so vicious an enemy. The anger Saul displays, however, is not his own, but supernatural: "When Saul heard this, the spirit of God took control of him, and he became furious" (v.6).

Christians are accustomed to Bible stories in which the Holy Spirit moves in someone to bring healing, prophecy, and the like—but listen to what He does in King Saul:

> [Saul] took two oxen, cut them in pieces, and had messengers carry the pieces throughout the land of Israel with this warning: "Whoever does not follow Saul and Samuel into battle will have this done to his oxen!" (v. 7)

What, indeed, occasions God's supernatural anger in a man? That is, what righteous purpose does Saul seek to achieve as with supernatural force he furiously hacks up huge oxen with his sword?

This story of King Saul proclaims that the Father God sends His Spirit of anger into a man when the people of God are being threatened by the Enemy, and the man otherwise would not be sufficiently motivated to execute God's saving action. The Father God's anger in a man focuses on saving and redeeming, not destroying and avenging.

Anger that motivates a man to save God's people from the Enemy's power of destruction would seem of God and thus, justified as a catalyst for action. In men submitted to Jesus, this might include anger against racism, abortion-on-demand, nuclear arms, crime, social structures that keep people poor, child abuse, and materialism.

Included as one of God's people myself, I might receive anger from the Holy Spirit either to defend myself from the Enemy's various attacks upon me through others, or to convict me and inspire repentance and counter-attack when I have myself allowed the Enemy to work in and through me.

Clearly, anger from the Holy Spirit of the Father God is not a secondary human emotion. It is God's call to action, and must be heeded faithfully. The man who has allowed the Enemy to delude him into thinking "Christians don't get angry," cannot recognize anger from the Holy Spirit. He cannot therefore mobilize his talents and energies to battle in behalf of God's people—not even, as Tim with his lying co-worker, in behalf of himself.

A man who fears anger—who suppresses and withdraws from every angry feeling—cannot discern the difference between his own self-centered anger and God's. When he runs from anger, either in himself toward another or in another toward him, he may avoid overreacting violently. But it costs him his manhood, for he misses the Father's call both to victorious arms and to redeeming conviction.

If indeed, "man's anger does not achieve God's righteous purpose," then a man dedicated to serving Jesus must diligently seek to distinguish his own selfish anger from God's. The problem of human nature itself, however, is that no man is capable of doing that by himself; human nature is just too subjective, too self-preserving. Such discernment is a supernatural gift of the Holy Spirit, who alone gives "the ability to tell the difference between gifts that come from the Spirit and those that do not" (1 Cor. 12:10b). Thus, a man must take his anger to Jesus before acting on it—not instead of acting on it, but so that his actions serve God's righteous purpose and not his own.

Human responses can be deceiving. Even the apparently righteous anger of many young men in the '60s who fought against racism and militarism, was at times just an arrogant effort to distance themselves from their fathers' sin and thereby avoid facing their own. On the other hand, what Tim took at first to be self-centered anger at his co-worker, turned out to be the Father God's anger at a son's being so mistreated.

Since denying anger places it in the Enemy's province of darkness, it builds up there and often explodes in violence, much as a dam without a spillway bursts under pressure. A major goal of helping men deal with anger is therefore to head off violent explosions and preclude their destructive effects on others in society.

This phenomenon is seen graphically among black males, who often lack fathers to guide them through the wounds of racism. The 1991 movie *Boyz 'N the Hood* portrayed ghetto wounds and violence negatively, but nevertheless gunfights and fisticuffs erupted at theaters around the country. As twenty-three-year-old director John Singleton responded, "It wasn't the film (that caused the violence). It was the fact that a whole generation (of black men) doesn't respect themselves, which makes it easier for them to shoot each other. This is a generation of kids who don't have father figures. They're looking for their manhood, and they get a gun. The more of those people that get together, the higher the potential for violence."[1]

If a man does not deal with his anger, it deals with him. If he does not take his anger to Jesus, the Destroyer takes it. That is, he either takes it to other persons and destroys them, or turns it inward and destroys himself.

The "curse" and destruction in Malachi 4:6 from the lack of father-son relationships, manifests not only in society at large, but in individual men. Statistics indicate that the American man today is three times as likely to commit suicide as the woman—largely, I believe, because he has learned through example and painful experience with his father to push down his feelings, and thus ultimately, himself.

Another word for "push down" is "depress."[2] Just as a clutch pedal when pushed down is said to be "depressed," a person who pushes down genuine emotions becomes, by definition, emotionally depressed. If we want most to push down feelings of pain, and if we seek most often to cover that pain with the secondary emotion of anger, then most emotional depression can be traced to suppressed anger, and then, pain.

The average man today, at some time in his life, has been troubled and puzzled by emotional depression. Popular expressions, such as "stuck in a rut," "bummed out," or "down in the dumps," may describe the sensation, but still he wonders what depression is, how it begins, and how to overcome it.

Christians know that depression does not indicate God's will, but a need for His healing. Indeed, Jesus said, "I have come in order that you might have life—life in all its fullness" (John 10:10). In depression, a man has lost touch with the God Who is Life.

Certainly, something must happen to a man in order to make him depressed. Medical science has determined that sometimes a chemical imbalance triggers depression, and in some cases modern drugs have been effective in alleviating it. But psychologists have discovered that often depression stems from particularly sad or painful life events. According to psychiatrist Arthur Janov, "Patients who do not report feeling depressed may have feelings of sadness at one event or another, but those feelings are always specific to a particular experience."[3]

That is, the key to unlocking the gates of depression is connecting what you are feeling to the specific event which caused that feeling. The depressed person has pushed down that painful event below consciousness as, "I don't know why I'm so down like this."

Contrary to popular belief, depression is not the absence of feeling, but rather, an unwillingness to feel—resulting not from an "empty nothingness" inside, but a reservoir of dammed-up feelings. "Depression is a mask," Janov says, "for very deep and painful feelings" which a person has not "connected with the event" which caused those feelings—a sort of emotional amnesia. It is "not a feeling . . . but a mood . . . a retreat from feeling."[4]

This definition allows that a man could retreat into depression from the Holy Spirit's call to godly anger. Thus, the prophet Elijah proclaimed God's fury against the wicked Jezebel—until she vowed to kill him:

> Elijah was afraid and fled for his life . . . a whole day into the wilderness. He stopped and sat down in the shade of a tree and wished he would die. "It's too much, Lord," he prayed. "Take away my life; I might as well be dead!" (1 Kings 19:3–4)

To push feelings down requires considerable energy; hence, exhaustion accompanies the emotional numbness. Indeed, Janov notes that when depressed persons are monitored on an electromyograph, they exhibit "a very high level of tension, which shows that depression is a disconnected feeling." He quotes a National Institute of Mental Health study demonstrating that "depressives begin their dream activity almost as soon as they fall asleep, and the sleep is truncated and fragmented"— further evidence that "tension is involved in depression."[5]

This tension comes from the inner struggle when deep and genuine feelings want to surface, but are pushed down instead out of fear. "Indeed," Janov says, "some persons are willing to kill themselves before they would feel those feelings."[6]

One survey has revealed that the nation's highest suicide rates are in Vermont, New Hampshire, and Maine. Mental health officials blame this on the very stoicism that so many men affirm. As Dr. Stephen Soffeff, Director of Emergency Psychiatry at Portland's Maine Medical Center, explains,

> It's the Yankee version of the "stiff upper lip." They try to keep it all in, try to be strong; hide their feelings until they do something drastic—like kill themselves. They feel that to get help for their depression . . . is not only wrong, but a symbol of weakness.[7]

Nowhere in psychology books, however, have I seen the origin of men's suicidal impulses more graphically demonstrated than in a student essay which I received in an adult class I once taught for men learning English:

> I was about fourteen years old. My father spank me real hard, because I did not do what he wants me to do. So I was really upset and angry to my father. But I didn't say any word to him, because I respect him very much in every way but the only thought in my mind, I am going to kill myself because my father didn't likes me.

This boy started with real feelings connected to a very specific event: pain at being whipped, not out of discipline but vengeance; and then, anger at his father. But he is convinced that his feelings, no matter how real, are unacceptable. He cannot feel his pain openly and drop all defense to his father's merciless anger, nor can he show anger back at his father, who must be "respected" at all costs—even, apparently, at the cost of his life.

The boy has been made to feel guilty for the simple, honest feeling of anger toward his father. The only course open to him is to suppress that. But his pain from and anger toward his father are so deep that, in order to suppress them, he must suppress his life itself.

The father-wound cuts into the very identity and being of the boy. It doesn't matter how widely recognized an authority demands a boy retreat so from it unto death—whether "village tradition," "Christian morality," or "manly respect." Still, the son dies: if he does not physically kill himself, he depresses his very life spirit.

Such internalized guilt, with no apparent release from it, is common in suicidal persons—who often cannot believe that the person in authority might be guilty of wrongdoing, and not themselves. Victims of incest and other child abuse commonly experience this.

The sensation of guilt can even be a cover-up to conceal the real feelings of hurt and anger toward the other person. It is safer, of course, simply to feel guilty for what happened than to say, "You hurt me"—especially if the one who inflicted the pain is much bigger and stronger, thereby holding the power of life itself, as a parent holds over a child.

The boy, therefore, tends to reason: "You hurt me, Daddy. I need you to recognize that and say you won't do it again, so I can trust you. But I'm afraid if I tell you that, you might hurt me even worse by ignoring, rejecting, or punishing me. That makes me angry at you. But if I show my anger at you, you'll hurt me more. Therefore, I'd better depress my hurt feelings, turn my anger away from you and focus it on myself instead."

As one author declares, mental depressives "usually have refrained from complaining," and have put themselves "under such long and rigid control" that they are "worn out from the effort."[8]

Catholic priests Dennis and Matthew Linn declare that

Much psychological depression is really swallowed anger and will disappear if I can answer the question, "Who or what is irritating me?" and then deal with my anger. . . . When I don't like my anger, I usually feel guilty about my anger.[9]

Similarly, another pastor has written,

I was so busy being self-critical . . . blaming myself for my sorry state, that I did not realize I was depressed. When I was able to stop feeling guilty at being angry at what happened, and to start getting in touch with my anger rather than turning it unconsciously against myself, then I began to feel better.[10]

The depressed man is therefore sitting on a powder keg of pushed-down feelings. What began as boyhood pressure to "control yourself like a good boy," becomes an adult habit that continues until so much pain, so many unpleasant feelings get dammed up inside, that he becomes afraid to deal with any one of them for fear that pulling one log out of the dam will bring the whole flood down.

One all-too-common response is to try and dull the pain with drugs when willpower eventually fails to hold it down. Alcohol, for example, is a "downer," a depressant—not an "upper," or stimulant. Its abuse is therefore often aimed at pushing down pains and subsequent anger.

Alcoholism is closely related to depression; the Linns conclude a chapter in their book titled, "Dealing with Depression," by saying, "This chapter could be summarized by the twelve steps of Alcoholics Anonymous."[11]

From this perspective, many well-intentioned efforts to help a man out of depression are often short-sighted. You may want to say, "Just try harder; work more at bringing yourself out of it!" But if depression is caused by too much self-control and biting the bullet in the first place, this advice only adds to the burden.

The basic assumption that leads a man into depression is "no one will share my troublesome feelings; what I'm feeling is too awful; anyone who heard me express my feelings would reject me!" He learned this as a boy, when first wounded and not allowed to express his pain and anger—that is, "Daddy won't love me if I feel this way."

A Christian, however, knows that in the life, death, and resurrection of Jesus, the Father God has demonstrated He is always with us. The very name Immanuel in Hebrew means "God with us."

Furthermore, in Jesus we know the Father God's love for us is so strong that it triumphs over death itself. "For I am certain," the apostle Paul proclaimed,

that nothing can separate us from [the love of Christ]: neither death nor life, neither angels nor other heavenly rulers or powers, neither the present nor the future, neither the world above nor the world below— there is nothing in all creation that will ever be able to separate us from the love of God which is ours through Christ Jesus our Lord. (Rom. 8:38–39)

In Jesus, our Father God has offered an alternative to covering our pain with anger and fearfully pushing it all down. With the help of a pastor, Christian counselor, and/or loving brother, we can let the Holy Spirit reveal our deepest feelings and take them to Jesus for His resolution.

Christians must therefore avoid invasive therapies such as hypnosis and "truth serum" drugs. Through His Holy Spirit, the Father God is well able not only to surface appropriate memories and feelings, but to respect the man's will and proceed at his own pace and depth.

This interrelationship between anger, depression, and God's intentions, is surprisingly well portrayed in the story of Jonah. Most people know that Jonah was swallowed by the monster fish, but few realize that his cries as he sank helplessly into the ocean depths closely reflect emotional depression:

> You [God] threw me down into the depths. . . . I thought I had been banished from your presence and would never see your holy Temple again. The water came over me and choked me . . . and seaweed wrapped around my head. I went down to the very roots of the mountains, into the land whose gates lock shut forever. (Jonah 2:3–6)

Certainly, we may feel sympathetic toward Jonah and any other depressed person. Yet we must not allow our sympathy to so blur the overall picture that we forget how Jonah got into his predicament in the first place. For Jonah chooses his fate. God called him to a task—to warn the enemy Ninevites. Angry that God would give Israel's enemy a chance to repent and be saved, he has chosen to run away rather than do what God commands (see Jonah 1:3).

When Jonah withdraws to the hold of his getaway ship, God brings a sea storm that threatens to capsize the vessel. But rather than beg God's forgiveness and surrender himself at last to God's calling, Jonah chooses self-pity—and thereby, guilt unto death instead. "Throw me into the sea," he tells the sailors, "and it will calm down. I know it is my fault that you are caught in this violent storm" (Jonah 1:12).

Jonah's depression stems not from his predicament, but from his own self-deception; he feels "banished" from God, while in reality, he has chosen to run away from God. The story suggests that we choose to be depressed insofar as we turn away from the Father God, because we do not trust Him to accept us as we are, hurt and angry.

This may sound harsh, as if simply to blame the person for being

depressed. But it is good news to discover your own role in your predicament: If we can identify particular choices that lead us into depression,
we can make other choices to avoid it. Certainly, a man may choose to
jump into a pit, but that pit may be so deep that he cannot simply choose
to climb out of it. He can, however, choose to humble himself, trust the
Father God, and cry out for help. This understanding underlies the non-
judgmental 12-step programs, which allow, for example, that a man
could choose to take a drink, but be helpless to stop.

We therefore choose depression insofar as, like Jonah, we decide to
turn away from God, to distrust Him and hide our pain and anger from
Him—and from others. Jonah may not be able to pull himself out of the
pit he's jumped into, but he could cry out to the One who can. Jonah's
choice to run and hide, however, only forces God to use drastic means to
reach him.

And so, when Jonah has cast himself into the merciless, guilt-ridden
sea of self-pity, God seizes him as if to say, "If you insist on casting yourself down, Jonah, that's fine! I'll take you all the way down: down into
the depths of your own broken self, down to where you must let go of
your life and cry out your pain at last, until you know that you belong to
Me and I am here as always to save you."

At last, therefore, "from deep inside the fish," Jonah prays to his God:

> When I felt my life slipping away,
>   then, O Lord, I prayed to you,
>   and in your holy Temple you heard me. . . .
> I will sing praises to you;
>   I will offer you a sacrifice
>   and do what I have promised.
> Salvation comes from the Lord!

Then, *the LORD ordered the fish to spit Jonah up on the beach, and it did.*
(2:7, 9–10, italics added)

Using life-threatening force, the Father God has jarred Jonah out of
his depressive self-pity and back into relationship, long enough to do
what He wants. In the vitality of restored relationship, the man no
longer chooses to depress his original feelings. For when the enemy
Ninevites heed Jonah's prophecy and repent, God pardons them. And
at last, Jonah "was very unhappy about this and became angry" (Jonah
4:1).

That is, the man knows what he is feeling and who has made him feel
that way—and he says so openly now, instead of depressing it and running away as before. His angry outburst shows that he has learned that

this God who delivered him from the gates of Hell itself is no unmerciful, unapproachable father-in-the-sky, whom he must respect even if it kills him. Indeed, a vociferous argument follows (see Jonah 4:9–10):

"What right do you have to be angry?" God demands.

"I have every right to be angry—angry enough to die!" Jonah shouts back.

Here the Bible portrays clearly the profound connection between the depressive, suicidal mood and anger. In knowing what he is angry about and speaking that out to the person who caused it, Jonah has moved further along the path out of depression. But he has not matured in his faith, remaining rather in that adolescent limbo between childish, self-centered pouting and maturely accepting and celebrating God's claim on his life.

Liberation from depression is a process of accurately focusing and expressing anger *and* surrendering your will to God. Jonah, however, has not grown beyond self-expression to the surrender that would allow him the full vitality of expressing the Father God with his life. He reaches to the Father when death threatens, but he withdraws when life beckons. That is, he recognizes the Father as merciful Savior, but not as Lord—as if childishly to say, "You can save my life, but you can't tell me what to do!" Although he has overcome his childish fear of getting angry at his Father God, Jonah has not moved beyond demanding what he wants for himself. And so he remains in the province of death—"angry enough to die," but not humble and faithful enough to live.

Nevertheless, all hope for Jonah is justified—as for any man, when honest and open relationship with the Father God has been restored. For the Father God did not resort to life-threatening measures against Jonah because he was angry, but because he turned away and broke relationship. Even when Jonah's cutting off relationship had led him to the doorway of death, the Father God did not punish him, but rather, used the occasion to call him back.

In allowing Jonah to get angry at Him, the Father God risks losing His son's respect in order to gain his love. Indeed, God did not receive Jonah's love in return for His effort. On the contrary, Jonah is last heard asserting his right to be angry at God. The story says that it remains to be seen whether Jonah—or any of God's people, unto ourselves today—will eventually appreciate and return His love.

On the Cross, Jesus demonstrated graphically that genuine Father-love respects the other's right to say No. It's always a risk. No father can be sure that his child will some day turn around and say, "Thanks, Dad, for hanging in there with me back then when I was so selfish and immature."

In the last verses of the book, after Jonah has lashed out at God for pardoning Israel's enemy, God responds simply by affirming how much "pity" (see Jonah 4:11) He feels for those innocent Ninevites who might have been destroyed along with the guilty. By the end of the story, we simply know that the Father God is merciful.[12]

But that is all we need to know, in order to have relationship with the Father—that is, to continue interacting with Him openly and honestly, instead of depressing our feelings and withdrawing from Him for fear of His judgment and punishment.

In Jonah, God portrays the vulnerability, the mercy, and the enduring faith required of the father who would save his child for God's purposes. If a boy is to fulfill his destiny as a man, his integrity must be honored, even as he must be held accountable for his actions.

The Christian man today must allow the Father God to save him from depression in order to fulfill his destiny in this world. He must dare to let Jesus connect his anger with the true persons and events which prompted it, even if that means letting God take him to the terrible depths—like Jonah—where God honors a man's surrender and delivers him at last into purpose and direction. For so Jesus blazed this path to destiny, in which resurrection to new life requires the Cross of pain and death.

But because Jonah continues to sulk in his anger, we see that the Father God's efforts to free us from depression do not focus on delivering us from all pain and anger. Rather, taking your pain and anger to Jesus promises the vitality of full, here-and-now feelings, so you can know who or what is hurting you or making you angry.

To connect feelings properly to the causing event and submit responses to Jesus, releases the chains on a man, but does not propel him into the fullness of life which Jesus offers. The Father God does not lift a man from the hell of depression into a heaven of bliss. Rather, He saves a man from the monstrous depths precisely so he can be spit out into the real world, where all his human feelings must at last confront and struggle with God's destiny and purpose for him.

Thus the Father God sets a son free to respond actively to Him; that is, He confers godly response-ability upon a man.

May we know God as so real a Father, that we might be so real as men.

Amen.

CHAPTER TWELVE

In Praise of Old Men

Caleb . . . said to [Joshua], "You know what the Lord said in Kadesh Barnea about you and me to Moses, the man of God. I was forty years old when the Lord's servant Moses sent me from Kadesh Barnea to spy out this land. I brought an honest report back to him. The men who went with me, however, made our people afraid. But I faithfully obeyed the Lord my God. Because I did, Moses promised me that my children and I would certainly receive as our possession the land which I walked over. But now, look. It has been forty-five years since the Lord said that to Moses. That was when Israel was going through the desert, and the Lord, as he promised, has kept me alive ever since. Look at me! I am eighty-five years old and am just as strong today as I was when Moses sent me out. I am still strong enough for war or anything else. Now then, give me the hill country that the Lord promised me on that day when my men and I reported. We told you then that the race of giants called the Anakim were there in large walled cities. Maybe the Lord will be with me, and I will drive them out, just as the Lord said."

Joshua blessed Caleb . . . and gave him the city of Hebron as his possession. (Josh. 14:6–13)

Recently a Christian radio producer in Los Angeles called and invited me to be interviewed together with Leonard LeSourd, who would be in town from Virginia promoting his recent book, *Strong Men, Weak Men.*[1] Now in his mid-seventies, LeSourd served as a pilot in World War II and then entered a long and distinguished career as an editor for *Guideposts* magazine, Chosen Books, and many of his late wife Catherine Marshall's bestsellers.

Though I had done joint interviews before, I sensed that the difference in our ages would make this one special. In my late forties, I am often one of the oldest men present as I minister to men around the country. Certainly, in order to seek God's strength, a man must be old enough to have experienced the limits of his own. Few men today over fifty, however, seem willing to look honestly enough at their own wounds to value the healing God is offering men today.

I have speculated that only men who might have graduated from college in 1965 or later—when the Viet Nam war escalated amid the social revolution of civil rights and women's liberation—would have been sufficiently jarred from the world's traditional view of men to seek change in their lives.

Whatever the reason, today's men-in-the-middle often feel abandoned by older men, even as by their fathers. "Where are the grey heads?" as one pastor in his late thirties lamented after I had spoken to his church about the need for older men as mentors.

Men of all ages today have been wounded by older men, whether through abuse or abandonment. But the social movements of the last three decades have freed younger men to begin moving through their pain more honestly and deeply, to a simple longing to be mentored that precludes resentment or vengeance.

At a recent retreat billed as "Healing for Men" which drew 155 participants, I asked for a show of hands from men 60 or older. Four went up. On impulse, I asked the four to stand. "I want to thank you, our older brothers," I said. "Your coming to this retreat to learn and grow gives us great hope that when we get your age, we can continue learning and growing then, too."

I found myself clapping—and was astonished at the thunderous, sustained applause that followed from the other, younger men. Far more than mere courtesy was being expressed in that release of applause, which fairly shook the sanctuary as the younger men recognized the old men who had come alongside them at last.

One man who had attended a men's retreat with Robert Bly, told me that, at the very outset before speaking, Bly had asked the younger men to clear the front row seats for older men, as a gesture of honor.

Thus I sat both uncertain and hopeful in the radio studio beside grey-haired Leonard LeSourd. Could I trust this guy? Would he discount me and try to take over? Indeed, would my own longing for a mentor betray me and encourage him to do so? As we waited for the interviewer's cue, I struggled to gather myself and prayed, *Father, I surrender all this to you. Keep me open to what you're doing here.*

Glancing at my fellow guest, it occurred to me how tired I'd been after my last cross-country flight, and I found myself impressed at this man's vitality and enthusiasm. Indeed, would I be willing thirty years from now to leave my quiet farm in Virginia to hit the asphalt in LA and promote anything, even my own book?

"Not long ago, I had pretty well figured I was retired, and that was just fine by me," LeSourd told our interviewer. "But in my daily prayers, I felt like the Lord was telling me to get ready for a new ministry, that he wanted me to do something for men. "I've edited dozens of other people's books, very successfully; why, I asked Him, would He want me now, at my old age, to write my own book for the first time? And why about men?

"As I began to read Gordon's book and some of the other work being done for men today, to look around at our society, and to recall the mistakes of my own early manhood, I realized what an awful shape we men have been in, and how terribly the Lord wants to heal us. I'm not exactly sure just what I'm doing in all this, but something about it grabbed me, and my spirit said, 'Yes, Lord, I want to be a part of what you're doing in men today.' So here I am."

I sat there transfixed by this boldly faithful old man, as he talked humbly and openly about his life struggles, what God had taught him over the years and what he sought yet to learn. Indeed, a strange peace had settled over me, as if a burden had been lifted.

Soon it struck me: I was no longer the elder spokesman, and at last, that was okay. I could indeed trust this man thirty years my senior, who had surrendered himself and his brokenness to the Father God as genuinely as I and any younger man I know.

Yes, I had many insights to share with the radio listeners, but did so appropriately, without compulsion. In fact, I felt encouraged by his presence in a way I had never felt from the numerous other peers or younger men who have supported my ministry so diligently.

I am and will forever be profoundly grateful for those younger men, and I will continue to need them. But sitting there beside seventy-three-year-old Leonard LeSourd was as if at last someone were walking beside me who knew a little more about this path—if only just the need to be on it—than I did. My fears of jealousy and competition had given way to trust and respect.

When our interviewer gave us each two minutes for concluding remarks, I took the opportunity to thank Leonard for his faithfully listening to the Father God and coming alongside us younger men in our struggle. "If you're really not sure why God's called you at your age to minister to men," I said, "let me tell you: we need you!"

When I got home, my wife Mary, who had listened to the interview, greeted me with a smile and enthusiastic hug. "I'm so proud of you!" she said.

"Why?" I asked—pleased, but genuinely puzzled.

"I was praying for you during the show, that you wouldn't feel competitive or threatened. I knew it would be so healing for the men listening if you could demonstrate a real camaraderie between men of all ages—and you did!"

"Thanks," I said, smiling. "I never thought about demonstrating that for other men—that's really good!" Then, I sighed. "I just know you weren't the only one praying to keep me open!"

For indeed, such harmony with old men has not been common for younger men in recent history. The Beatles' hit from the '60s, "Dirty Old Man," aptly served a generation which proclaimed, "Don't trust anyone over thirty." Today, however, many of us are older than John Kennedy when he became President—and so we struggle to re-gauge our parameters.

As a graduate student at Stanford in the late '60s, I embraced the liberal activism of the era. I was therefore jarred into new understanding when in 1970 black students there refused to support some eighty-five percent of white students who walked out of classes to protest the U.S. invasion of Cambodia.

As I noted in a subsequent *Christian Century* article, "The Great White Son Turns Left," the campus Black Student Union declared that the campus strike represented a mere "family squabble" between disillusioned white youth and their affluent parents:

> You have responded to the napalming of non-white Asians by throwing a temper tantrum as if suddenly discovering that your father was a liar, a racist and a murderer, after he told you that he represented the best humanity had to offer.[2]

White activist Jerry Rubin struck at the emotional core of much political activism when he declared, "Bring the war home: kill your parents." In the social protests of that era, many men tried desperately to cut themselves off from their fathers—and in doing so, cast themselves into an unreality which often bore tragic consequences.

Classic was the case of the Argentine medical student Ernesto Guevara. Enshrined by radicals as "Che," Guevara grew up in an upper-middle-class suburb of Rosario separated from the barrio, or slum, by a busy thoroughfare—much like its American counterpart "across the tracks."

In his *Che: The Making of a Legend,* Martin Ebon recounted the story, told him by one of Guevara's childhood friends, of how the young Ernesto once drove off a group of barrio children who had been taunting an old cripple. But the old man, himself a resident of the barrio, offered no thanks:

> Without saying a word, yet with a hatred so glacial that it made us shiver, he looked us over, especially Ernesto. In his icy silence he was telling us to save our good gestures, to keep our good intentions. It was not those barefoot kids who were his enemies. It was us. . . . Ernesto's whole life was a crossing of that street of his childhood.[3]

But even in his childhood it was too late for Che to cross that street. He never did resolve the gap between his universalistic ideals and his humanly parochial, upper-middle-class history. He made no attempt to radicalize his peers—his fellow medical students, his well-to-do neighbors—or indeed, his father. He chose rather—as the Stanford BSU said of white revolutionaries in its anti-strike declaration—to "turn the niggers loose on a trembling white society." As Ebon noted, the Bolivian peasants whom Che hoped to uplift looked on him as an outsider, an intruder—and they finally betrayed him.

Few people realize today, almost a generation after the Cuban revolution, that communist Fidel Castro was born into one of the richest families in that country, and when he took power his aides required that he immediately burn his father's sugar cane fields to demonstrate his solidarity with the poor.

In a graphic American example of the father-son split masked by political extremism, one Stanford radical interviewed in a National Educational Television documentary "Fathers and Sons" said, "My relationship with my father played an important part in the way I've turned out. He's one of the best opthamologists in the country and always in his three-piece suit. I always had a vast admiration for him, even held him in a kind of awe, never believing he could be wrong. Then I heard him talking of 'those niggers across town,' and it shook me to find that my father was not all he was cracked up to be."

Whereupon, the student said, he threw away his own suits, changed his major from physics to political science, and joined the left-wing Students for a Democratic Society.

The generational cycle of sin in men has been broken by Jesus. A man begins to walk in that freedom when at last he decides not to disown his father and embrace another heritage, but to claim his father's heritage as his own, for better or worse. Then, he must take his forefathers' sin to the Cross and die to the pride which fueled it. There on his knees, on the surgical altar-table, he must ask the Father God to show him what brokenness of his forefathers yet remains in himself, confessing that he cannot by his own human power set himself free from it any more than his father could. Such humble surrender teaches a man the Father God's mercy—which allows God to lead him into forgiving his forefathers, and thus break the hold of their sin upon him.

Killing your father does not make you a man, any more than it makes a white activist black. "Ours is a time not to curse the past, but to redeem it, in the true prophetic tradition," as Stanford's then Dean of the Chapel, Rev. Davie Napier, declared in 1970. The man who curses his father sacrifices his masculine heritage on the altar of his own ego. This only perpetuates the generational cycle of sin. Only surrender to the true Father can overcome wounds from the earthly fathers.

Most of us fancy that we do not forgive because we fear being vulnerable before and hurt yet again by our wounder. In reality, however, we simply do not believe, as James declared, that "mercy triumphs over judgment" (James 2:13). That is, we do not value forgiveness and see no power in it—because we have not recognized our own awful need for it enough to seek it and know its power. Thus pride not only keeps a man from seeking forgiveness himself, but from forgiving others.

Granted, you may not demonstrate every same wrong behavior as your father. But like him, you are a sinner before God, and just as much in need of God's saving power in Jesus.

"There is no difference at all," as the apostle Paul declares; "Everyone has sinned and is far away from God's saving presence. But by the free gift of God's grace all are put right with him through Christ Jesus, who sets them free" (Rom. 3:22–24).

A man must dare to face the wounds from his father and take them to the Father God through Jesus. In doing so, he will begin to see those wounds not simply "from" his father, but indeed, in and upon his father, from earlier generations. But having done so, a man must begin—as each generation of men before—not just to curse, but to build upon the history God has given him through his father, to redeem the uncompleted manhood of his heritage. That is what sons are for. We will want our own sons to do the same for us—and we will squirm in time as they discover our own uncompleteness.

Thus we had better teach our sons mercy.

A man who curses his father, therefore, curses his own manhood. Likely because this temptation of the flesh is so strong in all generations and its consequences so severe, God commands a man to honor his father "that you may live a long time in the land that I am giving you" (Ex. 20:12).

The truly revolutionary task to which the Father God has called men today is therefore not to reject your father, or even simply to forgive him. It is to forgive yourself for having loved your father idealistically and desperately as a child, so you can begin at last to love realistically and faithfully as an adult.

Too often, a man's drive to change—from political activism to religious fervor to professional ambition—becomes a desperate effort to prove "I am not like my father." A man might just as well try to prove he was never a child. Thus built on a lie, this effort only postpones his adulthood and thereby keeps him from identifying his own particular gifts and calling to foster God's kingdom of justice and peace.

The revolutionary work to which God calls men today will not be accomplished by the man who is waiting for the apologies or approval of his father, but only by the one who can accept his father as his own legitimate history. This frees him to begin the painstaking but authentic adult task of letting the Father God shape him in His image. Such humility opens the man at last to learn the Father's mercy—which restores him to authentic sonship to receive His strength to restore earth as it is in heaven.

That a man's forefathers were capable of lying to uphold their name, of defending their prejudice against the truth, of clutching after rigid standards amid whirlwind change—only reveals them to be human after all. They are not angels, but neither are they devils.

The break with the past, the revolution which brings lasting change, begins when one man dares to admit his own complicity in such human sin. This allows the Father "from whom all fatherhood in heaven and on earth derives its name" (Eph. 3:15 NIV footnote) to enter our lives and transform us at last. Sons need not panic at the revelation of their fathers' ungodliness. As human beings, we are not gods. None of us is perfect.

Finally, recognizing the sin in his heritage allows a man genuinely to let God overcome his human limitations and guide him toward a larger sense of brotherhood. Indeed, those non-poor white males who engage the Father in this growth and find that because of that limitation they cannot become what they want to be, shall finally have an authentic basis for understanding the predicament of the poor and non-white in America today.

"Parochial ethnic and community differences," as Chicano leader Eliu Carranza has stated, can only be resolved through such self-honesty. Young men commonly look to physical strength for saving power, because their youth affords them plenty of it. Men who recognize only physical power and not spiritual power cannot honor old men, who lack the former. Furthermore, young men often lack mercy because either they haven't sinned enough yet to recognize their own need for it, or they have the natural strength to run from the consequences of their sin.

The man who refuses to see the generational sin of his heritage often simply compounds it. When, for example, King Solomon's son and successor Rehoboam goes before the northern tribes of Israel to seek their allegiance, the people promise their loyalty if he will remove the oppressive burdens his father placed upon them.

Rehoboam first consults the older men who had served as his father's advisers. They tell him, "If you want to serve this people well, give a favorable answer to their request, and they will always serve you loyally" (1 Kings 12:7).

Sloughing the older men, Rehoboam goes instead to "the young men who had grown up with him," and these young hotbloods advise him quite differently, saying, "This is what you should tell them: 'My little finger is thicker than my father's waist!' Tell them, 'My father placed heavy burdens on you; I will make them even heavier. He beat you with whips; I'll flog you with bullwhips!'" (1 Kings 12:10–11). The biblical storyteller notes that the young new king "ignored the advice of the older men and spoke harshly to the people, as the younger men had advised" (vs. 13–14). Whereupon in one voice the people rise up in a revolt which destroys the United Kingdom of Israel and renders the people of God vulnerable to enemies for generations to come.

When young men break relationship with old men, nations fall.

In a segment titled, "Distrust of Older Men,"[4] Robert Bly refers to German sociologist Alexander Mitscherlich's thesis that "demons of suspicion" enter a boy when his father spends so much time away from home at work, encouraging "suspicion of all older men":

> The demons urge all young men to see *Lawrence of Arabia* and *Dead Poets Society* because they remind us of how corrupt all men in authority are and how thoroughly they betray the young male idealist. Mentorship becomes difficult to sustain; initiation is rejected. . . .
> In the next decade we can expect these demons of suspicion to cause more and more damage to men's vision of what a man is, or what the masculine is. Between 20 and 30 percent of American boys now live in a house with no father present, and the demons there have full permission to rage.[5]

In the Nigerian Igbo villages, the most honored spot at the weekly forest market is among the circle of old men. I recall one day entering the market, after having visited for a number of weeks since arriving in the village, and a young boy approached me. "The grandfathers would like to see you," he announced, smiling broadly—creating a stir among those near enough to overhear this honored invitation. The power in the moment seized me, and I followed the boy at once.

When I reached the circle of old men, one man—grey-haired but sturdy—rose with a flourish to shake my hand and welcome me. As the dozen others nodded, my host extended to me a glass of recently tapped palm wine. As I reached for it, he gestured for me to wait as he carefully spilled some on the ground. This gesture, he explained, honored the buried grandfathers of us all. Then, taking the glass carefully, I too spilled some wine on the ground to honor the men of our past, and took a swallow. The other men grunted and nodded in approval as I returned the glass. Thus I was invited to sit among the old men, and formally welcomed to the village.

In this land, so strange then to my dulled American sensibilities, old men are not merely honored—wonder of wonders!—but are acknowledged as bearing power to bestow honor upon others. Unlike in our own brave, new world, where the more "with-it" and "happening" society might occasionally deign to make room for old men, among Igbo people the old men themselves define and confer social acceptability.

Old Igbo men are not paid; they make the currency.

In America, when a man reaches the ominous age of sixty-five, he is told by his society that he is no longer capable of working, and therefore, is worthless. He is paid off, kicked out, and forgotten. Among Igbos, when a man no longer has the muscle-power to work on the farm, he becomes eligible at last to move in the dimension of real power, namely, the power of the spirit. He steeps himself in the traditions of his forefathers, and then turns to tutor the younger men—especially during the weeks-long initiation rite for boys.

In America, the older a man gets, the longer he hangs around, the more he becomes an obstruction to the young man's advancing career. Among Igbos, a man's increasing age grants him increasing authority to initiate and facilitate the younger man's calling. Not surprisingly, men in our society die soon after retiring. The new grain poisons old men.

Old women are at least valued for child care—erroneously seen among us as "a woman's job" anyhow. For our high-tech, high-powered "modern" society seeks primarily not to make men, but only to employ them.

Men dare not recognize the terrible need among boys for older men, because none have seen that need met in their own lives. Why open a wound that can't be healed—or if, indeed, the price for healing is surrender unto death to a God called "Father"?

Thus the American man is afraid to value old men. To do so would require that he confess his need for them. And the overwhelming evidence in his life is that they will not listen or respond to his need, because they have already abandoned him long ago when he was a boy.

The only hope in our society for honoring old men, for recognizing and affirming their gifts, therefore lies in the willingness of sons to grieve their loss of the father unto forgiveness. And only the Father God, who has revealed Himself among us in Jesus and is present today in His Holy Spirit, can lead a man against the flesh into that freeing mercy. No man can face the true and awful depth of his father-wound without knowing his true Father stands with him as he does. Nor can any man forgive from the heart in his own power. It is only human to avenge; to forgive is divine.

No schemes of the flesh, no humanly designed organizations, can offer the saving power men need today. The old fraternal organizations, such as the Elks and Masons, have never fostered the "brutally honest self-examination" required for genuine change, and therefore simply do not draw young men today.

A thirty-five-year-old businessman I know joined one such organization and dropped out a year later. "I thought it'd be good to know some older guys," he said. "But nobody really wanted to talk about anything really important. I hung in awhile, thinking at least it might at least be good for business—but it just got to be a waste of time. They're a bunch of old guys hanging onto another world that's long gone, and maybe never was real."

And what, then, of the church?

The common instance of older women's staffing the prayer chains and committees while the older men sit at home or occasionally water the church lawn, has been challenged boldly by Trinity Lutheran Church in San Pedro, California, in their "Caleb Corps." Biblically modeled on the fit and faithful eighty-five-year-old Caleb, the program recruits older men as mentors in the congregation.

A flyer decorated with baseball action pictures bears the headline: "Calling all veterans: Get back out with the players!":[6]

> One of the toughest decisions of a baseball player is knowing when to retire. He has loved the game but lacks the drive he felt a decade ago. He knows the game as well as ever but he is slowing down. . . . Many view retirement as the step just before the grave.
> What is the alternative?

Making coaches out of the many who have served so well in the Church and still have energy and vision. They have what the younger players lack—experience. The only way you get this is with time and output. Experience gives the veterans perspective, wisdom, and balance. The young ballplayers have talent, courage, and enthusiasm, but they lack the qualities that only come with time.

Acknowledging that "the church has not done a good job of either using its experienced players as coaches or bringing on those ready for the starting team," the pamphlet emphasizes "the need for development of personal relationships between the older and the younger":

Young people need the encouragement that can come from a solid friendship with one who has taken some risks they will take and made some mistakes they no doubt will too. They need the exhortation to stick with it. They need to hear the gentle rebukes from someone who has won the right to speak the truth in love. Too few have had that privilege, but those who have, know it to be a motivator of growth. The disciples knew it, men like Timothy and Titus experienced it, and those today who are given that kind of loving spiritual reinforcement will be like them.

Significantly, the pamphlet declares that "the coaches are like fathers fathering fathers."

Ministries listed on the back for Caleb Corps members range from visiting home-bound, hospitalized, or imprisoned persons to tutoring schoolchildren and helping with the inner-city food co-op. "When a man in the congregation retires, we give him one week," one member declared. "Then three or four of us are on his doorstep, calling on him to come out and minister with the rest of us that day."

Men in the church must reach out to the young boys to call them forth into the fellowship of men. But without a parallel reaching out to the older men, such an effort is tainted with a shade of dishonesty. The boys are safer. They ostensibly need us; we are the givers. To reach out to the boys may cost us a few hours of time here and there, but it basically affirms us, and protects our defenses.

But we ourselves need the old men. To reach out to them will cost us as much as we have invested in a self-image of defensive independence—which, for most men, is plenty, if not life itself.

I believe the finest a man can receive from a boy is not affirmation, but rejuvenation. Years ago at the age of thirty-five, I took my fatherless eight-year-old nephew out one afternoon. I asked what he'd like to do, offering him a movie, dinner . . . ? No. He'd seen another kid with a rubber-band wind-up balsa wood plane. Could we get some?

I balked, suggested a cops-and-robbers movie, and threw in a milk shake. But he would not forget the model planes. So off to Woolworth's we went, and bought two of the seventy-five-cent deluxe models. We took them to a nearby field, fit the wings together, and wound up the rubber bands to the propellers. Perhaps an hour of circles, banks, and spectacular crash landings later, as I was challenging the boy to see if he could loop his plane over a nearby tree limb, he paused and said matter-of-factly, "You didn't want to do this at first, did you, Uncle Gordon? But now you're really having fun, aren't you?"

I hesitated in mid-launch—and blushed. "Yeah . . ." I said finally. Quickly, I re-issued my challenge, and we were off and playing again—as I had not played for many years.

To receive from a boy, a man starts out doing for the boy. But to learn from an old man, a man must let the old man be for him. Even as he longs for it, today's unfathered man cannot readily receive from old men. But he must stay open.

At the end of a retreat, I was praying from the microphone for perhaps a hundred men between twenty and fifty, and I sensed that God was saying to them, "My son, I'm proud of you. You've sacrificed your pride, pushed through your fear of other men, and come here trusting Me."

When I said that into the microphone, a strange stillness settled over the men. I waited, then invited responses. Slowly, a man in his mid-thirties raised his hand. "When you said, 'My son, I'm proud of you,' it . . . just didn't register," he said, a confused sadness in his voice. "It sounded strange, even weird."

Glancing around the room, I saw the same confused sadness in a hundred men's eyes. "I'm going to say it again," I said gently, but firmly, "because I believe that's what the Father is saying. And I encourage you to write it out and stick it on your mirror at home."

Gil, a successful forty-year-old lawyer, told me about having lunch with a sixty-year-old grey-haired senior partner in his firm. At one point in the conversation, the older man matter-of-factly mentioned a praiseworthy accomplishment of one junior partner about Gil's age.

"Suddenly, I felt something sharp rise up in the pit of my stomach," he said. "I'm embarrassed to say it, but I felt jealous. Sure, I've gotten my own awards and all from the professional associations, but hearing that old man sitting in front of me praising some other guy my age just grabbed something in me."

I did what I had to do. "Did you ever hear your dad say he was proud of you?"

Gil looked down, shook his head. "No."

A younger man may wish it were not so, feel embarrassed by it, resent and fear it. But old men have power to lift young men up.

And in this fast-paced modern society filled with the new grain, a young man's respect and appreciation can lift up an old man. During break time at a retreat, a short, barrel-chested man with grey hair and sparkling blue eyes came up to me. "I'm almost seventy," he declared, shaking my hand vigorously, "and I really appreciate what you're saying. For a long time after I retired, I thought I was washed up. But then I got involved in this Head Start program—you know, going to help out with the little kids."

He flashed a wide grin. "Why, just this morning I went over there to the center, and when I walked in the room, all those kids dropped their crayons and paints and came running over to me. I had two or three with their arms wrapped around my legs, tugging on my trousers, while the others jumped around all happy. I'm telling you, there weren't many days I went to the office I could feel that good!"

Such vitality in old men recalls the story of the eighty-year-old who visited his doctor with a pain in his right leg. "Of course, at your age, you just have to expect such things," the doctor said; "after all, that leg's eighty years old."

"My left leg's eighty years old and it's just fine!" huffed the old man—and got another doctor.

Harry, thirty-eight, told me his father has always lived about twenty miles from him, and he had spent years grieving for the emotional distance between them. Not long ago, the father—a former businessman now in his mid-sixties—called him. Expecting some business at hand, the younger man was astonished at what he heard.

"I'm not getting any younger," Harry's father said. "I'd like to spend some more time together, and get to know each other better. What would you say about maybe scheduling in once a month just for the two of us to have lunch or something?"

Harry had already yielded up his father-wound to Jesus, and had therefore been able to forgive his father and stay open amid his pain rather than close himself off in anger or rejection. He was therefore quick to find his calendar and sweep it clean for those monthly father-son times.

The "new grain" today makes us believe that the goal in life is to get younger. Television and magazine ads tout wrinkle-free, hard-bodied, energetic youth. What's "new" sells. A diabolical corollary to this belief is the youth-culture emphasis on "now," and its implicit denigration of history as well as future. The young man-of-the world's password to freedom is that the past is "dead and gone." Most say, "I don't care what happens; let the Devil take tomorrow." But response-able behavior requires history, that is, a sense of position within a larger continuum to which we must respond.

Yes, we live only in the present. But time is real; we have a history, live in and struggle with its consequences, and thus shape our future. Yet amid life's myriad uncertainties, clearly every one of us will be "old" some day. If only as a critical investment in our own eventual welfare, we must begin learning to bestow honor upon old men.

A man old enough to be reading this book is old enough not only to have suffered life's wounds deeply enough to seek healing, but to anticipate aging himself. Let this be an occasion for us not to gulp the new grain, sever ourselves from our history in old men, and despair, but rather, to face honestly our need for old men and the Father God of the history we share.

CHAPTER THIRTEEN

The Commandment To Remember

To portray the tragic loss of masculine heritage today, at retreats I invite men in the first small-group exercise to introduce themselves to each other like this: "I'm *(your full name),* son of *(your father's full name),* grandson of *(his father's full name),* great-grandson of . . . etc." Typically, about seventy percent of the men know their paternal grandfather's name, but barely ten percent know their paternal great-grandfather's name. Significantly, the percentages are often higher for knowing the mother's line.

"I was stunned," one man who did not know his father's father's name told me, "to think that my boy's son wouldn't know my name."

Stuffed with the "new grain," men today must realize that this severing from the men of our past is virtually unprecedented in human history. Never has a society of men been so cut off from their masculine heritage.

Significantly, the New Testament opens with Matthew's "list of the ancestors of Jesus Christ, a descendant of David, who was a descendant of Abraham," naming explicitly forty-two generations (see Matt. 1:1–17).

Years ago, upon entering seminary, I decided to start at the very beginning and take a "History of the Jews" course from Rabbi Murray Rothman, then of Temple Shalom in West Newton, Massachusetts. On the first day, he declared that "Judaism is the only religion with a commandment to remember," pointing to Deuteronomy 8:2 as a model: "Remember how the Lord your God led you on this long journey through the desert these past forty years."

In the movie *Norma Rae,* a young woman working in a southern textile mill organizes the other workers with the help of a labor organizer from New York, who is Jewish. In one scene, when victory is assured and the organizing staff has left to celebrate, Norma Rae turns to her benefactor, with whom she has shared rich moments of play, deep thought, and hard work. "You're Jewish, aren't you?" she asks, puzzled.

He nods—whereupon she tells him she's confused, because he looks pretty much like everyone else.

Laughing good-naturedly, he asks if she thought maybe he should have horns or something.

"What makes you different?" she persists.

He pauses thoughtfully for a moment, and then offers a short, but powerful answer: "History, I guess."

As God commands His chosen people,

> Tear down their [pagan] altars . . . and burn their idols. Do this because you belong to the Lord your God. From all the peoples on earth he chose you to be his own special people. The Lord did not love you and choose you because you outnumbered other peoples; you were the smallest nation on earth. But the Lord loved you and wanted to keep the promise that he made to your ancestors. That is why he saved you by his great might and set you free from slavery to the king of Egypt. Remember that the Lord your God is the only God and that he is faithful. (Deut. 7:5, 6–9)

The God we worship reveals Himself primarily not in nature, wise sayings, metaphysical consciousness, or even rituals, but in history, through His acts in human affairs. Even nature points back to God's creating the world, and rituals—such as communion and its link to the Exodus Passover meal unto the Crucifixion—point to something God has done in history. Those who worship the God of Israel—and Jesus—therefore testify to His existence, love, and power by proclaiming what He has done in their lives, precisely so God's purposes may continue to be fulfilled in the future.

As the psalmist declared,

> Write down for the coming generation what the Lord has done so that people not yet born will praise him. (Ps. 102:18)

And so God commands His people,

> In the future, when your son asks you, "What is the meaning of the stipulations, decrees and laws the Lord our God has commanded you?" tell him: "We were slaves of Pharaoh in Egypt, but the Lord brought us out of Egypt with a mighty hand. Before our eyes the Lord sent miraculous signs and wonders—great and terrible—upon Egypt and Pharaoh and his whole household. But he brought us out from there to bring us in and

give us the land that he promised on oath to our forefathers. The Lord commanded us to obey all these decrees and to fear the Lord our God, so that we might always prosper and be kept alive, as is the case today. And if we *are* careful to obey all this law before the Lord our God, as he has commanded us, that *will be* our righteousness. (Deut. 6:20–24 NIV, italics added)

How do you answer your son when he asks you, "Daddy, why do we pray and go to church and try to do things like God wants us to?" Will you be able to tell him what God has done in his past, because you remember God's work in your own?

A man's character is revealed in his actions. We therefore know the Father God's character by remembering His acts in our past. The thrust of the biblical faith is not to trust in the future—which, in this broken world, is always uncertain—but to trust in the Father God, who is Lord of all time.

The Christian man who has not honestly and humbly submitted his father-wound to Jesus cannot distinguish between his earthly father and the Father God. Without an expressed relationship, he may say, "I know my father loved me"—if only out of his desperate longing to see that love borne out in hugs, words, and actions. Similarly, in only one-way interaction with God, he can read the Bible, commit his life to Jesus, and cite his ultimate future in the Father God: "I know I'm going to heaven."

But for such a man, daily life in this world can remain a painful, lonely confusion. Confessing your destiny in this world and discerning your unique calling while alive, requires give-and-take interaction with the Father God here and now. Blind faith and memorized Bible passages—however helpful at times—cannot substitute for relationship with the Father. It's one thing to say, "I know I'm going to heaven because the Bible promises that to anyone who gives his life to Jesus," but quite another to say, "I know I'll always be in my Father's hands, because He's always been doing things in my life, and we talk it over together all the time."

And so Jesus, when He was on the brink of death, did not smile blissfully and quote reassuring scriptures, but rather, sweat blood and shouted out to His Father the agonizing question of Psalm 22:1, "Why did you leave me here alone to die?"

That's trust in the Father, not in the future.

That's relationship with your Father, not religion.

Hence, in his farewell address as the people begin at last to occupy the Promised Land, Joshua does not give the people of God a five-year plan for the future. Rather, he inspires new faith for the monumental task ahead by reminding them of what God has done in their past, even in this as-yet-unconquered land of Canaan. Gathering the tribes together at Shechem, he proclaims God's word to them:

> Long ago your ancestors lived on the other side of the Euphrates River and worshiped other gods. One of those ancestors was Terah, the father of Abraham and Nahor. Then I took Abraham, your ancestor, from the land across the Euphrates and led him through the whole land of Canaan. (Josh. 24:2–3)

After reviewing God's saving acts in their common history—the exodus from slavery in Egypt, the crossing of the Red Sea, the defeat of Jericho and other cities—Joshua then commands the people to "decide today whom you will serve" (v. 15). Uplifted, the people replied, "We would never leave the Lord to serve other gods!" (v. 16).

Once aware of their history, the people of God remember whose they are and, therefore, where they are going: children of the Father God—who has promised to restore them to a land of their own and who has demonstrated He is faithful by His saving acts in their past. Knowing thereby the Father's faithful character, frees men of God to their future, that is, to be faithful to Him in return.

The average man today, however, does not know his history. Consequently, he is confused about where he is going, and fearful that he may not get there. As one Christian college professor declared, "I wept during my year of teaching undergraduates as I came to terms with how few of my 260 or so students had any sense of themselves as truly special, as gifted, or as people of destiny and vocation."[1]

We ask God, Where am I going with my life? What is my purpose? Will I fulfill it? and the God of the biblical faith answers, "Remember." Translation: "More than to know your future, I want you to know your Father. And you will know Me by the things I've done. If you now engage Me in relationship—talk to Me, listen to Me, cry, shout, ask Me questions, trust Me—the rest will follow."

Seek first the Kingdom of God, the place where the Father God rules as King. Seek to let Him have all power and authority in your life. To focus on the future, as suggested in an earlier chapter, is to seek a fortune teller, not a Father—and the Enemy stands ready to mislead any man who thereby allows his fears to close off his trust in God.

That is, the future which God has planned for us unfolds precisely insofar as we are faithful to what He has done for us in the past. As another has noted, the biblical faith moves us into the future much like rowing a boat: fixed on our ultimate destination, but facing to the rear and gauging direction with landmarks passed.

We are naturally concerned about our future. But until we have confessed His work in our past, the Father can only tell us, "You haven't recognized what I've already done for you; how then can you see what I'm going to do?" Any parent knows how to deal with children like us: "You haven't appreciated what I've already given you; how can you ask me for more?"

No man can become an authentic leader, either in his family or his community, without a sense of vision for the future. But the biblical faith understands that leadership is not gathering people to follow you in your own plan, but helping people recognize and surrender to what the Father God is doing among them. Thus Jesus tells his followers, "Nor should you be called 'Leader,' because your one and only leader is the Messiah" (Matt. 23:10). To recognize God's fingerprints and footprints, a man must know the character of the Father—which is revealed in history, both his own and that of those he would lead.

This does not mean that a man is held captive by his past—at least, no more than a tree is held captive by its roots. He may wish he did not have his particular father or cultural background. But, however painful, these are the soil in which he has been planted, the crucible in which he has been placed to learn and offer the fruits of forgiveness, grace, and commitment in this world. By thus engaging his history faithfully, a man discovers himself at last as a son of the Father God.

Certainly, a locomotive can travel faster without cars behind it, but when the trip is finished, it has little to show for its efforts. Moses was safe in the Pharaoh's palace and family, but when he saw a Hebrew slave being mistreated by an Egyptian foreman, he remembered his own Hebrew blood, and lashed out and killed the oppressor. After running, he was safe in the desert with his new wife and wise father-in-law, far from Egypt, where he was wanted for murder.

But the God who had saved Moses in the past, even as a baby in the bulrushes, called him to return to his own people and lead them. And in that bond with his history and the God who had shaped it, Moses fulfilled his destiny as a man.

Your authenticity as a man is comprised of what you have allowed the Father God to do in your life. In order to fulfill your destiny, your calling, you must know that you belong to the Father.

When I was a boy about ten or eleven, I had some friends who began staying out after dark and running around the neighborhood. This sounded like great fun to me, and they all said their fathers didn't mind.

So I went to my father and asked if I, too, could stay out and play at night. To my surprise, he said no.

Of course, I protested that my friends' fathers all had said it was okay for them; why, then, was it wrong for me?

"Because you are my son and not theirs," my father said simply. "I know those boys, and sooner or later, they're going to get into trouble. I don't want you to be a part of that" (see Amos 3:2).

Jonah offers a graphic biblical illustration of a man who flees his identity in God, and in the process of returning becomes shaped for his destiny. The very first verses burst forth with the story's premise:

> One day the Lord spoke to Jonah son of Amittai. He said, "Go to Nineveh, that great city, and speak out against it; I am aware of how wicked its people are." Jonah, however, set out in the opposite direction in order to get away from the Lord. (Jonah 1:1–3a)

The Father has called His son Jonah to the terrifying task of speaking out against Israel's deadly enemy Assyria—not in Israel, where he might be cheered, but in the enemy's own stronghold, its capital city!

We can understand Jonah's balking, but wish he would trust the Father enough to express his feelings and argue it out with Him. For we know that, when a man thus turns from relationship with the Father, death lurks ahead.

Jonah runs from the Father's call, boarding a ship headed for Spain with men from many countries aboard. When God sends a storm against the boat, the men pray to their various gods, to no avail—until finally they are led to Jonah, who is forced to confess to them who he is: "I am a Hebrew . . . I worship the Lord, the God of heaven, who made land and sea" (Jonah 1:9).

As the ship threatens to capsize, the story suggests that when the man of God refuses to confess who/whose he is before men and move faithfully in the Father's call, other men pay for it, even with their lives.

Jonah tells the men to throw him overboard, since the storm has risen because of his unfaithfulness to his God. Reluctantly, the men do so; at once, the sea calms, and God commands the whale to swallow Jonah.

Deep in the belly of the monster, Jonah is forced to realize that he has no life but what God has given him. At last, he surrenders—whereupon God orders the fish to deposit the prophet on the Assyrian shore.

Listen to the story: Do men today still run from the Father's call and flee their destiny, forcing God to send us into the storm and monster's belly to confess Him and remember who we are? Might a divorce, job layoff, illness, or other severe loss become such a crucible?

Now listen to how the Father God shapes Jonah's destiny in his particular crucible:

> Once again the Lord spoke to Jonah. He said, "Go to Nineveh, that great city, and proclaim to the people the message I have given you." So Jonah obeyed the Lord and went to Nineveh, *a city so large that it took three days to walk through it*. Jonah started through the city, and *after walking a whole day,* he proclaimed, "In forty days Nineveh will be destroyed!" (Jonah 3:1–4, italics added)

Jonah does not begin to proclaim his dangerous message until he is a whole day's journey into the city, that is, so deep into the belly of the Assyrian monster that he cannot escape. Only one kind of man would undertake such a do-or-die mission, namely, one who had already been in the belly of a monster and discovered there the saving hand of God. That is, the man's past suffering and trial has surfaced his identity in the Lord and shaped him quite specifically and appropriately for his calling, his vocation, his destiny.

Two points determine a straight line. If you want a better sense of God's purpose in your life, look back over your past and pick two or three major struggles or turning points in your life. Can you see any common thread or theme in what you have learned? What gifts were being drawn forth in you? Can you extrapolate from this, as if to extend the line through and beyond the points of your past, and sense what tasks the Father has been shaping you to perform today? Talk it over with Him.

The world says that a man's mistakes and brokenness disqualify and make him unworthy. This judgment compels him to repress and forget them at all costs—to overwork, drink, smoke, chase women, run from all wounds. The Cross, however, proclaims that nothing qualifies a man for God's service, reveals his created purpose in life, and frees him to his destiny and calling in this world, except brokenness surrendered to the Father. Just as my father forbade me to roam the neighborhood at night with my boyhood friends, the Father God is calling to His sons today, "Remember who you are!"

At first glance, these words seem contradictory. Remember means to focus on the past; doesn't God mean, instead, "Remember who you were"?

No. Because who we are is what God has done.

In the Last Supper, Jesus commands His followers to eat the Host "in memory of me" (Luke 22:19). Is He saying here that at communion today, He wants us merely to bring into our minds a thought of Him, even as we might in nostalgia remember last year's office picnic?

Rather, I believe Jesus is calling us as my mother would tell me, "Remember your grandmother on her birthday." I knew what she meant: not simply to let a thought of Grandma come into my mind for a moment, but to recall the many times Grandma did nice things for me, and therefore, to send a card, make a phone call, buy her a gift. The biblical commandment to remember is not just a mental exercise, but a commitment to act now based on how God has acted in your past.

If we look at a man's bloodline as a chain through history, his father is the closest link. The man's father guards the gateway to his masculine heritage; he cannot pass into that heritage—connect with it, celebrate it, draw upon, or extrapolate from it—without relating to Dad. The father and all uncomfortable feelings associated with him cannot be circumvented; he is the most important link in the chain of a man's masculine heritage, without which a man remains unlinked to his manhood, lost and adrift in the present.

Alex, whose father died when he was a boy, heard many stories from his mother about how "kind and good" his father had been. In high school, he liked P.E. wrestling, and decided to go out for the school wrestling team—but performed half-heartedly. One day, his uncle happened to mention that his father had been an amateur boxer as a young man. Though no world champion, nevertheless the father had never been knocked down, because, as the uncle put it, "he just would never give up."

This was the masculine view of his father that Alex needed.

By the end of his four-year wrestling career in high school, the son had lost his share of matches by points, but had never been pinned. "I just couldn't get that idea of Dad out of my mind," Alex told me. "No matter how hard a wrestling match got, I just wouldn't give up, ever."

For most men today, however, forging the father-link beckons considerable pain and fear. Unless he knows the Father God and His determination to heal men, the wounded man will readily reject his father. He will try to forge his own identity—not realizing that in doing so, he has cut himself off from his masculine heritage and the avenue to his true identity. Later, he wonders why he feels so insecure, so cut off from other men, so unable to feel as if he belongs in this world, and thus, so lacking a sense of destiny in his life.

Some men cannot move through the father-wound toward their destiny because they are anchored to their need for Dad's approval.

The late pop singer Marvin Gaye is a tragic example. Writer Chip Brown tells the story in an article, "Do We All Become Our Fathers?"

> When . . . negotiating to re-sign with Motown, [Gaye] demanded a million-dollar bonus, requesting that it be delivered in cash in a briefcase. He wanted the money, he told a friend, "so I can take it to my father and say, 'See that? That's a million dollars. I just want you to know how successful I am.'" He didn't get the million, and he died by his father's hand, shot to death during an argument. Would a million have made a difference?[2]

A man wants his father's approval so desperately because his father is literally in him, whether he likes it or not, and he needs to make peace with that part of himself. For better or worse, Brown therefore notes,

> There is hardly a man who has not marked a moment when he recognizes his father in himself. He catches himself thinking like his father, acting like him, feeling like him. Little gestures, tiny habits. . . . More often than not, it comes as a shock . . . for the vast majority of men have problems with their fathers.[3]

The mystery of feeling your father in you hints at the greater mystery of the Father God's longing to fill men with His Spirit. The worldly man, however, cannot make that connection. His secular vocabulary will not allow him to see a son's longing to be one with his father as beckoning the Father God.

Writer Brown therefore struggles in confusion as he describes his growing sense of similarity to his own father. "We may be our father's antithesis on one level," he says, "only to uncover his likeness on another, the sense of being part of a larger design, the instrument of some cultural or genetic force that transcends generations."[4]

He even reaches a clear point of humility, confessing, "I cling to the idea that I am self-invented, that I rise and fall on my own authority. And yet when I see my father, the conceit is shattered. I am in relation to a man. His legacy flows into me."[5]

But he cannot break spiritually from his earthly father to grasp his proper destiny as a son of the Father God. "What's most haunting," he concludes, "is the spiritual sense that my fate is rehearsed in his. As my father gets older, his attachment to the world grows simpler, purer, less concerned with what he can create than with what exists. Already, I hear that echo in myself. I peer at the road ahead. The dark hour that rushes toward him rushes toward us both."[6]

All the secular programs in the current "men's movement" today ultimately reach this spiritual impasse. Robert Bly, for example, can portray the father-wound brilliantly and draw forth the grief. His drums, the dancing, the shouting, can tap a natural, hitherto unrecognized strength in a man. Lacking authentic "re-ligion," however, he cannot "re-connect" a man to the true Father of all men, even Dad. Only Jesus can do that, in men who surrender to Him.

Sadly, the historic Church has sought to cover up the father-wound by portraying Jesus as feminine, complete with long silky hair, white uncalloused hands, and a dress. The largely anti-Christian leaders of the current men's movement have predictably seized upon this caricature. Christians, therefore, dare not judge Bly for declaring that the key to strength in manhood cannot be found "in the force field of an Asian guru or even . . . of a gentle Jesus."[7]

Like most men today, Bly has searched our so-called "Christian culture" in vain for guideposts to authentic manhood. But—or perhaps, therefore—he has not surrendered to Jesus, and thus cannot know the Father. And so, understandably, he turns not to the Bible, but to the ancient pagan myths, because "mythology helps to give weight to our private wounds"[8]—wounds, that is, which the Church has largely ignored and given no weight at all. Thus men simply don't bother with churches, and either stuff the pain and wreak destruction, or go instead to secular spokesmen like Bly for healing.

Exegeting myths and fairy tales as his holy texts, Bly draws forth truths remarkably relevant to men's wounds. His truths, however, are so remarkable not because—as he implies—the Bible simply lacks witness to such truth, but because no Christian men have dared look honestly enough at their wounds to seek those truths in the Bible. Bly is telling men's story as no Christian has. But all that he says—and far more to heal men's wounds—can be drawn from the biblical accounts of God's acts in human history.

For example, in a chapter titled, "The Road of Ashes, Descent, and Grief," Bly declares that an essential step in masculine development is what the Greeks called "katabasis," that is, for the "golden boy" to lose his charmed life of comfort and affirmation, and "sink through the floor" into "a mean life of ordinariness, heaviness, silences, cracks in the road, weightiness, and soberness . . .":

> There is something more than a little frightening about this Drop. Our ego doesn't want to do it and even if we drop, the ego doesn't want to see it. . . .
> When "katabasis" happens, a man no longer feels like a special person. He is not. One day he is in college, being fed and housed—often on someone else's money—protected by brick walls men long dead have

built, and the next day he is homeless, walking the streets, looking for some way to get a meal and a bed. People know immediately when you are falling or have fallen: doormen turn their backs, waiters sneer, no one holds the subway car door for you, . . .

We remember Oedipus in his katabasis: one day an arrogant, demanding king, the next a blind man led around by others.[9]

Even the most biblically ignorant man knows that Jesus died on a cross mocked by the authorities, rejected by His own people and abandoned by His followers. The entire thrust of the biblical faith, from the Fall in Genesis to slavery in Egypt to the Babylonian Exile to the Cross to persecution in the early Church is a chronicle of God's people's being thrust into crushing defeat as a means or pathway to the Promised Land, Resurrection, and abundant life in the Holy Spirit.

So Oedipus was blinded into humility? Big deal. What about God's blinding the apostle Paul for refusing His call (Acts 9:1–19) and then restoring his sight to preach God's salvation to humankind for all time? Any man who dares to remember his need for the Father God and trust Him enough to seek historical confirmation of His healing love in the Bible, can find therein stories far superseding the pagan myths in human insight, healing power, and revelation of destiny.

Why then, do men raised in a country filled with churches, flock to hear Robert Bly talk about Oedipus and "katabasis," instead of to hear Christian men talk about Jesus and the Cross?

Because the men of God, who have read God's stories in the Bible, have not dared walk themselves in those stories, and thus do not know what they're talking about—that is, have not surrendered to the Father God and let Him lead them into their own "katabasis"/belly-of-the-monster/cross to starve and kill their pride.

Men respect honesty, integrity. If you're going to tell me to follow a God who dies on a cross, I want to see the scars in your palms. And I want to see in your own life example not a model of perfection, but rather, what it's like to engage this "Father God" in relationship.

Again, from a fairy tale, Robert Bly draws the redemptive truth that "we have to regard as a gift" any wound that drives us to seek healing, and contrasts this with the lies of the world:

Men are taught over and over when they are boys that a wound that hurts is shameful. A wound that stops you from continuing to play is a girlish wound. He who is truly a man keeps walking, dragging his guts behind.

Our story gives a teaching diametrically opposite. It says that where a man's wound is, that is where his genius will be. Wherever the wound appears in our psyches, whether from alcoholic father, shaming mother, shaming father, abusing mother, whether it stems from isolation, disability or disease, that is precisely the place for which we will give our major gift to the community.[10]

Is this not the direct, life-upending, life-renewing message of Jesus, namely, that the true life of meaning, the Resurrection to glory, requires the Cross of death to self—in every man's life, that we discover our calling and destiny insofar as we surrender our lives to God? (Rom.12:1–2).

God will judge Christian men—not a Robert Bly—for depreciating His acts in history. Jesus never spoke against the pagan Romans, but reserved his judgment for God's people—who from their history of God's acting among them should know better. Indeed, however ultimately ineffective his efforts at healing, Bly is an intelligent, sensitive, gifted man. God has tried with only limited success to get Christian men to live and tell His story. Bly is doing that better than most Christian men today, for the considerable truth he speaks can only come from the Living God.

Indeed, the leaders in the men's movement today are insightful enough to know that authentic masculinity requires a spiritual life-view. Here is the great danger, the fork in the road at which men of God must begin to take the lead: that because the secular spokesmen reject Jesus, they reject the Father God (Luke 10:16). In their spiritual journey, therefore, they must eventually mislead men into false and manifestly destructive powers. They look not to the Father God's acts in human history for witness to healing truth, but to pagan myths and fairy tales—which can well reveal the heart of a man, but not the character of the Father who created him. Their goal is relating to yourself better, not walking in full relationship with your Father God.

John Bradshaw is another fine secular writer and lecturer whose work has helped many men struggling with shame and fear. Once a Catholic priest, he nevertheless eschews a Christ-centered perspective. As one Christian psychologist remarked after hearing Bradshaw's teaching on healing father-wounds, "He portrays the wound well, even understands the need for self-honesty, forgiveness, and surrender. But he ends up embracing himself; he just doesn't know who to surrender to."

Do we Christian men?

While the secular movement forges ahead, the Church remains in a polarized limbo. The mainline "liberal/universalist" churches refuse to call God "Father" for fear of appearing sexist; the evangelical/fundamentalists rigidly demand God be called "Father" because "the Bible says so," and the pentecostal/charismatics are too often "dominated by the desire . . . to have their felt spiritual, emotional or physical needs satisfied, or by the pursuit of charismatic power" instead of "obedience to the universal purpose and will of the Father."[11]

The leaders of the secular men's movement, meanwhile, cannot tell us who we are, because they cannot remind us Whose we are. To know that you are a son of the Father God, it is not enough simply to yield to "katabasis" and trust some natural process of growth; you must yield to Jesus and trust the Father who acts in history to restore men as His sons.

This takes tremendous courage—the kind that no milquetoast "gentle Jesus" could conjure. Putting His life on the line before the arrogant secular authorities, the self-righteous religious leaders, and His own cowardly followers, required far more than mere gentleness. Sweating blood in the garden at night, Jesus begged off; He prayed three times, when His followers abandoned Him in their fear and slept. He was naturally terrified, but He pushed through His fear to do what He had been called to do, because He knew His history and His destiny in the Father.

Christian men today must rescue Jesus from Christianity. That is, regardless of how men of the past have twisted the faith to avoid facing the father-wound, Jesus Himself remains the avenue to a man's authentic heritage and destiny in the Father God.

Today's secular "men's movement," therefore, is really an imperfect reflection of "the Father God's movement among men." It stirs with the ancient longing of a Father proclaiming amnesty and crying out, "Come back!" to sons who have turned away from Him to the path of death. It does not proclaim that men are politically oppressed or otherwise disenfranchised, but rather, wounded unto death—and thus, blinded to our true calling as men.

A wounded animal lashes out dangerously. If the deep and genuine wound in men today is not taken seriously in the church—that is, named clearly and brought diligently to the Father God for healing—men can only continue displacing their pain destructively onto others.

This book is not designed for men seeking techniques, "principles of manhood," or any other Band-Aid, quick-fix solution to specific problems. Rather, I have aimed here at men seeking genuine transformation, that is, who have given up on the question, "How can I do it right?" and have begun at last to cry out, "Who will save me when I can only do it wrong?"—like the apostle Paul in Romans 7:24.

I have sought not to portray "right action," but rather, the loving Father God and the relationship which He has been offering men in Jesus for two thousand years. I have therefore focused on the problem Jesus came to address: not men's destructive behavior, but the deeper problem of which that is but a symptom, namely, broken relationship with the Father God—reflected in and exacerbated by broken relationship with the earthly father.

In a 1990 "Tonight Show," host Johnny Carson noted that guest Burt Reynolds had so often been cast in strong, manly roles. What, Carson therefore asked him, is a real man?

"You're not a man 'til your father says you're a man," Reynolds replied.

Lacking a spiritual perspective—having forgotten the Father God—Reynolds can only declare that salvation lies in the earthly father, who retains ultimate power to confirm manhood. To the extent that a man lives in the natural realm, without memory of the Father God, he will believe that.

In fact, most men today will never hear their fathers say "You're a man," simply because Dad never heard that from his own father, has not listened for it from the Father God, and therefore, doesn't know how to say it. In the face of such profound loss, the man who has forgotten the Father God can only seek someone else to confirm his manhood: the woman, the gang, the boss, the team, even his own son.

Since no man wholly transcends the natural realm until he meets Jesus in death, every man will carry a portion of the father-wound with him in this present life—which will draw him into the arms of either Death or the Father God. That is, a generation so severely cut off from the earthly father's blessing will either burn out unto death chasing false substitutes, or give up at last to the true Father. Thus, even as the Father God wounded His Son on the cross, the earthly father-wound becomes the avenue to salvation among men today, the pain which forces men to choose life or death (Deut. 30), and thereby, to know the Father God from whom all life comes.

When a man gives up on his own energies and surrenders to Jesus, he becomes not just "a man," not even his own man, but a true son at last, eligible to receive the inheritance of the Father God's very Spirit. Thus the apostle Paul declares,

> To show that you are his sons, God sent the Spirit of his Son into our hearts, the Spirit who cries out, "Father, my Father." So then, you are no longer a slave but a son. And since you are his son, God will give you all that he has for his sons. (Gal. 4:6–7)

This reality does not instantly transform the man so that all his problems go away; rather, it makes him eligible at last to call upon the Father confidently to come and heal him from past wounds, strengthen him in present ones, and walk thereby with him in future ones.

I have tried herein to demonstrate a genuine respect for men, trusting that most of us know all too well how disobedient and sinful we are, and don't need anyone else commanding us to be obedient or moral. Such Pharisaic religion is the worst form of male-bashing, namely, kicking a man when he's down (Matt. 23:24).

We know we're broken, weak, and lost—and those of us who haven't faced that yet are simply not ready to be healed. What we have forgotten is that we have a Father who loves us, who has come in Jesus to pour out the mercy that not only "triumphs over judgment" (James 2:13), but allows men to receive the Father's own Spirit, and thereby be transformed at last.

God is not, as Freud once scoffed, simply "a father substitute," but the true Father we long for. Indeed, we forget this precisely insofar as we naturally make the earthly father a God-substitute. To see God accurately, we must see our fathers accurately—for better or worse. But in order to let go of Dad as saving idol—to see Dad as human and God as true Father—a man must become human enough to remember his own sinful condition and the Father who has come in Jesus to save him from its deadly effects.

Thus, as for thousands of years, the Father God is even now calling men to Himself and to His purposes in this broken world.

And thus the apostle Paul knelt "before the Father, from whom all fatherhood in heaven and on earth derives its name" (Eph. 3:14–15 NIV footnote) and offered this benediction for us all:

I ask God from the wealth of his glory to give you power through his Spirit to be strong in your inner selves, and I pray that Christ will make his home in your hearts through faith. I pray that you may have your roots and foundation in love, so that you, together with all God's people, may have the power to understand how broad and long, how high and deep, is Christ's love. Yes, may you come to know his love—although it can never be fully known—and so be completely filled with the very nature of God.

To him who by means of his power working in us is able to do so much more than we can ever ask for, or even think of: to God be the glory in the church and in Christ Jesus for all time, forever and ever! (Eph. 3:16–21)

Amen.

Notes

Introduction.
1. Marvin R. Wilson, *Our Father Abraham* (Grand Rapids, MI: Eerdmans, 1989), 56–7.

Chapter 1.
1. Elie Wiesel, *Souls on Fire* (New York: Random House, 1972), 202.
2. Roosevelt Grier, *Rosy's Needlepoint for Men* (New York: Walker & Co., 1973).
3. Richard Rohr, "A Man's Approach to God," tape series produced by St. Anthony Messenger Press, Cincinnati, OH.
4. Paul Ciotti, "How Fathers Figure," *Los Angeles Times Magazine,* June 18, 1989, 10.
5. Rohr, tape series.
6. Robert Carmichael, "Is the Price Too High? Payment for Playing Football Can Be Debilitating Injuries, Lingering Physical Problems," *Los Angeles Times,* January 1, 1992.
7. Associated Press, "Chang Follows Instructions in 6–1, 6–1 Victory," *Los Angeles Times,* August 15, 1989, C8.
8. Ciotti, 10.

Chapter 2.
1. Robert Bly, *Iron John* (Reading, MS: Addison-Wesley, 1990), 93.
2. Scott Ostler, "Canseco Really Appreciates a Good Bash, Even One by Gibson," *Los Angeles Times,* October 16, 1988, III–6.
3. "Can Homosexuals Change?" *Christianity Today,* September 1989.
4. John and Paula Sandford, *The Transformation of the Inner Man* (South Plainfield, NJ: Bridge, 1982), 29.
5. Paul Vitz, "The Psychological Roots of Atheism," tape series produced by Allies for Faith and Renewal Conference 1988, P.O. Box 8229, Ann Arbor, MI.

Chapter 3.
1. Sue Horton, "Mothers, Sons, and the Gangs: When a Gang Becomes Part of the Family," *Los Angeles Times Magazine,* October 16, 1988, 8.
2. Ciotti, 10.
3. Prentice Tipton, "The Crisis of Black Manhood," *Pastoral Renewal,* March 1987, 4.
4. Tipton, 4.
5. Bly, 94.
6. *Time,* July 18, 1988, 61.
7. *Los Angeles Times,* March 10, 1991, A1.
8. Mike Clary, "Kennedy Nephew Surrenders, Denies Charges," *Los Angeles Times,* May 12, 1991, A4.
9. Paul Richter, "The Two Images of Kennedy," *Los Angeles Times,* June 7, 1991, A18.
10. Rohr, tape series.
11. *Los Angeles Times,* February 25, 1991, A23.
12. Aubrey Beauchamp, *Aubrey* (Orange, NJ: Promise, 1988), 249.
13. Beauchamp, 251.
14. Beauchamp, 251.
15. Bobbie Reed, Ph.D., *Single Mothers Raising Sons* (Nashville, TN: Thomas Nelson, 1988), 80.

Chapter 4.
1. "Man to Man," Focus on the Family Radio Series, February 22–23, 1991. This tape can be ordered for $5.00 from Focus on the Family, 102 North Cascade, Colorado Springs, CO 80903.
2. Clarence Tucker Craig, "Introduction to 1 Corinthians," *Interpreter's Bible* (New York: Abingdon, 1952), Vol. X, 34.
3. Arthur Crudup, "All Shook Up," RCA Records, 1958.
4. Michael Martin Murphey, "You're Talkin' to the Wrong Man," Timberwolf Music, Inc., 1988.
5. John Bradshaw develops this notion in his *Healing the Shame that Binds You* (Deerfield Beach: Health Communications, Inc., 1988), viii, stating that shame as a healthy human emotion can be transformed into shame as a state of being . . . to believe that one's being is flawed, that one is defective as a human being.
6. Sandford and Sandford, 278.

Chapter 5.
1. Tim Kurkjiam, "Tommy's Team," *Sports Illustrated,* March 4, 1991, 23.
2. Dean Merrill, "None of Us Are Sinners Emeritus," an interview with Bruce Larson, *Leadership,* Fall 1984, 18.
3. Melissa Healy, "In Face of Death—What Makes Soldiers Disregard Instinct?" *Los Angeles Times,* February 26, 1991, A8.

4. Healy, A1.
5. Merrill, 15.
6. Merrill, 14–5.
7. Merrill, 16.
8. Merrill.
9. Bob Spichen, "The Inner Warrior," *Los Angeles Times*, March 19, 1991.
10. Spichen, E4.
11. Spichen, E4.
12. Gordon Dalbey, "On Becoming Thirty: The Season for Love," *The Sign*, July/August 1975, 32–5.
13. Merrill, 23.

Chapter 6.
1. Steven M. Wolf, "Coming of Age," *Vis a Vis*, March 1991, 12.
2. Lee Green, "Like Father, Like Son," *Los Angeles Times Magazine*, June 18, 1989, 11.
3. Reg Lansberry, "The Son Also Rises: Brett Hull," *Vis a Vis*, March 1991, 74.
4. Richard P. Feynman, *What Do You Care What Other People Think?* (New York: W. W. Norton, 1988), 12.
5. Feynman, 15–6.
6. Gordon Dalbey, "The Shoes of the Upholsterer," *The Priest*, January 1991, 34.
7. Moishe Rosen, "Rejoicing in the Lord," *Jews for Jesus Newsletter*, 1991, 1.

Chapter 7.
1. This chapter includes portions of my article, "The Procrastinator, The Rebel, and the True Child of God," *The Christian Ministry*, September 1984.
2. Hugh Missledine, *Your Inner Child of the Past* (New York: Simon and Schuster, 1963), 101.
3. Missledine, 105.
4. S. Adams Sullivan, *The Father's Almanac* (New York: Doubleday, 1980), xv.
5. Benjamin Spock, M.D., *Dr. Spock Talks with Mothers* (New York: Fawcett World, 1974).
6. Missledine, 102.

Chapter 8.
1. John and Paula Sandford, *Healing the Wounded Spirit* (Tulsa, OK: Victory House, 1985), 292.
2. Oswald Chambers, *My Utmost for His Highest* (New York: Dodd, Mead, 1935), 155.
3. Robert A. Raines, *To Kiss the Joy* (Nashville, TN: Abingdon, 1983).

4. Raines.

5. E. James Wilder, *Just Between Father and Son* (Downers Grove: InterVarsity, 1990), 9.

6. Lloyd J. Ogilvie, *Discovering God's Will in Your Life* (Eugene, OR: Harvest House, 1985).

7. Dudley Hall, "What Is Legalism?" audio tape produced by Successful Christian Living Ministries, Box 101, Euless, TX 76039.

Chapter 9.

1. Dudley Hall makes this specific point in his tape "What Is Legalism?"

2. My interpretation of Joseph's story is from my article "When the Man of Principle Becomes a Man of Faith," *The Christian Ministry,* September, 1979, 25–6.

3. Clyde Besson, "Suddenly Single," video produced by The Sampson Co., 1980. Available through Word, Inc.

4. Portions of page 137 were originally published in my article "God's Greatest Enemy: The Inactive Believer," *The Church Herald,* March 5, 1982, 9–10.

5. Stephen Arterburn, "What Is Toxic Faith?" *New Life,* Vol. II, Issue I, 1.

6. Portions of pages 141–42 are taken from my article "Receive God's Blessings," *New Covenant,* April 11, 1985, 23–5.

Chapter 10.

1. J. B. Phillips, *Your God Is Too Small* (New York: Macmillan, 1961), 8.

2. Portions of this chapter are taken from an article by the author, "God and Flight 191," *The Church Herald,* October 19, 1979.

3. I drew this insight on Joshua's inner struggle from an excellent essay by Max Apple in *Congregation: Contemporary Writers Read the Jewish Bible,* David Rosenberg, editor (San Diego, CA: Harcourt Brace Jovanovich, 1987), 61–9.

4. C. S. Lewis, *Mere Christianity* (New York: Macmillan, 1952), 65–6.

5. Rohr, tape series.

Chapter 11.

1. John Leland with Donna Foote, "A Bad Omen for Black Movies?" *Newsweek,* July 29, 1991, 48.

2. The discussion on depression in this chapter is taken from "Depression, Depressed Feelings—A Christian Approach" by Gordon Dalbey, *Pastoral Life Magazine,* November 1986, 18–26.

3. Arthur Janov, *The Primal Scream* (Huntington Beach, CA: Putman, 1981).

4. Janov.

5. Janov.

6. Janov.

7. *Los Angeles Times,* March 23, 1978.

8. Agness Sanford, *The Healing Gifts of the Spirit* (San Francisco, CA: Harper, 1984).
9. Dennis Linn and Matthew Linn, *Healing Life's Hurts: Healing Memories Through the Five Stages of Forgiveness* (Farmington, PA: Paulist Press, 1978).
10. Rev. Margaret Crockett, "Depression and Middle-aged Women," *Journal of Pastoral Care.*
11. Linn and Linn.
12. William Scarlett, "Exposition of Jonah," *Interpreter's Bible* (New York: Abingdon, 1952), Vol. VI, 576.

Chapter 12.
1. Leonard LeSourd, *Strong Men, Weak Men* (Old Tappan: Chosen Books, 1990).
2. Gordon Dalbey, "The Great White Son Turns Left," *Christian Century,* June 9, 1971, 716.
3. Martin Ebon, *Che: The Making of a Legend* (New York: Universe, 1969).
4. Bly, 94–6.
5. Bly, 95–6.
6. "Are You a Candidate for the Caleb Corps?" Trinity Lutheran Church, 1450 W. 7th Street, San Pedro, CA 90732.

Chapter 13.
1. James W. Fowler, III, *Becoming Adult, Becoming Christian* (New York: Harper & Row, 1984), 142.
2. Chip Brown, "Do We All Become Our Fathers?" *Men's Life,* October/November 1990, 50.
3. Brown, 48.
4. Brown, 48.
5. Brown, 52.
6. Brown, 52.
7. Bly, 8.
8. Bly, 45.
9. Bly, 70.
10. Bly, 41–2.
11. Thomas A. Smail, *The Forgotten Father* (Grand Rapids, MI: Eerdmans, 1980), 16.

About the Author

Gordon Dalbey, author of the widely acclaimed *Healing the Masculine Soul,* is a popular speaker at retreats and conferences around the country. He is a graduate of Duke University and holds the M.A. in journalism from Stanford University and the M.Div. from Harvard University. He was a news reporter, a Peace Corps volunteer, and a high school teacher before pastoring churches in Southern California.

He has appeared on many radio and television progams, including "Focus on the Family," "The 700 Club," and "The Minirth-Meier Clinic." His articles have been published in a wide variety of journals, magazines, and newspapers, including *Reader's Digest, Los Angeles Times, Catholic Digest, Leadership,* and *Christian Herald.*

He lives in Los Angeles with his wife, Dr. Mary Andrews-Dalbey, and their infant son, John Miguel.

For information on speaking engagements or further resources, contact:

Gordon Dalbey
Box 24496
Los Angeles, CA 90024